They Took the Kids Last Night

They Took the Kids Last Night

How the Child Protection System Puts Families at Risk

Diane L. Redleaf

 PRAEGER™

An Imprint of ABC-CLIO, LLC

Santa Barbara, California • Denver, Colorado

Library of Congress Cataloging-in-Publication Data

Names: Redleaf, Diane L., author.
Title: They took the kids last night : how the child protection system puts
    families at risk / Diane L. Redleaf.
Description: Santa Barbara, California : Praeger, [2018] | Includes
    bibliographical references and index.
Identifiers: LCCN 2018023512 (print) | LCCN 2018024434 (ebook) | ISBN
    9781440866296 (eBook) | ISBN 9781440866289 (hardcopy : alk. paper)
Subjects: | MESH: Child Protective Services | Child Abuse—legislation &
    jurisprudence | Family Relations | Mandatory Reporting | Civil Rights |
    Illinois
Classification: LCC HV6626.5 (ebook) | LCC HV6626.5 (print) | NLM WA 320 AI3
    | DDC 362.76—dc23
LC record available at https://lccn.loc.gov/2018023512

ISBN: 978-1-4408-6628-9 (print)
        978-1-4408-6629-6 (ebook)

22 21 20 19   2 3 4 5

This book is also available as an eBook.

Praeger
An Imprint of ABC-CLIO, LLC

ABC-CLIO, LLC
130 Cremona Drive, P.O. Box 1911
Santa Barbara, California 93116-1911
www.abc-clio.com

This book is printed on acid-free paper (∞)

Manufactured in the United States of America

To the families, colleagues, supporters, and allies with whom I have been privileged to work over many years of advocacy for families in the child welfare system.
To Melissa Staas, whose 10 years of work on the cases presented here forged her outstanding leadership as a family defender and made this book her story too, and to Carolyn Kubitschek, whose brilliance lit the path I have followed.
To my husband, Anatoly Libgober, and my parents, Paul and Rhoda Redleaf, who are a source of support, inspiration, and courage.
To my own children, Brian and Jonathan Libgober, who are my greatest source of joy and my teachers on the meaning of the precious right to raise a family.

Contents

Preface

This book comes out of my 38 years of practice as a lawyer in Chicago, 33 of which have focused on the Illinois child protective services (CPS) system. While Illinois' system, like each state's, has its own peculiarities, I've tried to make this book as generic as I can. Cases like the ones I talk about happen in every state, for child abuse hotlines have been federally mandated since 1974. But each state has its own statutes, rules, policies, and practices, so readers must be aware that this book's descriptions may not strictly translate to the way things are done in another state. This book is no substitute for specific legal advice or guidance.

I've had a front-row seat and sometimes been in the driver's seat in the reform efforts this book discusses. I've been a part of national, state, and local child protection advocacy for families. In 1984, Chicago's largest legal services agency, the Legal Assistance Foundation, allowed me to start a child advocacy project. I wanted only to represent children, not their allegedly abusive parents. It took just one first case to turn me around. I've been a family defender ever since.

That case involved two sisters, a 10-year-old and a 13-year-old. The older sister alleged that her stepfather had fondled her. Both girls were removed from their home. A disabled younger brother was left at home, not because the State believed he was safe but because the State had no available foster homes for his special needs. When the mother sought my help, she had lost contact with her 10-year-old daughter after the child had repeatedly run home from successive foster homes. Eventually, the child was placed into a residential facility, Maryville, far from her family in Chicago. While the mother was a monolingual Spanish speaker, none of the facility's staff spoke Spanish and so no one had called the family to let them know the girl was all right. At this point, the mother had already endured a month of no contact with the girl.

After a few phone calls to CPS officials, I found the girl. I drove her family out to see her at Maryville. It was a joyous reunion, so I vowed to help the family reunite permanently. The 10-year-old girl said that nothing inappropriate had happened to her and that she longed to be back home. When I prepared the girl to testify in the Cook County Juvenile Court, I focused some initial witness-qualifying questions on her understanding of the judge's role. In our prep session, she answered well: a judge, she said, was someone who listens and makes a decision after hearing from everyone. But when her case came into court, the judge refused to let the girl testify. He dismissed out of hand my request to return her home. I watched a little girl's view of justice dim before my eyes.

A few weeks later, however, the State dropped its case against the mother, and suddenly the children went home. The State had no evidence showing the mother had failed to protect her 13-year-old daughter. The 13-year-old waffled about what had happened, too. I concluded that while the mother was quite powerless, it was her perceived guilt or innocence that mattered to the court. But her legal representation had been, if anything, less vigorous than the children's. Her court-appointed lawyer didn't make any of the arguments that needed to be made.

This first case of mine taught me why child advocates need to defend families—not at all costs but vigorously and effectively. I'm not naive. Some parents commit terrible abuse. Some child abuse cases are notoriously difficult to figure out. Sexual abuse cases, like this first case of mine, almost always turn on whom you believe. This book steers clear of sexual abuse cases. It focuses, instead, on cases in which the children are brought into the child welfare system solely because of an unexplained injury or a symptom that might be due to either child abuse or an accident or a medical condition. These stories are easy for those who never have encountered CPS themselves to appreciate, since no family is immune from a childhood accident that could be misinterpreted as child abuse. It's also easy to relate to parents' concerns when something mysterious causes their children bleeding, seizures, or a previously undetected fracture.

As this book discusses, there are many more cases of wrongful allegations than commonly touted child abuse statistics suggest. And between innocence and guilt lie a range of parenting mistakes, misjudgments, and misunderstandings that should be addressed through means less drastic than taking the kids one night.

The stories here, coming from my own docket as a lawyer, are meant to provide an up-close and in-depth description of the CPS system in cases where the parent's innocence no longer is in any reasonable doubt. Each of the stories involves parents first accused and then eventually exonerated. In the course of taking the kids, CPS systems frequently seem out of control. Lest I be misunderstood on this point, I want to emphasize that I do not advocate keeping children with parents who are genuinely abusive. Nor do I claim that CPS is always in the wrong. Rather, CPS systems need to do a vastly better job of distinguishing heinous abusers from reasonably good parents who deserve protection from the risk of losing their kids one night. If this book generates discussion as to how to better protect loving families from having their children taken one night, it will have served its primary purpose.

I could not have written this book without the inspiration and support of the parents I call Ben and Lynn here, along with Lynn's father, Richard. They have chosen to change their names here in order to protect their children's privacy. Mary Broderick (chapter 1) and Tony L. and Tiffany W. (chapter 16) have agreed to use their real names, but Tony and Tiffany's children's names have been changed, as have Thomas and Daniel's names in the last story (chapter 17). These families, as well as Crystelle and Joshua Hernandez, the plaintiffs in an important civil rights lawsuit (chapter 14), have been enthusiastic and generous in this project, sharing with me the hope that telling their stories will help to prevent other families from experiences like those that happened to them one night. The story in chapter 15 uses the names as they appear in the published appellate court opinion in *In re Yohan K.*

Apart from the already-published names of the doctors, lawyers, and judges in the *Yohan K.* case or in published federal court opinions (*Dupuy* and *Hernandez*, chapters 4 and 14), the names of participants in the trial court actions also have been changed. It is not my purpose to single out any specific individual or group for criticism but to paint a detailed picture of how the CPS system operates at times to the detriment of families. As in any large system, there are many CPS players in specific roles with sometimes correct and sometimes wrong ideas.

Stories where the right call was made, where the family was treated with dignity and respect, and where the courts never had to intervene may be the substantial majority of cases in the CPS system, but those cases don't typically come to the attention of family defenders like me. One thing is clear: unless the stories of the families whose kids were taken one night are told, the child welfare system will continue to make mistakes like the ones that changed the lives of the families in this book.

Opinions and recommendations in this book, except where attributed to another, are my own.

Introduction

"Not everything that is faced can be changed, but nothing can be changed until it is faced."

—James Baldwin

"They took the kids last night," the mother on the line tells me. It is 5:15 p.m. on a chilly Friday afternoon. Shaken and scared, she has reached out for legal help, hoping that a lawyer can make her nightmare go away. She sounds almost too tearful to talk. Somehow she gets through to me even though the receptionist has left already. But the mother on the phone needs legal advice from a family defender right now. By early next week, she must be ready for an emergency court hearing, though she doesn't know that yet.

The words "they took the kids last night" bring up many questions. A narrative leads to the State's child protection system (CPS) decision to take the kids from their home last night. A family defender who helps this mother will need to know the whole story. At the same time, these words don't suggest any good answers that will restore the children to the unfortunate mother's care this weekend. Whenever a parent calls to say, "The kids have been taken," the CPS agency has already done its most immediate damage: pulling the trigger on the family. Undoing the damage will take much more time than it took for the State to seize the kids and place them into an emergency foster home or shelter.

This evening the mother's desperate question is, "Where are my children right now?" The children don't have any belongings other than the clothes they wore when the CPS caseworker came for them last night. No special blankets, no cuddly bear. For all I know, the children now are in a distant foster home with older system-savvy kids. Worse, they may be in

an overcrowded emergency shelter with children aged 0 to 18, waiting for
another placement into a longer-term foster home or group home. Since
the State chose not to put these children with a relative, news about their
whereabouts won't be good news. The State CPS system has left the
mother powerless, at least for the moment, unable to prevent the children's
removal into state protective custody and unable to direct them to a familiar home. The mother is sick with worry. Who could blame her for that?

Unfortunately for her and the kids, though, it will be impossible at this
hour for anyone outside the CPS system to find the kids. It's possible to
call the State's local emergency shelter, of course, but information about
the children's whereabouts almost certainly won't be shared. That's understandable. The CPS system assumes the worst and then treats the parents
accordingly. The emergency-shelter personnel aren't about to tell a mother
who might be accused of serial battery of her children or a father accused
of molestation where that parent can find their children before the first
dependency court date. Besides, the emergency-shelter staff aren't told the
specific child abuse allegations against the parents. Those staff members
are not about to take any chances that could lead them to be featured—and
not in a good way—on the evening news.

So even if this mother is entirely innocent of hurting her kids, it will be
nearly impossible to find out who is taking care of the children right now.
Though the mother is desperate to find her children, she has no idea when
she will see them next. It will be nearly impossible for this mother to see
or talk to the children before the weekend is out.

No one who works for CPS will talk to an attorney who hasn't formally
appeared in the court action that has yet to begin, so I'm not even going to
try to reach anyone to inquire. The mother might do better by making some
calls herself to phone numbers I give her, though I am not betting on it.

Giving the mother a few phone numbers helps to calm her, though. It
tells her where to start, at least, in her quest for information. Now she can
begin to focus on the next steps. While there is no legal magic that will
bring the children home right away, that doesn't make legal help useless; it
is important for the mother to know what to expect during the legal process
that's about to begin. So we start to talk about the recourse the legal system
does provide. I spare her the details about how that recourse inevitably will
be too little, too late, and too costly, even for an obviously innocent parent.

It helps her to learn how she can prepare for the legal action that's about
to commence. She's grateful for information about the uncertain world she
will soon have to navigate. For example, she will need to gather the

children's medical records, especially the most recent ones. She needs to spend the weekend finding family or friends who might keep the kids temporarily if the court rules that she can't retain custody. A strong support network can be key to survival in the CPS world.

The suggested to-do list gives the mother a modest sense of control and distracts her slightly from the shock of not having her children with her. Even a tiny ability to influence what is happening to her family helps, because her children's future is no longer up to her. A judge she doesn't know, along with attorneys for the State, will soon be deciding whether her kids will come home next week or ever.

While the mother is grateful to learn what to expect, it's obvious that she is in a fog of confusion and panic. She asks me several times for addresses for my office and the court building, where a hearing should take place on Monday afternoon. Monday is the State's legal deadline for bringing a petition to a judge following an emergency CPS child removal.[1] While I explain this legal requirement, it's clear that much of what I'm saying isn't registering. She doesn't ask any questions about the court hearing, though she clearly has no idea what to expect. She isn't legally savvy. Nothing like what is happening now to her family has happened before. Moreover, it's doubtful that she has slept more than an hour or two since the kids were taken. She's already exhausted by today's search to find a family defender. She is coping the best she can but not well.

Adjusting emotionally to the sudden loss of the precious, intimate connection to her children will take a long time. Really, it could take her a lifetime, depending on what the courts and CPS caseworkers decide next. But adjustment will not mean acceptance, especially if she is innocent of wrongdoing, as she insists.

It feels as if an earthquake struck her home, toppling every structure and creating rubble. She hears in her own mind, as only a mother hears, her children's cries for her. If she is able to sleep over this coming weekend, she will be luckier than many parents who temporarily lose their kids to CPS. There is no getting around it. She soon will hear plenty of euphemisms about the CPS system's benign intentions to ensure her children's safety, but her family will not be the same after this weekend. The CPS action has shattered the family's sense of safety in their own home. Repairing that damage will take a long time.

The mother starts to tell me how the CPS system got called in the first place. Soon, it becomes apparent to me how the investigation turned against her.

The CPS investigation started after the mother took her younger daughter, a 20-month-old toddler, to the doctor's office after noticing the child wasn't using her right arm. When X-rays found a humerus fracture, the mother first tried to explain to the nurse that her child must have fallen out of the crib. The doctor took a look at the swelling arm and then huddled together with the nurse. After that, the nurse told the mother that the State's child abuse hotline had been called.

The mother had told the nurse that her daughter "couldn't run or climb." She meant to explain that the child wasn't running or climbing now that her arm was hurt. But the medical staff must have thought the child could not run or climb at all and must have concluded that the mother's suggestion about a possible fall out of the crib was a made-up story, designed to cover up child abuse.[2]

Like most parents who call me, this mother didn't fault the doctor or the nurse who made the hotline call. In their position, she might have done the same thing. She didn't know, of course, exactly who reported to the hotline. She worried that a negative comment she made about her child's recent tantrum had been misunderstood or taken out of context. She understood that an investigation would be undertaken, although her understanding of the difference between the police and CPS was foggy. She wanted to cooperate, but she also wanted to be cleared of wrongdoing quickly.

While the mother wanted to answer the CPS caseworkers' questions, the truth was that she really wasn't certain how the fracture occurred. Under the circumstances, a fall from the crib made the most sense. But maybe the fracture happened before the child's afternoon nap, not after, when her older sister had pushed her down while chasing the family dog.

Her younger daughter had briefly cried but then quieted and went to sleep. After the nap, the mother found her daughter had gotten out of the crib by herself and was nursing her arm. But the mother hadn't heard any crying. When the mother first came into the room, her daughter was sitting on the floor, playing with a toy and smiling. She realized that the crib mattress needed to be lowered now that her daughter could get out of the crib but didn't think much more about it.

When she handed her daughter a banana as an afternoon snack, however, the mother noticed then that the child wasn't using her right arm, even to grab the banana. She also noticed some swelling on the arm that she hadn't seen before. The mother called the doctor's office right away. If she had abused the child, she wondered out loud, would she have been so quick to call the doctor? Wasn't it obvious that she would never hurt a child?

The mother was already frustrated that no one from CPS seemed to believe her denials of wrongdoing. Showing frustration to CPS caseworkers isn't recommended, however. It usually makes matters worse. She now could vent her concerns to me; lawyers can help clients simply by serving as an outlet for their frustrations. I could help her navigate the child protection maze. Thousands of parents who go through similar ordeals every year are less fortunate. There is no right to have counsel appointed in any state in the union *before* a court case starts. Parents under investigation by CPS are on their own.

Over and over, the CPS system gets hotline calls exactly like this one. This story itself is a composite of recurring fragments of my experiences representing parents in child protection cases for the past 33 years. The CPS system has grown dramatically during this same period. In 2016 alone, 7.4 million children were reported as suspected victims of child abuse or neglect.[3] Of this number, 4.1 million had a case referred for some CPS responsive action, ranging from finding no merit to the allegations and closing the case, to referring the family for social services, to a placement of the children into foster care.[4] At the conclusion of a CPS investigation, 676,000 children were then labeled the victims of abuse or neglect.[5] In 2016 alone, 273,539 children came into foster care.[6]

Physical abuse, the category that any claim that a parent inflicted a fracture on their child would come under, makes up a relatively small fraction of the overall caseload of CPS—18.2 percent of the total cases that result in findings of abuse or neglect.[7] But it's a wide-ranging fraction, spanning cases of heinous abuse to the sorts of minor childhood injuries that could happen to any active child, including scratches, scrapes, bruises as well as fractures, head injuries, and burns.[8]

No parent is immune from the possibility that ordinary childhood accidents could be misjudged as due to child abuse, and at the same time, everyone is rightly concerned about serially beaten and battered children, the classic victims of physical abuse. According to federal government statistics for the most recent year, 1,750 children in the United States reportedly died from abuse or neglect of a parent or caregiver.[9] But the number of parents who haven't committed abuse, even though someone suspected them and an investigation ensued, dramatically dwarfs the number of parents who are truly dangerous. Overall, 29.4 percent of the CPS hotline calls that weren't immediately screened out ended up with a finding of abuse or neglect.[10] As this book will show, that figure masks a range of errors that the overall statistics don't tell.

It's important to figure out which parents are as safe and loving as Ozzie and Harriet and which are as dangerous as John Wayne Gacy Jr. Since children can die from physical abuse,[11] it is especially important for the CPS system to make the right call when they see an injury that could be due to physical abuse. But it's also important to the family that the CPS system not presume parental guilt and proceed to take the children from loving homes. Where the balance of risk of error should lie is a question at the heart of this book. Proof beyond a reasonable doubt may be too high a threshold, but operating under a principle of "when in doubt, take them out" is, if anything, worse.[12]

For the CPS system, policies and practices have sprung up in abundance, starting with federal statutes that allow children to be removed from their suspected parents and evidence gathered later.[13] Public demands for swift action in the face of child abuse have led to a climate of quick-trigger responses. Woe to any governmental official who is perceived as soft on child abusers! But even being separated for a couple of days can be life altering for a child and family in ways that are just beginning to be documented in social services and legal studies.[14] "Better safe than sorry" is often safer for the CPS caseworkers than for the children removed from their homes. Of course, some children say that their lives were saved when they were taken from their abusive parents and placed into foster care. But others will say that they don't know why they were taken and that they wish above all else that they had never heard of CPS.

In physical abuse cases, CPS needs to gather medical evidence, including expert opinions of doctors who treat the child's injuries. It is common, and some child protection administrators argue it's essential, for CPS caseworkers to assume that the doctors evaluating children for abuse are reliable. In fact, the system trusts certain doctors and discounts the opinions of others. When a doctor reports abuse, even when other doctors later disagree, the CPS caseworker focuses on the question, "Who did it?" Sometimes there was no "it"; the reporting doctor could have been wrong in the first place about the abuse claim. Or CPS might blame the wrong perpetrator. All this may get sorted out months after the CPS system took the children. That's when the system "works."

Heaven help any parent who can't explain how an infant got a fracture or bleeding on his or her brain! The hypothetical mother on the phone with me was in a classic form of legal peril. The CPS system put everyone who had ever been near her child under suspicion. Because all of her nearby relatives had recently watched the child, CPS decided not to place her children with any of them. As long as child abuse is a remote possibility, it doesn't have to be an especially likely cause for normal daily contact with children to be restricted for parents and grandparents alike.

Overstressed CPS hotline call centers sort out millions of hotline calls every year, sending about half the calls for investigation or social service responses. CPS caseworkers in field offices make the life-and-death decisions for children and families then. When these caseworkers don't make the right assessment and a child dies, blaring headlines and public demands for accountability often follow. But when they take kids who were not abused or neglected or when they label an innocent parent guilty of abuse in the State's child-abuse register but never press charges, there are rarely any headlines concerning these types of mistakes. Often, no one outside the immediately affected family is the wiser, but the family can be devastated.

Overall error rates in issuing false abuse labels are not reported in the national child abuse statistics. Court cases tell a different story. Federal court decisions have shown error by caseworkers in their assessments of abuse and neglect at rates that are "staggering," to quote one of the federal judges who opined on CPS system malfunctions.[15] It should not surprise anyone that the CPS system's most glaring errors have a disproportionate impact on minority communities, especially African Americans.[16] One well-known study found that prenatal drug use for pregnant African American women was reported to authorities at a 11 times higher rate than for Caucasian women, even though their actual substance use was the same.[17] These overreporting, overinvestigating, and overlabeling errors often have serious, harmful consequences of their own. In most states, CPS abuse decisions go straight into child-abuse registers—no prior court hearing is necessary—and these registers operate as employment blacklists. A system that so broadly sweeps in the innocent in order to catch a few guilty should at least take account of the harm that its practices cause to the innocent. Yet the CPS system rarely acknowledges its false-positive errors or their harmful impact on the children whom the system is supposed to protect.

Secrecy adds to the system's lack of accountability. CPS officials shy away from revealing how often their caseworkers intervened when the family was innocent of wrongdoing. For the mother on the phone, the accusation alone, even though untrue, is terrifying. Shame prevents her from complaining publicly about the injustice of taking her children from their home. Some of her closest family members might be willing to help if they knew of a child abuse investigation. But she is too afraid to tell them.

I leave the mother with clear instructions. I tell her that I'll check in over the weekend, and we set a time to talk when my office opens on Monday morning. Since the State will have to get a court petition filed by Monday afternoon,[18] we have just a little time to get ready on Monday morning.

Terrible as it is to hear from the mother who just had her kids taken the night before, the pressure is off me until my office reopens on Monday. What happens next is out of my hands; there is nothing more I can do right now to prevent the CPS action from taking its course. But if the mother had used some other words when she first reached me, it's more likely my own weekend plans would have been derailed. Sometimes a family defender can stop the kids from being taken. Sometimes legal work late into the night or the weekend can stop a CPS mistake from changing the course of a family's life.

When Ben, the father in the primary story I'm about to tell, called my office on October 1, 2009, he used words that pushed me into high gear. Ben told me that the caseworker had asked him and his wife, Lynn, to come to the CPS office with their kids the next day.

An investigation had started a few weeks before. The caseworker said she was "inviting" Ben to "bring the kids to the office tomorrow morning." When Ben told me about this "invitation," he needed legal help to interpret the signs. As a family defense lawyer, I knew what this "invitation" meant. The CPS team was about to take Ben and Lynn's kids and put them into foster care. Only some legal intervention would stop the action, and if I failed to advise Ben and Lynn correctly, the kids would be taken.

The words "bring your kids into the office tomorrow morning" were code words. The CPS caseworker certainly didn't warn Ben that he would be leaving the office without his children. She made the meeting sound routine. Nor did she advise him to pack any bag of belongings for the children. To be sure, she made the meeting sound important; she promised a chance to discuss the direction of the investigation.

While she presented the meeting in this matter-of-fact way, her words flagged what CPS was planning to do. There was no reason for the CPS caseworker to see the children *at the CPS office* during a hotline investigation. During investigations, CPS sees children at home, at schools, at daycare centers—all settings where children may be comfortable talking to a stranger and where the child's telltale interactions with adult caregivers can be observed.

The CPS office might be a reasonable setting for interviewing a parent who works full-time, but children should be seen in a more natural and comfortable setting than a CPS office.

Ben and Lynn were about to lose their kids. They would be blindsided, unaware of the caseworker's true plans. Ben had been trying his best to put this investigation behind him as soon as possible, so he was primed to comply with the caseworker's request. A final wrap-up meeting with the kids at the office sounded promising. He was wary, however, so he called for legal advice right away. Parents often believe that the caseworkers are on their side. Ben and Lynn had learned not to be too trusting. Still, without some on-the-spot legal intervention, parents, like the hypothetical mother on the phone with me, may go to a CPS office and leave without their children. They start to call for legal help only after they realize what has occurred, when it's already too late for a family defender to prevent a nightmare from coming to pass.

The family defense field is complex, fascinating, and distressing. When wrongly accused parents' rights to keep their kids are violated, it can often seem as if no one is listening. Parents' rights advocates can feel vilified themselves, pejoratively labeled as the defenders of child abusers or as "child abuse deniers," even when arguing about basic precepts, like the importance of the State's having evidence of wrongdoing before children are taken from their parents. The mantra "best interests of the child" is often self-righteously invoked to silence family advocates who question the assumption that the State knows better than the parents what is best for the children. The battleground in the fight for the fundamental right of families to raise their children has no clear political lines or sides, except that the resources in the fight are heavily on the State's side. For the three decades in which I've been a family defender, I've never felt it was a fair fight.

The face of legal advocacy for families is starting to change, however. That's long overdue. I hope this book will help to continue to advance the cause of justice for families, explaining why our society needs to protect children by defending their families.

The primary story in this book—why Ben and Lynn needed the help of a family defender—fits a paradoxical mold: while theirs is an exceptional and unique family, the investigation and court action that followed became "business as usual" for the child protection system. Ben and Lynn are skilled and patient parents whose infant son's mysterious injury led to a nightmare no one could have predicted. The parents of two-year-old twins, they had just welcomed their newborn son, Robert, into their family. But suddenly, at age four weeks, Robert showed signs of an injury to his left leg that neither parent could explain.

Soon, Ben and Lynn were both accused of abusing Robert. They were separated from their three children with out-of-state relatives coming in to substitute for them, and the ensuing battle to exonerate Ben and Lynn from the abuse allegations took months. It involved a slew of lawyers and doctors with conflicting agendas and opinions. The mystery of how Robert got his fracture was never solved, but developments months after the court case ended shed light on why Ben and Lynn couldn't explain it.

Many elements of Ben and Lynn's story will seem familiar to professionals who work in the child welfare system in America. Though heartbreaking, Ben and Lynn's story is like many that do not end as well. At the same time, they are unusual among those families of kids taken into CPS custody. Lynn is a social worker herself, and Ben is an executive. Both of them come from prominent families who are leaders in their home communities. Lynn's mother was a federal judge.

It's rare to find parents defending themselves in child protection court cases who have such education, professional accomplishment, and social support networks. Their story is told in part because it demonstrates that what happened to them *could* happen to just about any family in America: no race, class, or profession is entirely immune from CPS intervention into their family life. Many people react to CPS stories with the thought that what happened to another family couldn't happen to them. But that's what the families in this book believed, too. Not understanding what they were up against added to their shock.

What happened in their families *does* happen to thousands of other families—across races, religions, income levels, and professional status—who are equally exemplary. The child protection system most disproportionately intervenes against families of color and those who lack other forms of privilege. But the experiences of the families as described in this book show that all American families with children are at some risk from the CPS system. A system that is supposed to protect children *from* their parents ends up too often harming children's precious attachment *to* their parents. Nowadays, due to many of the CPS policies and practices this book describes, no one can take fundamental family rights for granted.

The families profiled in this book are also unusual in the ways that they fought back, armed with legal counsel well versed in the dynamics of family defense. Many families—including those with financial means but especially those without—have trouble finding experienced counsel who work in this unusual hybrid area of law. Jobs in family defense are usually poorly paid and dramatically under-resourced. Some of the lawyers in this field carry hundreds of cases at a time, when 20 to 30 cases per attorney would be more reasonable.

It's tragic that unless a parent has some of the advantages of the families profiled here, he or she may lose the battle to keep his or her children or to return them home even though they are innocent of wrongdoing. An unjust system, like the CPS system in America, punishes, especially harshly, those who are disadvantaged from the start. The risks families run when they raise and love a child demand that we change the CPS system in this country to protect children and families from the harms CPS causes when it gets hotline investigations wrong. For all the system's good intentions, the unintended consequences for millions of children and families are too severe. It is imperative that we make the system safer for children and families.

The stories here are drawn from fragments of each parent and each child's life, fragments that turned their life experiences and health concerns into cases. Their personal ordeals turned into the stuff of legal analysis and legal adjudication. These are *legal* as well as family stories. From the sometimes-jaded vision of a family defender, the case and the client can blur into one. The lawyer works several steps removed from the reality that the family faces. That's by design, for the lawyer who actually felt all of his or her client's pain quickly would be incapable of effective advocacy. At the same time, any lawyer who doesn't appreciate or understand the client's experience will fail to secure justice for the client who has sought legal help. It's a delicate balance between caring sufficiently to be effective and keeping enough distance so as not to become incapacitated.

To the extent that this book's stories come out of a long legal career of working to keep children in their own homes, this is my own story too.

ONE

Today the *Brady Bunch* Kids Could Be Taken Too

Ben and Lynn called me on September 22, 2009, 12 days after their brush with CPS first began. Their good luck in finding legal help followed a string of disruptions to their family's stability that had occurred over the previous 12 days. Now Ben and Lynn needed a family defense lawyer themselves.

Ben got my name from Mary Broderick. Mary's own tangle with CPS had started more than six years earlier. The investigation against her and her husband, Tom, took 43 excruciating days to resolve but ended with a sigh of relief. The case against Mary and Tom came from an allegation that one of them, or maybe both of them, had shaken their infant son, Ryan, until his brain bled. The medical term was "subdural hematoma" (literally bleeding under the "dura," one of the three membranes that surround the brain). While both Mary and Tom were accused of causing their son's brain bleed, anyone who had cared for their son before the bleeding occurred was viewed with suspicion.

Actually, nothing was suspicious about the initial injury to the couple's four-month-old son that caused him to need medical attention. Tom had been on the family's porch holding the baby. Tom suddenly fell backward, and in his efforts to avoid falling onto his 18-month-old daughter standing nearby, Tom let go of the baby, who tumbled onto the grass. A neighbor and Mary heard Tom cry out. 911 was immediately called. When a small hematoma was found in the baby's head, there was no suspicion—not yet. Tom had some injuries to his shoulder, too, so doctors accepted the fall as a reasonable explanation for the bleeding.

The problem emerged when a second precautionary brain scan showed an older, chronic subdural hematoma. Now, suddenly, there was suspicion. Doctors decided that the State's child abuse hotline must be called. A CPS caseworker came to the hospital and notified Mary and Tom that they were child abuse suspects. The caseworker announced that the couple's two children could not continue to live with them; Mary and Tom would have to find alternative caregivers for the children. In fact, if they didn't quickly find relatives to step in, their two children would be put into foster care.

Such threats are common.[1] CPS caseworkers will tell parents they must enter into agreements to allow someone else to take care of their children while the investigation proceeds. If the parents refuse to agree, they face the real possibility that their kids will be placed with strangers, and they may not be allowed to see them for days or even weeks. The agreements they sign are called "safety plans" in Orwellian CPS newspeak. But if the parents have done nothing wrong, there is nothing safe for the children about ejecting them or their parents from the home.

Like 99.9 percent of parents faced with a demand for a safety plan, Mary and Tom would do anything to keep their children safe from removal by CPS. They cooperated fully. They agreed to have their kids go live with relatives during the investigation. They were unable to resist if they wanted to keep the children with family members rather than with foster parents who were strangers. Agreeing to a safety plan was a much better alternative under the circumstances. Though an unwelcome imposition, the safety plan at least allowed them to visit their children as much as they wished, on the condition that designated relatives supervised all of their contact with their children.

While her kids were living with a chosen relative, Mary worked hard to expedite the medical review for CPS to finish its investigation of the hotline call. She started to read voraciously about shaken baby syndrome, which is what CPS claimed had caused her son's subdural hematomas.

Mary's worry was not limited to a fear that her children would be taken and put into State-run foster care. Mary was anxious about what would happen to her son if he had further sudden unexplained bleeding, given that no one knew the cause of the old chronic bleed. Mary knew that her baby hadn't been shaken, so she genuinely was concerned that he might have a serious undetected medical condition. Subdural hematomas are not a joke, but they can go unnoticed and disappear. Her son's bleed, fortunately, was in this category. He never did have a recurrence.

After 43 days of waiting, the CPS caseworker told Mary and Tom that their children could come home; their safety plan was over. But in the same breath, the caseworker told them that the CPS team had determined that baby Ryan *had* been abused; the CPS team just didn't know *who* had abused him. The hotline call investigation would register a final finding of "indicated to an unknown perpetrator." In other words, their son would be listed as an abused child in the Illinois State Central Register, but Mary and Tom were not being labeled responsible for causing that abuse. Indeed, no one would be named as an abuse perpetrator.

Mary and Tom were relieved that they were no longer targets of State action to take their children and gratified that they finally could bring their children home. But this news left them confused and anxious. Of course, they disagreed with the conclusion that their child had been abused. At the same time, they had no recourse to challenge the "abused child" label that the State had given their child. The only people allowed to challenge investigation findings through Illinois' complex administrative appeal system were people named as child abuse perpetrators in the register.[2]

In Illinois, CPS investigations are supposed to be completed within 60 days. Other states have different time limits. To keep an investigation open for longer than 60 days, CPS caseworkers are supposed to have "good cause," but the deadline could be extended another 30 days for just about any legitimate reason. In Mary's and Tom's case, on the 61st day, the CPS investigative team changed its decision from "abused" to "unfounded." It turned out that the older chronic subdural hematoma on their son's second brain scan had been misinterpreted. The baby never did have an earlier subdural hematoma predating the fall from the porch. The new conclusion was that neither Mary nor Tom—nor anyone, for that matter—had abused their son. The investigation was over, and the "abused child" label would not be attached to their son in the register, after all.

After the CPS caseworkers marked the investigation "unfounded," the State of Illinois left the family alone. No one apologized to Mary and Tom for turning their lives upside down for 43 days or for making them wait another 18 days to reverse the abuse label. Mary and Tom's family was separated for more than six weeks, and they were left hanging for another two and a half weeks beyond that, all the while living under the suspicion of having committed the heinous action of violently shaking their son. These effects were routine collateral damages following a hotline call investigation. None of the doctors involved in Mary and Tom's case viewed their family's treatment as out of the ordinary. In fact, nothing about their status as a family *had* changed in the eyes of the State, except that Mary and Tom now felt acutely that their family life was fragile and could be shattered anew the next time their children needed medical care.

Ryan is now a teenager. To this day, Mary remains bothered by the question of how Ryan's reported chronic subdural hematoma appeared and then disappeared. What made the doctors who read these scans think that such bleeding had been present, and then what made them decide later that the baby didn't have a chronic hematoma after all? Fluid collections for children with large heads like her son's weren't uncommon, Mary learned. These collections could be mistaken for bleeding. But why wasn't this noticed at the time? And why did it take so long to correct? Mary doggedly asked doctors for explanations, tracking down several child abuse doctors who worked on contract with the State CPS authorities and who lectured other doctors on detecting child abuse. She tried to show them the scans from the hospital and ask for an explanation of how the mistake occurred. None of these doctors was willing to sit down with her.

Frustrated by her inability to get answers to basic questions about the health and safety of her child, Mary acquired a ready sympathy for other parents who told her they weren't getting answers from doctors and CPS caseworkers, either. Whenever she heard about a medical case in which the child abuse hotline had been called, she was quick to offer to help the parents understand medical research that might help when health care providers brushed them aside.

Mary was feisty and tenacious, with a fury at injustice. Plus, she was a doer, not a talker. She was very active in her kids' preschool and Catholic elementary school, juggling many school activities with running her own small media-research company. A Chicago native, Mary hailed from a large Irish family filled with cops and firefighters. Her husband, Tom, worked for the city. It came naturally to her to give positive words of encouragement to such parents as Ben and Lynn, who, like her, had an unexpected encounter with the CPS system. Eventually, Ben and Lynn would come to play a similar role as friends-in-chief and peer counselors for dozens of similarly wrongly accused parents. But that role came much later and only after a longer, more terrible legal battle than Mary and Tom faced.

Mary hadn't kept the CPS investigation against her family a secret; friends and neighbors in her residential Chicago community knew that she was someone who had tangled with CPS and won. Mary's CPS ordeal had long been over when the mother of a child at her daughter's preschool stopped her during a routine child pickup in the school's parking lot. This mother was married to a colleague of Ben.

The mother told Mary, "This family needs help. What do you suggest?" Mary answered right away, "Tell him to call me." Soon after that, Ben called, and they talked for a long while. Then Mary alerted me to expect Ben's call. Within a few hours, Ben had left a message on my voice-message system. He and his wife, Lynn, needed the help of a family defender.

When Ben called, he reported that his four-week-old baby son, Robert, had an unexplained fracture. The CPS investigation had been going on for 12 days already. Ben and Lynn had been expelled from their home on the first night of the investigation. Ben's parents had come from another state to take care of their three children while they waited for decisions by the CPS investigative team about their family's future.

On the terrible first night of the investigation, after a night in which she got 45 minutes of sleep at most, Lynn went through an exhausting interrogation by a child abuse pediatric fellow, a doctor in a special training program to become a board-certified child abuse pediatrician. Just as Mary had experienced a few years before, a CPS caseworker threatened Lynn that if a relative didn't immediately come to their home to care for their kids, the children would go to a foster home. Ben and Lynn's safety plan was similar to the one CPS forced upon Mary and her kids for seven weeks.

Safety plans often eject the parents from the home rather than the kids. Whether the parents or the kids would leave the home was up to the CPS caseworker to decide. Under the safety plan, Ben's mother served as the children's primary caregiver in the family home, while Ben and Lynn lived with neighbors. Luckily, Ben and Lynn were allowed unlimited contact with the kids during the day, as long as Ben's mother supervised.

From the very first phone call, Ben and Lynn stood out to me. Though they were still young parents, they were solid and well established. The majority of my clients live at or just slightly above the poverty line. The parents who seek help in CPS cases are often in school or training programs, or they may work in jobs that pay little more than minimum wage. But Ben was a team leader at an insurance company. While most of the family members investigated by CPS don't have college degrees, let alone graduate degrees, Ben and Lynn had met in college, and Lynn had a master's degree in social work. She had worked for five years as a school social worker, and she had been a social worker with the State's program for disabled children before she took time off to raise her own kids.

Like Mary and Tom, Ben and Lynn were doing everything they could to give their children a stable and happy home. The picture that these families presented could not have been further from the common media stereotype of a child abuser. Moreover, as people who made the common assumption that CPS didn't involve families like theirs, nothing in their past experience had prepared Mary, Tom, Lynn, and Ben for the treatment they encountered when they found themselves under suspicion for child abuse.

In fact, Lynn never would get over being a target of a child abuse allegation. As a social worker, she had made hotline calls herself about genuinely troubling cases where child abuse appeared to be ongoing and no one was protecting the child. It was especially heartbreaking when a disabled child had been mistreated. Lynn took her duty to report suspected child abuse seriously. If she had reason to believe parents were abusive, she expected the State to step in to protect the vulnerable young person. She had never imagined that the CPS system would go out of its way to accuse parents of obviously healthy, well-cared-for children of being secret child abusers. Indeed, she often had been bothered by the opposite response: the CPS system sometimes had been slow and cavalier when she had reported real abuse.

Lynn was familiar with the cases that make headlines: stories of children killed by their parents, where the child protection caseworkers ignored marks of abuse, deplorable conditions in the home, or dangerous mental instability of household members, conditions that cried out for some form of intervention or at least a serious investigation as to whether the children were safe. Lynn was stunned to learn that the system could turn against a person like her, who so obviously cared about keeping children safe from harm and whose children were the picture of attentive parental care.

"Is this really happening in America?" she asked me, newly aware that the presumption of innocence had no apparent application to CPS. She was shocked, too, by the speed and certainty with which CPS acted against her and Ben, when neither of them had done anything wrong and when all they wanted were answers from medical and child protection authorities.

Lynn and Ben's professional backgrounds aside, they both possessed intangible qualities of integrity and decency. A dozen support letters from friends, including doctors and lawyers, soon would attest to their character as parents. There was something seemingly old-fashioned, and charmingly naive too, in Ben's belief in the legal system. Ben had never even been in a schoolyard fight. Like Lynn, he was aghast at being accused of any unlawful conduct, much less child abuse.

Both Ben and Lynn had Midwestern roots, and they shared the central goals of being the best parents they could be, putting their family first. Lynn was modest and focused on her children; she considered her greatest strengths to be her love for them and her dedication to providing them a happy, loving home where they would thrive.

In the run of cases that pit the CPS system against families, another feature of Ben and Lynn's background was even more unusual. Both Ben and Lynn had grown up in families who were leaders in their communities. Indeed, I had never represented anyone from such prominent families on both sides. Ben's dad was a high-level executive and lawyer at a major corporation. And I had never before represented the family of a judge.

When I first heard about Lynn's mother's position, I must have asked her three times, "Are you sure she's a *federal* judge?" Lynn wasn't making it up. Not only was her mother a federal judge but also her family's closest friends and colleagues included other federal judges, law professors, and corporate executives. Clearly, the CPS system was tangling with an atypical family when it decided to accuse Ben and Lynn of abuse.

Both sides of grandparents were close to their grown children and grandchildren, and the grandparents would defend them as vigorously as they could. The family's closeness was tangible; the grandparents traveled hundreds of miles each month to help out with the growing children. Lynn's father, Richard, who was more reserved than her dynamic, acerbic, and intense federal judge mother, would eventually become a special friend and supporter of legal and medical defense advocacy. Ben's mom was as fiercely dedicated to her grandchildren as a grandmother can be, telling Ben from the beginning that she didn't want to be a "refrigerator grandma" whose grandkids only saw their picture under the magnet on the refrigerator door. She came to visit as often as possible and little realized how essential her devotion to her grandkids would become in the months ahead.

It was curious that the CPS system would single out the family like this one, especially without a shred of specific evidence of wrongdoing by either Ben or Lynn. Why had Ben and Lynn been accused? Was it possible that the system was so lacking in judgment that it couldn't tell the difference between *Leave It to Beaver* model father Ward Cleaver and a mass murderer like Charles Manson? In the topsy-turvy world of CPS, would the *Brady Bunch* kids be taken into foster care nowadays if the hotline got a call?

Ben and Lynn were married in the fall of 2004, after they had known each other for nine years. A few years later, Lynn became pregnant with twins, a boy and a girl, who were born in June 2007. When the twins were two years old, around Thanksgiving, Lynn got pregnant again, and she gave birth to their third child, Robert, in mid-August 2009.

The twins were excited to have a younger brother. After Robert came home from the hospital, the twins wanted to hold him and be around him as much as they could. They wanted to feed Robert his bottles, though Lynn and Ben wouldn't allow it. The twins could be rambunctious. As newborns, the twins had been more of a handful than Robert, probably because they were smaller and hadn't slept well through the night. Robert, by contrast, rarely fussed. Ben and Lynn agreed that Robert was the easiest baby they had ever seen.

Robert quickly blended into the family's well-established routines. Now, the twins napped and went to bed on schedule, rising early with Ben, who would let Lynn and Robert sleep in for an extra hour. From their new suburban home they had moved to two weeks after Robert's birth, Ben left for work between 7:30 a.m. and 8:30 a.m., and he usually took the 4:53 p.m. train home. Sometimes Lynn would greet him at the park, where the twins loved to watch the nearby trains, and they would all head home together for supper. Bedtime at 7:30 p.m. involved stories, one chosen by each twin to make it fair. Bedtime was usually pretty easy.

Ben was usually the one to put Robert to bed, rocking him on his chest and sometimes falling asleep himself on the sofa. When that happened, Lynn would gently transfer them both into their beds for as much of the night as Robert could sleep through.

By now experienced parents, Lynn and Ben adhered to a clear and consistent disciplinary technique called "One-Two-Three Magic," with a time-out lasting one minute for each year of the child's age. When the twins occasionally misbehaved, they got a two-minute time-out. Of course, Robert was too young for any discipline. His days were filled with feedings and naps. But just as Ben and Lynn had done with the twins, just about every new milestone in his life, from the first hug by each grandma to the first bath, was documented in photos. Later, these family photos proved useful in exonerating Ben and Lynn, though CPS caseworkers never asked Lynn or Ben to see their photo album.

From the beginning, Lynn saw Robert as the "sweetest boy" and a "very chill"[3] baby; nothing fazed him or changed his sunny, calm disposition. Robert cried very little and soothed easily; he was even-tempered. Lynn nursed him every two hours. Other than a few trips to the bathroom, she never left him except when he napped or when Ben took over to watch him. Robert would sometimes be in a Pack 'n Play or a baby swing in the living room. An easy baby was a relief, because the twins were very active and could demand attention.

The weather during the Labor Day weekend was beautiful, so Ben and Lynn took the kids outside to start to get to know their neighbors. They also wanted to check out possible gyms to join, and so they took the twins out to swim at two nearby gyms with pools. To go outside, Robert was strapped into his Snap-N-Go car seat, which was attached to a stroller. Otherwise, he would be draped over Ben's belly in a Babybjörn carrier, in a fashion that Ben later would have to demonstrate in the juvenile court. Nothing seemed remarkable about the Labor Day weekend other than the good weather and the chance to get out into the new neighborhood as a family. Robert gave no hints of any discomfort. It never would be clear if something already was wrong with his leg.

September 10 shaped up to be an especially full day, peppered with appointments. It would be Lynn's first outing with Robert alone. Ben offered to stay with the twins for a special "dad's day." Because Robert had failed an at-birth audiology test, he first went with Lynn to a follow-up appointment with an audiologist at the children's hospital. Fortunately, Robert slept through the entire appointment and passed the test while he slept in his car-seat carrier.

Following that appointment, Lynn had a first-time post-childbirth appointment at her favorite hair salon in Chicago. Exactly when in her appointment-laden day, surrounded by other people, Lynn might have gone on a violent rampage against her son Robert without anyone noticing was a question that naturally surfaced later on, when Lynn and Ben's life during the week of September 10 was put under the CPS and juvenile court's microscope.

It was during Robert's late-afternoon diaper change, when she was already back home awaiting Ben and the twins' return for dinner, that Lynn first recalled noticing that Robert's leg seemed slightly swollen. The possible swelling wasn't alarming, but she thought it bore watching. She couldn't be sure anything was wrong, because Robert did not seem to be in any pain. Ben and the twins arrived home a few minutes after the diaper change. Soon Lynn was preparing dinner, and Robert went into his swing and happily watched as his siblings played nearby.

Shortly after 7:00 p.m., Lynn changed Robert's diaper again while Ben started to put the twins to bed. Alarmed, Lynn suddenly called out to Ben. Robert's leg was extremely swollen. The leg looked very different than just two hours earlier. Something was seriously wrong. The leg looked painful to the touch. Robert seemed a bit irritable, but he wasn't bawling.

Lynn's first thought was that Robert had gotten a bee sting. Ben agreed, for he had seen lot of bees out in their suburban town. Lynn hadn't been outside much with Robert, so she and Ben started to wonder aloud if a spider rather than a bee had bitten Robert. Lynn had seen a spider or two in their new home. Regardless of cause, Robert's left leg now was unmistakably much more swollen than the right.

Lynn immediately worried that he might have a deathly allergy to an insect bite. Her thoughts were racing. She thought, *Holy smokes! If we don't get this kid to a hospital, he might stop breathing.*

Lynn worried that if she moved Robert, she might hurt his leg more. She gently dressed him as she and Ben conferred about getting Robert to an emergency room doctor as soon as possible. They called a new neighbor to ask where to go. Within minutes, Ben headed for the recommended hospital with Robert.

Ben waited about thirty minutes before a nurse examined Robert. The car-seat carrier came in handy, as Robert could stay put until his medical exam. Within another hour, a doctor came to take a look, this time manipulating Robert's leg enough that he started to cry in earnest. An X-ray was prescribed.

By 10:00 p.m., the news came back. Robert's left femur was fractured. Ben was stunned. He immediately asked how the leg could have been broken. The doctor replied tersely, "Force." Telling Ben nothing about what *kind* of force had caused his son's leg to break or when that break likely had occurred, the doctor announced that the State's child abuse hotline had to be called. The police would be called too. The doctor told Ben that this was "standard protocol" for any fracture in a newborn. Ben understood. He had nothing to hide.

The suburban hospital had no orthopedist on duty. And while it also did not have a specialized child abuse team, the staff didn't mention that as a reason why Robert should transfer to a Chicago hospital that night. In fact, three Chicago area hospitals had specialized teams to handle suspected abuse cases.

Lynn decided to spell Ben at the hospital. Relying on the neighbor to watch the twins, she came to be with Robert. Thinking they were going along with a sound plan to get Robert the best orthopedic treatment available and not realizing that the suburban hospital might have had reasons of its own for shifting Robert's care to Chicago, Lynn and Ben quickly agreed to transfer Robert back to the same hospital Lynn had visited that morning for the audiology appointment. Lynn decided to ride with Robert in the ambulance so that she could nurse him on the way.

Unfortunately, Lynn's plan to nurse Robert during her trip into the city didn't work. Paramedics blocked Lynn from feeding her son while they were in transit to the hospital. Ben went home for the night, but he didn't get much sleep. Neither did Lynn—because what awaited her when she got to the hospital with Robert at 1:00 a.m. was not an orthopedic specialist to attend to her son's fracture but a series of child abuse interrogations and threats going to the heart of her role as a mother.

TWO

A "Multidisciplinary Pediatric Consortium" Means Doctors Help Police and Caseworkers to Take the Kids

By the time Lynn got to the children's hospital with Robert, it was 1:00 a.m. When he was finally examined, Robert, the ultracalm baby, was screaming. Lynn hadn't been able to give her baby a proper feeding in the ambulance, so Robert's most recent meal had been at 4:00 p.m. He had missed three feedings. He hadn't been breastfed since Lynn's 2:00 p.m. hair salon appointment, so Lynn was feeling very uncomfortable herself.

Lynn begged the emergency room staff to let her feed her son. She asked the pastor, each nurse, and the first doctor she saw. Each person told her, "No, you can't feed him yet." No one explained why she and Robert needed to wait.

Soon Lynn and Robert were assigned a private room where a hospital social worker could interview Lynn about Robert's injury. Lynn cooperated. She had nothing to hide. She wanted answers herself as to how Robert's leg was fractured.

Lynn reviewed her own eight-year employment history as a social worker. The hospital social worker pressed her for mental health, substance use, and criminal history, but Lynn had none to report. Lynn described how she had spent her day with Robert, mentioning that she had barely taken him out of his car seat, except for his regular feedings at 11:00 a.m. and 2:00 p.m. No traumatic event came to mind, although she mentioned that Robert had seemed a bit fussier than usual during diaper changes since Labor Day. Recalling an odd incident in which Robert had screamed out in his sleep, she still couldn't identify a specific fall or slip. She told the social worker that Ben and she were already "racking their brains." They had come up short.

The social worker wrote a file note stating that the case had been discussed with the "medical team," but it mentioned just one protective service team member: the child abuse fellow (a child abuse pediatrician-in-training), Dr. Sandra Felix. Lynn had yet to meet her. Dr. Felix soon would assume the primary role in providing a medical opinion about the cause of Robert's fracture to the caseworkers assigned to investigate the hotline call. The social worker's note described Lynn as "tearful and very concerned" about how her son could have sustained the injury because he had constantly been in her care. The note also asserted that the social worker advised Lynn "what to expect from CPS" and how the hospital would "contribute."

The social worker did *not* disclose to Lynn, however, that the hospital would be cooperating with the CPS and police investigations *against* Lynn and Ben. Nor did Lynn have any inkling that the doctors on the hospital's CPS trauma team from whom Lynn assumed Robert would get treatment for his injury would eventually become the lead State witnesses against her in a court of law.

Dr. Felix's involvement as a consultant to the CPS agency came through a joint contract between the State of Illinois, the State's child advocacy centers, and the Chicago children's hospitals. The contract called for hospital child protective team doctors to provide opinions to the State in suspected child abuse cases. Although Lynn and Ben were unaware of it, this contract operated in the background through their entire experience with CPS.

No hospital protocol required hospital staff to disclose the existence of this contract to Lynn, even though American Medical Association ethical standards clearly specify that doctors who hold third-party contracts need to disclose those relationships to patients. For example, when a patient gets an insurance evaluation from a doctor, that doctor must disclose that he or she works for the insurance company, too, and not just for the patient. Neither the social worker, Dr. Felix, nor any administrator expressed any concern about a conflict of interest when hospital staff members from whom Lynn sought treatment for Robert's fracture seamlessly shifted to the side of the police, the CPS caseworkers, and the State prosecutors who soon arrayed themselves against the family.

Lynn, therefore, remained unaware of the minefield she was stepping into. Had she been told of Dr. Felix's role in child abuse investigations and had she known the legal peril that faced her and her family, she would have immediately called the two lawyers in her family, including her federal judge mother. But Lynn didn't want to alarm anyone in middle of the night. Ben was the only person she called.

At 1:41 a.m., a resident in the emergency room examined Robert and reported his temperature, weight, lack of bruises, and normal muscle tone. The protective services team ordered a skeletal survey, a head CT scan and an ophthalmology consult, all standard protocol in a child abuse case (although hardly necessary to treat a fracture).

No one explained the purpose of these tests to Lynn. No one asked her for further permission, beyond the initial blanket consent Lynn had signed when she came in with Robert for care of his fracture. No orthopedist came to see Robert. The "treatment" that the protective services team was ordering for Robert was not orthopedic care for Robert's broken leg but a child abuse assessment, with Lynn herself the primary suspect. The additional tests might tell the doctors whether Robert had other suspicious injuries, letting them know how serious an abuse case they had on their hands.

With an increasingly hungry child on her lap, Lynn tried to calm Robert. Lynn didn't question the members of the medical team about the reasons for the additional tests. She assumed that the doctors knew what they were doing and that they had Robert's well-being uppermost in their minds, just as she did.

At 2:00 a.m., an emergency CPS caseworker arrived at the hospital, looking for Robert. The caseworker's supervisor had already instructed him to prepare a safety plan for Robert's siblings. Because of that instruction, the caseworker knew, even before he met Lynn, that Lynn would not be leaving the hospital with Robert. Someone else would have to take over as the primary caregiver for the three children. The caseworker made cursory notes of his "good faith" initial contact with Robert: Robert had been "crying on the bed" and "had been admitted to the hospital."

As the caseworker started to talk to Lynn, nurses streamed in and out of the room. The caseworker handed her a form notification of her "rights" during the CPS investigation, but Lynn barely glanced at it. She was eager to finish the interview quickly, and she was tired.

The caseworker asked Lynn to recount her day—her third retelling. The caseworker's interview notes later would be transferred into the computerized CPS investigation file that the State had opened in Lynn's name. While accurate for the most part, there was one odd note in the file Lynn eventually saw. The caseworker's note stated that Lynn had gone into the city to "sell her condo" right after the audiology appointment on September 10. That was false. Lynn had been to the condo building to give Robert his morning feeding at a friend's home, but the condo had been sold a few weeks before.

Odd notes like that one are hardly anomalies in CPS files. Parents don't get the right to review the notes of CPS caseworkers for accuracy until weeks or months later, after an investigation is over or if a court case begins. Because parents can't see these notes right away, it is impossible to correct misinformation quickly. In the scheme of things, this particular mistake was inconsequential, but another mistaken note about Lynn's family history, made later in the evening by Dr. Felix, would prove much more significant.

At the conclusion of this first round of questions, the caseworker told Lynn that she had to find someone else to watch all of her children. Indeed, she had to find someone other than her husband to care for her twins at home *immediately.* By now, the twins were sound asleep in their beds, unaware of any drama at the hospital. The caseworker gave her an ultimatum: find someone within 20 to 30 minutes, or else he would go to their home and take the twins into State protective custody.

The perfectly healthy twins were suddenly at risk of being seized from their beds and placed into the custody of the State of Illinois that night. These happy-go-lucky children would then go to an emergency shelter or be put with strangers in foster care. Lynn was at a complete loss as to what to do.

In his own notes of this 2:00 a.m. meeting, the CPS caseworker dutifully and accurately wrote that Lynn was "very emotional and began to cry when discussing the safety plan" that would separate her from her children.

A few minutes later, the caseworker reported back to his own supervisor that Lynn and her husband had no family members in the Chicago area. The supervisor told the caseworker to inquire about friends and neighbors. The caseworker's 2:00 a.m. note explicitly recited the ultimatum that an appropriate friend or neighbor must be found, stating, "If not, PC [protective custody] of the children would be taken."

It seemed possible, even likely, that the family would be torn apart in the middle of the night.

By now, Lynn was in a waking nightmare. The neighbor who had watched the twins while Ben went to the hospital with Robert had returned to her own home for the night. Lynn called Ben right away. She reported the CPS caseworker's ultimatum that Ben also could no longer be alone with his children. If they didn't find someone quickly, the children would be picked up and taken from their home that very night.

Frightened but full of resolve, Ben and Lynn breathed a momentary sign of relief when their new neighbor was willing, at 2:00 a.m., to let the twins come to her home to stay overnight. For the moment, Ben and Lynn averted disaster, if only until morning.

The caseworker was temporarily satisfied that he didn't need to initiate the protective custody action. But he still had to go out to Ben and Lynn's home as soon as he finished up with Lynn and Robert at the hospital.

After the caseworker left the hospital, Robert went for his full skeletal survey. No other injuries besides the left femur fracture were noted. At 3:13 a.m., the CT scan was taken, and it showed no evidence of any bleeding or other concerns. The tests that Lynn had allowed without having been told their real nontreatment purpose showed nothing more than the single, isolated femur fracture to Robert's leg.

At 4:15 a.m., the overnight caseworker arrived at Ben and Lynn's home in the suburbs of Chicago. He questioned Ben, who, like Lynn, couldn't provide a clear explanation for Robert's fracture. Ben told the caseworker that his mother was already driving in from out of state—several hours away—to care for the children in Ben and Lynn's home. The caseworker looked in on the sleeping twins at 4:30 a.m. and mercifully let them sleep through the night. The caseworker allowed the neighbor to stay to watch the kids while they waited for the paternal grandmother to arrive.

By 4:35 a.m., the overnight caseworker had run a mandatory background check, making sure that all the substitute care providers for the children had no recorded history of abuse or neglect known to the State of Illinois. Now it was Ben who had to leave his house, the caseworker announced. Ben's separation from his children was necessary, the caseworker said, in order to allow the twins to remain in their beds. He claimed that those were the "rules."

In reality, there weren't any such rules. Caseworkers operated under an assumption of power that gave them broad discretion to act on a variety of assumptions, hunches, and customs with a smattering of laws and policies in the background. There was a custom of dictating to families that they had to separate from their children during physical abuse investigations where a specified perpetrator had yet to be pinpointed. No one in the family knew that the demands the caseworker made were mere customs. None of them knew the actual legal rules under which the CPS caseworkers operated. With two lawyers in the family, Ben's father and Lynn's mother would ask questions soon enough about the caseworker's legal authority to issue these demands, but neither Ben nor Lynn was in a position to argue against the caseworker that night.

The CPS system liberally authorized its caseworkers to decide on an appropriate safety plan, even without first having definite evidence pointing to child abuse. Through a series of constitutional cases and legislative reform proposals beginning in 2000 and continuing to the present time, I worked with teams of lawyers to try to outlaw exactly the sort of ultimatum that the emergency caseworker delivered to Ben and Lynn. (How these legal cases and proposals fared in the courts and legislature is discussed in chapters 4 and 14.)

But there were no court precedents on the books in Illinois to stop the case-worker from telling Ben and Lynn that suddenly, on the strength of the hotline call alone, they couldn't live in their own home with their children. The legal precedents necessary to help a family in Ben and Lynn's position only began to take shape in 2011, and even then, the State's implementation of those prec-edents would be spotty at best.

Ben understood that if he wanted to save his children from being seized that night, he had better leave the house and trust his neighbor to watch the twins until his mother arrived in the morning.

At 5:30 a.m., as Ben was leaving his home and the neighbor was dozing during her overnight shift with the twins, the hospital staff finally gave Lynn permission to feed her son.

At 8:10 a.m., the attending emergency room physician filed a request for an "orthopedic consult" and a "social work recommendation." According to these notes, Robert was to be discharged "when safe," without specifying how Robert's safety was to be determined.

At 8:45 a.m., a medical student examined Robert, who was by now sleeping soundly. The sole prescribed treatment for Robert was Tylenol for pain, a future "orthopedic consult," a "follow up with the protective services team," and a "consult with ophthalmology" to test for retinal hemorrhages (to rule out other signs of child abuse).

Soon after 8:45 a.m. (the specific time was never recorded in the medical file), Lynn finally met with the child abuse pediatrician-in-training: Dr. Sandra Felix, the doctor who would assume the lead role in the child abuse investigation under the hospital's contract with the State CPS agency. Dr. Felix, whose official title was Child Abuse Fellow, had a medical license and had completed her general pediatrics training although she had not yet taken her pediatric board exam. Now she was in a two-year subspecialty training program with the hospital's child protective services team. She hoped to run a child abuse team at a major hospital herself someday.

The brand-new subspecialty, child abuse pediatrics, was growing. Indeed, the field's subspecialty board-certification process, approved by the American Academy of Pediatrics and other medical-board examination authorities, wouldn't begin examinations for another two months, in November 2009.[1] While no doctors yet held the coveted board certification, the children's hospital caring for Robert offered one of the nation's leading child abuse fellowship programs. By the time she questioned Lynn, Dr. Felix had already been involved in 1,000 child abuse evaluations.

Though assigned to Robert's case, Dr. Felix did not put all her notes into Robert's medical file. That was typical of her team; they kept their own notes for their reports in separate confidential files. The protective services team of social workers and doctors might make occasional notes in the child's medical chart, too. Dr. Felix's calls with CPS caseworkers were not recorded anywhere in Robert's medical file, even though the CPS file documented calls to Dr. Felix.

By the time Lynn spoke to Dr. Felix, she was exhausted. Lynn had snatched only 45 minutes of sleep all night. For Dr. Felix, the day was just starting. For Lynn, the night had never ended.

Like all the residents and other doctors who came in and out of Robert's room that night, Dr. Felix presented herself as part of Robert's treatment team. She didn't let on to Lynn that she was in a training program to become a board-certified child abuse pediatrician. Nor did she or anyone else who spoke to Lynn that night explain that Dr. Felix worked under a contract with the State of Illinois CPS system. Eventually, Dr. Felix would prepare a Multidisciplinary Pediatric Evaluation and Education Consortium (MPEEC) report, which she would provide exclusively to the CPS investigation team,[2] not giving a copy to Lynn or Ben. When Lynn and Ben later asked to get a copy of Dr. Felix's report, she refused, telling them to get it from the CPS team. This exclusive reporting to CPS, not the parents, was part of the MPEEC protocol.

Dr. Felix was not, strictly speaking, a regular member of Robert's medical treatment team. The sole medical treatment Robert ever needed was orthopedic care. As of 8:45 a.m., he had yet to see an orthopedist. But pursuant to its MPEEC contract with the State, the hospital assigned Dr. Felix to examine Robert, question Lynn and report her conclusion to the police and CPS team that would investigate the hotline call. It was the State of Illinois that sought her opinion as to whether Robert had been abused. Lynn wasn't asking for such an assessment. Ordering additional abuse-focused tests and questioning Lynn while she was at the hospital seeking treatment for her son was convenient for the State and certainly furthered its interests in investigating whether Lynn or Ben had abused their son. Had the child abuse doctors or hospital staff notified Lynn of the true purposes of these additional tests and Dr. Felix's inquiry, Lynn might have balked, refusing consent while she sought independent advice and counsel.

It would have been hard to explain Dr. Felix's role to Lynn. The head of the hospital's protective services team would later testify in another case (discussed in chapter 17) that he held "dual" roles as a protective services doctor. He claimed he functioned as both as a treater for the child in his hospital's care and as a forensic consultant. When pressed, he elaborated that the "treatment" component of his role was "providing consultation to CPS caseworkers."

That's an odd definition of treatment. Medical ethics, like other professional ethics systems, prohibits practitioners from having two conflicting masters or from acting on behalf of another master against the interests of the patient, unless the role of the second master is disclosed and accepted by the patient. The MPEEC program placed child abuse pediatricians into children's treatment teams caring for the child at the behest of their parents and at the same time made them prosecution team members whose master was the State of Illinois. It was an uneasy combination, to say the least.

It was impossible to pinpoint when, on the night of September 10 and the morning of September 11, Lynn, lacking any notification or clarification of her right to refuse to speak to Dr. Felix, lost the rights to direct Robert's medical evaluations, diagnosis, and treatment or to consent to tests that had no obvious treatment benefit to him. Exploiting Lynn's interest in getting answers to questions about how Robert's leg got fractured and her interest in cooperating with medical authorities presenting themselves as his treaters, the CPS system—now working hand in hand with the hospital's child abuse doctors—moved quickly to restrict the family's rights in the name of protecting Robert from his parents, who had vigilantly sought medical care for their son.

Exhausted but still eager to get answers, Lynn responded to every question that Dr. Felix asked. Dr. Felix found Lynn to be very cooperative.

Like most pediatricians, Dr. Felix started her interview of Lynn by taking a family health history, including general mental health questions. Lynn had nothing to hide, so she answered honestly that she thought a grandparent had a mental health condition although it had never been formally diagnosed.

Dr. Felix misunderstood. She put a note into her own file stating that it was *Lynn* who had a mental health issue. This same mistaken note would become the basis for hours of testimony and arguments, the sort of foray that lawyers call a "fishing expedition."

Without requesting any of Lynn own medical records and without giving any consideration to Lynn having been up all night at the time she was being questioned, Dr. Felix soon provided to the CPS caseworkers, courtesy of her mistaken note, her own arm chair diagnosis: Lynn had "mental health concerns." Dr. Felix was no psychiatrist, and Lynn hadn't been notified that *she* was being evaluated for anything related to her own health or functioning.

Dr. Felix's claim that Lynn had a mental health condition was not just unsupported; it was false. Not a single person who knew Lynn, who treated her medical conditions, or who worked with her ever reported any mental health issues whatsoever. But if Lynn seemed stressed, exhausted, and anxious on the morning after the worst night in her life, it would have been reasonable to conclude that no parent is immune to signs of stress.

Dr. Felix's note came with no such disclaimers. There was no acknowledgment of Lynn's sleepless, interrogation-filled night of worry about her son, conditions that would make the most stable parent seem frazzled and distressed. Also, the report Dr. Felix gave to the CPS team did not mention her own lack of training in adult psychiatry.

Of course, Dr. Felix asked Lynn about possible explanations for Robert's leg fracture. Lynn tried her best to answer, but again she came up short. After all, getting answers to that very question and finding out if a genetic condition could account for Robert's fracture were the main reasons Lynn had wanted Robert to be transferred to the children's hospital.

By 9:00 a.m. on September 11, Robert was cleared to go home. By now, Ben's mother and father had arrived in Illinois, having driven through the night. The State wasn't looking for any evidence to contradict its suspicion that either Ben or Lynn had abused Robert and caused his fracture. Fortunately, the caseworker agreed that Lynn and Ben could come home during the day, but they had to stay elsewhere overnight. Moreover, they would be allowed into their own home only if they remained under the watchful eye of a grandparent at all times.

Although Ben and Lynn's family life had been turned upside down over-night, the CPS system had just begun its investigation. The overnight CPS caseworker who had required Ben to leave the home was not the regular CPS caseworker; he was just the first responder. Known as a "mandate worker," this first caseworker's limited responsibility was to attempt within 24 hours to see any child who was the subject of a hotline call.

At least in Illinois, any CPS caseworker has authority under state law to seize children from their parents if there are reasonable grounds to believe the child is in immediate danger. Doctors and police, too, have the same extraordinary power under the state law.[3] States have differing rules on who can seize children without parental consent. Several states limit that power to police.

The mandate worker hadn't seen any immediate danger to Robert. He did not have any specific suspicion that either Ben or Lynn, or both of them together, had been responsible for causing Robert's injury. Nevertheless, he clearly had threatened Lynn and Ben in succession with taking their children into State protective custody if they did not quickly make alternative plans for their three children's round-the-clock care.

Soon, a new caseworker would be assigned to conduct the full CPS investigation. Ben and Lynn had no idea what to expect next, but they knew that their ordeal and their quest for answers had just begun.

THREE

The Investigation Begins in Earnest with "Hurry Up and Wait"

Ben and Lynn didn't have to wait long before they heard from the primary investigator, Janelle Green. The overnight caseworker had completed a Child Endangerment Risk Assessment Protocol form—a mandatory assessment required at the beginning of an Illinois CPS case.[1] The form was to be completed every five days whenever a safety plan separated parents from their children during an investigation. But the five-day review policy wasn't followed religiously. Janelle Green would be the first to admit that she didn't meet that particular requirement in Robert's investigation. More conscientious than some caseworkers, however, she started in on her investigation of the hotline call soon after it was assigned to her on the morning of September 11.

The mandate worker's supervisor took just one more step in the investigation before passing it on Green. She wrote a series of standardized directives applicable to any "bone fractures by abuse" investigation (as to Robert) and any "risk of harm due to environment injurious" investigation (as to the twins). The allegation of "environment injurious" arose from the theory that *if* Robert had been abused by his parents, then his twin siblings were also living in a dangerous environment. The supervisor pulled up the directives from the protocol in the CPS Rule and Procedure Manual.[2]

The supervisor listed eleven specific instructions, the most significant of which directed the assigned caseworker to do the following:

1. Secure documentation that a fracture exists and an exact description of the fracture. Interview all physicians directly involved with the treatment of the reporting injury (e.g., attending physician, radiologist or orthopedist).

2. Get all medical records and X-rays/films.

3. Do a timeline for the injury. Obtain detailed explanatory statements from each person with knowledge of the injury. Interview the parents regarding where they were at the time of the injury and which other children were present.

4. Get all police report history on the family.

The full list was reasonable but barebones; it skipped the required step of asking the parents for their own list of witnesses, including character and witnesses who might have observed Robert at the time his injury was likely to have occurred. It also did not seek any family history, birth history, or social history for Robert. For that sort of social history and context, it was the CPS's custom to rely on hospital social workers' accounts.

The list of tasks Green was expected to complete also was thin regarding any required assessment of the relatives who were to become the children's full-time caregivers. As long as Ben's mother passed a minimal background check showing she had no reported prior history of abuse or neglect, she could care for the children with the CPS system's blessing. An in-depth interview of Ben's mother to learn how she approached caring for her grandkids was not performed. Fortunately for Robert and the twins, however, their grandmother needed no special instructions.

There wasn't a hint of concern about the disruption the CPS agency caused the grandmother by demanding that she stop living her own life for an unspecified period of time to become the full-time caregiver for her grandchildren. As for the delicate balance of becoming the monitor of her son and daughter-in-law's interaction with their children, including the expectation that she would report to the State CPS caseworker if anything went wrong, there was no discussion whatsoever.

Under safety plans, it was routine to expect grandparents to care for children. Disrupting their lives was not part of the caseworker's concerns—unless and until the grandparents refused to continue to help out. If the grandmother started to say she couldn't care for the children any longer, another arrangement—possibly taking the children into foster care—would have to be made. Unless that occurred, without so much as a thank-you, the grandmother was expected to do everything asked of her, ask no questions, and make no demands.

These omissions aside, had Caseworker Green followed the task list that the mandate worker's supervisor provided, the course of the investigation into Robert's fracture might have been different. While it was expected that she would talk to Robert's treating doctors, this requirement was not something that Caseworker Green or her primary supervisor, Kirby Long, took seriously. What they intended to do was to talk to the child abuse doctor, Dr. Felix, period. And ultimately, that's exactly what they did.

At about noon on September 11, after first calling the hospital social worker, Caseworker Green's next call was to Ben's mom in order to confirm that she would supervise the children under the safety plan. Ben's mom informed Green that the copy of the safety plan that the mandate worker left them was illegible. Green promised to come out with a legible one quickly. After providing all information necessary to run both child abuse and criminal background checks, by 4:00 p.m., Ben's mother was cleared to become the children's full-time caregiver. The responsibility for the children's care was transferred by oral approval. Ben's signed agreement on the safety plan was not considered essential, apparently.

Janelle Green's initial investigative calls started with the child abuse team at the hospital. According to Green's first note, a hospital social worker told her that Robert had "a large injury for such a small child." It is hard to know if the social worker really said such a thing or if that note represented Green's interpretation. Referencing Robert's audiology appointment on the morning of September 10, the social worker mentioned that since Robert had stayed in the car-seat carrier through the entire exam, "they may not have noticed an injury."

The social worker told Green that Dr. Sandra Felix was now completing a "multidisciplinary review" of the case, the MPEEC report. As for Ben and Lynn's alleged responsibility for the fracture, the social worker simply told Green that the parents "could not explain how the injury could have occurred."

Now that the parents were no longer living in their own home, it seemed that the CPS caseworkers were no longer in a hurry to investigate the possible explanations for the child's injury. As far as the CPS caseworkers were concerned, child abuse pediatricians were the experts whose opinions mattered. It would be inappropriate for CPS caseworkers, not trained in medical science, to second-guess a medical expert's opinion. Gathering and synthesizing other medical opinions to reach a conclusion as to whether a child had been abused was something Green and her supervisor viewed as the responsibility of the child abuse pediatrician.

While such deference to the child abuse pediatrician was the practice, it contradicted the CPS agency's own rules; those rules explicitly required direct CPS caseworker consultation with other treating doctors. In a bone fracture case, for example, the CPS rules expressly said that caseworkers were supposed to obtain confirmation of the fracture from an orthopedist or radiologist.[3]

For the CPS caseworkers, having a child abuse pediatrician on a case made their job fairly straightforward; it was largely a matter of waiting for that final child abuse pediatric opinion. Once the CPS team had the opinion in hand, they would be in a position to make decisions about formally taking the kids into the state foster care system—a strong possibility if the child abuse pediatrician believed the child had been abused and was willing to testify about her conclusion. The CPS team would also then be able to decide if the parents or other individuals should be listed as child abuse perpetrators in the State's child-abuse register. At the conclusion of the investigation, they would decide whether the allegations were "indicated" or "unfounded" and mark the register accordingly.[4] A court decision wasn't necessary to label a child "abused" and the parents responsible for that abuse.[5]

Before proceeding to juvenile court or issuing an indicated finding of child abuse against the parent in the register, however, it was essential first to get the child abuse pediatrician's written MPEEC report. Often that required a bit of a wait. Without the MPEEC report, the CPS caseworker couldn't make a final decision as to whether the evidence supported a conclusion that the child's fracture was due to abuse, an accident, or a medical condition. If the CPS team decided to take the children into State protective custody, the State's Attorney would need to see that report, too, before filing a petition in juvenile court at the required 48-hour mark after the children were formally taken from their parents.

It didn't matter how eager Ben, Lynn, and Ben's mother were for Caseworker Green to get the final report from Dr. Felix. The family would just have to wait.

While "MPEEC" stands for Multidisciplinary Pediatric Evaluation and Education Consortium, it's a misleading label as well as a mouthful. It sounds lofty and important, a solid team effort to get a cross section of doctors from different medical disciplines together to review records and share their opinions. But at Dr. Felix's hospital, the MPEEC disciplines do not include medical specialists in areas like radiology, orthopedics, neurosurgery, or genetics—doctors whose training and experience might enlighten the discussion by providing the latest research on bones, tissues, injury mechanisms, diseases, and new treatments for injured children.

The MPEEC's consortium *does* include the hospital's child abuse doctors and social workers. But the other disciplines it includes are those responsible for prosecuting parents for child abuse: the police and CPS, all coordinated by the Chicago Child Advocacy Center. What sounds like a broad attempt to get medical consensus operated in effect as a prosecution-focused task force. Nor do the doctors from other specialties typically review MPEEC reports. Indeed, these other doctors rarely are asked to verify the information that the child abuse doctors attribute to them.

I have won a couple of cases—meaning that child abuse charges against my clients were dropped after trials—after I have called another doctor from the child abuse pediatrician's own hospital to testify only to discover that this doctor held a different opinion than the child abuse doctor had ascribed to him or her in an MPEEC report. Once, not knowing what her ultimate opinion would be, I took a big chance when I called a radiologist to testify. But it turned out she believed that a child's injury was due to a direct impact (banging the head) and not shaking, contrary to the child abuse pediatrician's claim. That disagreement came as a nice surprise. Since the toddler involved in that case had been seen banging his own head on his high chair, the radiologist's disagreement with the child abuse pediatrician helped convince the judge that the parents were innocent of shaking the child, which the child abuse pediatrician had claimed.

This experience provided a telling example of a child abuse pediatrician shading another doctor's opinion in order to support her abuse conclusion. Likely aware that such an opinion might differ from her own, the child abuse pediatrician had studiously avoided asking the radiologist for any opinion about the injury's cause.[6] I quickly learned that child abuse pediatricians, like other professionals, could be fallible and might, at times, operate under motives that were not quite as benign as their lofty titles suggest. Unfortunately, there was no available process other than in the courtroom for parents to challenge child abuse pediatricians' medical opinion or to correct their error. That was the job I had to do, but I always needed the explanations of other doctors to be able to convince a judge.

Caseworker Green did not have to take any action in order to get a formal MPEEC assignment. The hospital's child protective services team automatically took on the MPEEC-reporting responsibility as soon as they knew that the CPS hotline had been called.

Ben and Lynn would later ask why, when Dr. Felix had questioned Lynn after her sleepless night at the hospital, no one had told them about the hospital's MPEEC contract, which called for Dr. Felix to report to the State of Illinois CPS system and not to them. Why had a secret medical consultation with the State happened behind the parents' backs? Who had created this system of medical advocates working at the behest of the CPS system, and whose actions led to their children's removal from their loving care?

When Ben learned later that Dr. Felix's primary function was to consult with CPS as to whether she thought Robert had been abused, he became livid. With his training in handling complex insurance policies, where disclosure of third-party relationships is essential before any policy can be issued, Ben wondered how a hospital from which parents sought care for their child could work hand in hand with State agents trying to take children from their parents. It was galling, too, that Ben's insurance was billed for the tests the hospital's child protection doctors decided were needed for the child abuse assessment, when those tests had nothing to do with treating Robert's fracture. It felt like a giant trap.

After learning of Dr. Felix's role, Ben reached a critical juncture; he started to shift from feeling like the victim to becoming an advocate. Anger can be therapeutic, and so it was with Ben as he began to realize how he and Lynn had been set up. Ben started to focus on what he could do to stop the assault on families that he now understood had its roots in the hidden State MPEEC contracts. Lynn, on the other hand, was just trying to hold it together so that the kids would not be taken from their home.

Into the afternoon of September 11, as Janelle Green began her initial contacts on the newly assigned investigation, Robert and Lynn remained at the hospital. They had to wait for Janelle Green to tell a hospital social worker that Robert could be discharged to his grandmother's care. As evening approached, they eventually were allowed to leave with Ben's parents. Just 24 hours had passed since the discovery of Robert's swollen leg, but it felt like an eternity.

A pediatric orthopedist, Dr. Miller, finally saw Robert that afternoon, just before the family left the hospital. She answered their questions about Robert's injury, assuring them that a speedy full recovery was likely. She adjusted Robert's splint, which had been put on at the suburban hospital.

That splint, plus some Tylenol, remained the only treatment Robert received for his broken leg.

Unbeknown to them, as they were leaving the hospital, Dr. Felix was giving her first oral report to Caseworker Green. Green's note of the conversation recounts that while "Lynn was very cooperative and very nice" in her interview with the doctor, Lynn "could not give any history for the injury at all." Lynn reported that Robert never cried in pain and he was never inconsolable. The note recounted the tests that Robert had been given and that he had a fresh "spiral femur fracture" with no signs of healing in the last three to four days. Dr. Felix also shared the information that Robert had a pediatrician in Chicago but didn't provide the name.

Caseworker Green's initial contacts sufficed for her first day. She didn't make it out to the family's home to provide a more legible safety plan, leaving the family to its own devices for the next three days.

Ben and Lynn didn't consider flouting the safety plan by staying in their home overnight. Trying to make the best of their precarious situation, Ben and Lynn stayed with friends. They were not about to take any risks. Going against CPS's directives could land their children into foster care.

Never thinking he had anything to hide, Ben willingly talked to the police on September 11. That interview went well. The police officer told Janelle Green, when she resumed her investigation on September 15, that he "did not have a sense of abuse" in the family's home. She went to meet Ben and Lynn at their home. At 2:30 p.m., she noted contacts with each person in the home, including each child. She provided a required written CPS notice of investigation to Lynn and Ben.

This notice was the same version my colleagues and I had hammered out in federal court in 2003. Prior to our successful litigation in the first phase of *Dupuy v. McDonald*,[7] the CPS system misleadingly would tell parents and caregivers who work with children that investigative findings were entirely confidential. To their dismay, oftentimes CPS immediately notified these parents' employers that CPS had registered child abuse findings against them. Parents would be summarily fired before they had any chance to prove their innocence. The prior notices hadn't explained parents and caregivers' rights to a neutral review of the evidence against them in order to protect their careers. Fortunately, the notice Ben and Lynn got was a marked improvement over the prior misleading notices that the CPS system used for many years before the federal court intervened.

As a licensed clinical social worker, Lynn already knew that a child abuse finding could ruin her career and prevent her from going back to work as a social worker, as she planned to do when the children were older. Lynn was already on guard, but the notice identifying her as a target of a child abuse investigation shocked her nevertheless.

During Green's home visit, Robert was asleep in his grandmother's arms. She noted simply that she saw him in a leg cast. Her notes from interviewing Lynn consumed two full single-spaced pages. Green recorded how Lynn reported spending September 10 before she noticed Robert's leg had swollen up. Lynn told her that when she had changed Robert on the floor of the salon, he was "a little fussy." She mentioned she had handed Robert to her hair stylist, Susan, but could see him the whole time. There is no verbatim account in the notes, however, and no recording. Lynn repeated the account of noticing Robert's swollen leg at about 7:00 p.m., noting that Ben already was reading to the twins before bedtime.

Lynn had only one small request of Green: could she be allowed to be alone when she breastfed Robert? While she loved her mother-in-law, Lynn viewed the feeding time as a special time to be with Robert alone. Green was quick and firm in her response: "No." The family's safety plan, supposedly a voluntary agreement, had to stay in place, according to Green, because Robert's injury "could not be explained."

With that modest request turned down, Lynn signed the updated safety plan, and Green left a copy. The paternal grandmother was expected to supervise the parents' contact with their children at all times, including during Lynn's breastfeeding, lest Lynn snap and batter her baby boy. The CPS system simply couldn't afford to take the chance on this breastfeeding mother of a newborn baby.

Caseworker Green next went through the house with Ben. It passed the safety inspection. She observed that the twins had no signs of abuse or neglect—no bruises or scars of any sort. She talked to the grandmother, who asked, reasonably enough, how long the investigation would take, for she had left her own life in another state. She loved her grandchildren but hadn't planned to live with them indefinitely. Caseworker Green's answer was evasive: the law gave her 60 days to complete the investigation.

The final interview of the afternoon was with Ben. Ben highlighted what an easy baby Robert had been. If Robert ever cried, he consoled immediately. Ben gave Green names of his kids' pediatrician, the neighbors who helped them on the evening of September 10, and another new friend he had met in the area, as Green had forgotten to ask Lynn for any character references. Ben confirmed that he had no history of violence, no medical or mental health issues, and no issues with alcohol or drugs—all standard but intrusive questions that he willingly answered, eager to get the investigation done as soon as possible.

When Ben heard that the safety plan would continue for at least the next two weeks while the caseworker waited to get a final report from Dr. Felix, he became visibly upset. Not willing to put the children at risk of being taken from the home, he also signed the safety plan. Like Lynn, he had become a parent the State didn't trust to be alone with his own children. Concerned about what Dr. Felix was telling Janelle Green, he decided to call Dr. Felix himself.

As a final demand, Green told Ben that the twins had to go back to the hospital's affiliate office for full skeletal survey exams. Ben asked who would be responsible for paying for the radiological tests. She told him that the family would have to assume the cost. Ben politely responded that cost sharing with CPS might be "more appropriate." Green then modified her language, clarifying that the skeletal surveys weren't a "requirement"; they were a "request to ensure the safety of the children." In other words, Ben was free to thumb his nose at the request for the skeletal surveys, but at his peril. The State now viewed the twins, who didn't have a scratch on them, as potential abuse victims. Ben was being told to subject his twins to radiation in order to disprove the State's baseless suspicion that they, too, had unexplained injuries due to abuse.

By now, the burden had inexorably shifted to Ben and Lynn to prove to the satisfaction of CPS caseworkers that their children were safe and healthy in their own home with their own parents. The parents' rights to choose medical providers and to determine when their children needed to have X-rays were slowly being stripped from them—at least if they wanted to cooperate with the investigation in order to keep the kids. Nothing Ben or Lynn said or did seemed to make a difference. It was Dr. Felix, who had never talked to Ben, who held the key to their family's fate.

Ben completed the interview with Janelle Green. He saw no reason for the intrusive skeletal X-rays for the twins, but he needed time to think.

The next day, September 16, Green's supervisor, Kirby Long, reviewed the notes from the investigation with his own superior, Kim Ford. Under CPS policy, this level of review was appropriate because the children had been deemed "unsafe" and had been living under a safety plan since September 11. Kim Ford's notes directed the team to update their case notes, to submit their information to the hospital's child protection team, and to interview police.

Later that same afternoon, Green called the nurse at the suburban hospital where Ben had first taken Robert. This nurse was the not-so-secret hotline caller. Because the nurse had told Ben that the hotline would be called, it was easy enough to figure out who had called, even though the caller's identity was confidential under state and federal law. The nurse noted that Robert had cried when his leg was repositioned but not when he was resting. Green got no description of how long Robert had cried when his leg was moved, a critical omission of an important detail.

The next day, the police officer confirmed that he had interviewed Ben. Police, CPS, and the Chicago hospital's child abuse team by now were working hand in hand on the investigation of the possible abuse that caused Robert's leg to be broken.

Over the next several days, Ben and Lynn started to tire of their over-nights away from home, the new restrictions, and the uncertainty about the investigation. Wanting to plan for appointments back home, Ben's mother was getting a bit restless too. So Ben and Lynn requested that Green add some friends as new safety plan supervisors who could watch them with their children. This step would give Ben's mother a short break.

On September 22, Green went to the home again and noted that the family was managing "as well as could be expected." While Robert's leg swelled some at night and he was fussy at times, his disposition otherwise was excellent. Lynn authorized Green to talk to the kids' regular pediatrician. When Green observed Robert in his grandmother's arms, other than the broken leg, he looked just fine. So did the twins. The family appeared picture perfect.

On September 23, 2009, Ben's dad decided to send a four-page letter to Green, first introducing himself to her and then vouching for his son and daughter-in-law. Noting first that he had seen them once a month since the twins were born, he referred to them as "ideal parents" who were "caring, loving and patient even when the twins are 'acting out.'" He mentioned his own and his wife's excitement when Lynn became pregnant with Robert and noted how easy Robert was to care for.

While everyone wished that Ben and Lynn could have provided a history of how Robert's injury had occurred, Ben's dad wrote that Ben had been genuinely surprised and confused when he had learned of the fracture. The letter advanced a series of potential causes for Robert's fracture, from having his leg accidentally tangled in car-seat straps to being stepped on inadvertently by one of the twins. He urged the CPS team to consider that "these are credible, trustworthy young professionals who care dearly about their children. Their lives, their accomplishments, their upbringing, and their family all argue strongly that they are telling the truth." Because the investigation had been the most traumatizing event in Ben's and Lynn's lives, Ben's dad urged the caseworker to conclude her investigation quickly.

Despite this eloquent plea from Ben's father, the parents' credibility didn't receive a moment's attention from Green or her superiors. It would take another two months before the answer to the question of whether Ben and Lynn were truthful people would matter to anyone. Ben's dad did not hear back from Janelle Green. The next time anyone in the family saw or spoke to Green was on a night she and the other members of the family would never forget—nor will I.

By the time Ben's dad sent this letter to the caseworker Green, Ben had called my office. The family had decided it was time to get legal help.

FOUR

It's Fine to Take the Kids, Unless the State Is Lying

Was what had happened to Ben and Lynn and their kids so far lawful? Clearly, both the CPS mandate worker who interviewed Lynn at the hospital and demanded the initial safety plan and Janelle Green acted as if there was nothing improper about requiring the parents to leave their home. Indeed, they behaved as if they were just following established protocols. After all, the first safety plan had been directed by the mandate worker's supervisor. Green's pat answers to Ben's questions and her instructions concerning the family's expected behavior during the investigation suggested that her own chain of command at the CPS agency approved of the steps she was taking. If anything, because the CPS caseworkers had allowed the kids to stay home with their grandparents, the CPS caseworkers saw their actions as benign and reasonable. They knew they could have caused the family more disruption if they had taken the kids into foster care.

Ben or Lynn had been effectively ejected from their own home by State authorities and separated from their very young children, and Lynn had been denied the ability to breastfeed Robert at night. Operating under claims of Illinois legal authority, the caseworkers nevertheless had offered them no information as to their rights to refuse the safety plan, no real choices in the matter, and no recourse to object through proper legal channels. The CPS caseworkers assigned to the investigation had targeted them as child abusers, effectively telling them to do as they were told if they wanted to keep legal custody of their kids and prevent the children's removal into foster care. No one from the CPS system had yet come before a judge to prove a case against Ben or Lynn. No one in any neutral role had reviewed the evidence the caseworkers had amassed against Ben and Lynn, if such evidence existed. After Ben and Lynn had been living for weeks under orders and instructions by caseworkers, they started to wonder about the CPS team's legal authority to compel them to sign the safety plan.

I'm often confronted with exactly this sort of question. As soon as Ben and Lynn hired me as their family defense attorney, they asked me this question themselves. Reasonably enough, clients like Ben and Lynn think I should know families' rights and recourse in this situation. Clients ask that I explain the State CPS caseworkers' legal authority for their actions, usually starting with the question, "Can the State really do this to us?" They expect me to know since I'm a well-trained and experienced lawyer who specializes in family defense.

In a way, I *do* know the legal answers; I can cite constitutional decisions about the fundamental rights of parents to raise their children and the requirement that no constitutional right can be abridged by state officials, including CPS caseworkers, without "due process of law." I can explain that "due process of law" includes the right to be heard by a neutral decision maker before essential rights lawfully can be forfeited.[1] In fact, I've litigated quite a few due process cases, and it isn't terribly hard to give an answer about what the law on the books provides.

But the law on the books is not the law in practice. The conflict between the law on the books and the law in practice makes such questions about the legality of CPS's actions toward Ben and Lynn exceedingly murky.

The constitutional right of families to raise their children is considered "fundamental," according to U.S. Supreme Court holdings since the 1920s.[2] The rights at stake, according to the highest court, are "more precious" than property rights.[3] It follows that a commanding State justification must be given before parents can be compelled to modify their parenting decisions. Legally, fit and able parents are entitled to call the shots about where their children live, what medical care and education the children receive, and with whom the children are allowed to associate. The parent's rights are strongly protected, as the Supreme Court declared in a landmark decision 2000 decision, even where the person a parent doesn't want his or her children to associate with is the child's own grandparent.[4]

It follows that a State CPS caseworker cannot take children from parents without possessing evidence establishing legally sufficient grounds. State officials—including CPS caseworkers—cannot break up the family simply because they view that result as "best" for the children.[5] To remove children from their homes without parental consent, State officials, like Janelle Green, must possess specific evidence showing that Ben or Lynn, or both, were reasonably likely to have abused Robert. Such evidence would afford the State probable cause. But probable cause is not enough to take a child without a court order first, except if there is no time to get a court order. Federal due process decisions and statutes on the books in Illinois require a genuine emergency that makes it impossible to get in front of a judge before the child is likely to be hurt.[6]

It was easy to tell clients that all of these procedures were what due process law and statutes required—in theory. But the State's practices did not conform to these requirements. The theoretical explanation of what constitutional law required would do Ben and Lynn little good.

In practice, the State used clever devices to circumvent its duty to gather sufficient evidence to establish probable cause and to bring that evidence to a judge before removing children from their parents. Safety plans were one of the clever devices. When the State secured safety plans, it treated these plans as entirely different from nonconsensual removals, for which formal legal process was required.

When the State itself seized a child from the home and put the child into a foster care placement, caseworkers called it "taking protective custody." But when caseworkers told parents that they had to "agree" to a safety plan under which the parent approved the child staying with a known relative, the caseworkers were taught to label such transfers of responsibility for the children as "voluntary agreements." It was only *involuntary* separations that needed to meet the established due process requirements.

In legal speak, the State's legal position was that safety plan agreements were valid waivers of parents' fundamental constitutional rights to direct the care and custody of their children. But there was a serious flaw in the State's legal position, as the constitutional waiver standard established a heavy burden of justification: any waiver of a fundamental right was supposed to be "knowing, intelligent and voluntary."[7]

Ben and Lynn hadn't been given information about their choices or the basis for the CPS demand that they leave their home. They certainly hadn't been told their options. These factors made their "choice" to leave their home far from "knowing and intelligent." And they had been threatened with having the kids put into foster care if they refused to leave their home, making any claim that they "voluntarily" agreed to the safety plan seemed like sophistry.[8]

Families like Ben and Lynn's (or Mary and Tom before them) did not decide of their own accord to separate from their children during the CPS investigation. The safety plan Lynn signed was foisted on her. The sole reason Ben and Lynn had agreed to leave their home was that the CPS caseworkers had used their "awesome power"—their authority backed up by the State of Illinois—to "coercively intervene" in their family life.[9] But if the safety plan was a forced separation at the hands of the State's caseworkers, it followed that Ben and Lynn should have had the right to compel CPS to present evidence against them in a court of law before they could be directed to leave their homes.

Common sense, logic, and legal doctrine all would suggest that Ben and Lynn should have had a right to challenge the demand that they leave their home. But a 2006 decision by the federal court of appeals in Chicago, in the second phase of the *Dupuy* class action case that I had been working on worked on since 1997, stopped me from telling Ben and Lynn that they had any such rights.

Directives and so-called safety plan agreements requiring parents or children to leave their homes during a CPS investigation were nothing new to me. I had met Mary Broderick, after all, because she learned of my work on the federal class action lawsuit, *Dupuy*, that challenged safety plans as violations of due process rights of families protected by the Fourteenth Amendment to the Constitution. Mary provided an affidavit as to her own family's experience as part of the extensive court record we amassed in our challenge to safety plans. Since Mary Broderick was the person who had referred Ben and Lynn to my office, in effect, *Dupuy* was the case that had led to Ben and Lynn to seek me out for legal help in the first place.

I worked as a legal services attorney at the Legal Assistance Foundation (LAF) from 1979 until 1996. But in 1996, Congress restricted federally funded legal-services program attorneys from working on any class action suits. As a result of this restriction, I left LAF with its deputy director for litigation, Robert Lehrer, and formed an unusual public interest and civil rights law firm, Lehrer and Redleaf. We took seven pending class action cases—involving foster care, housing, homelessness, unemployment insurance, mental health, and jail conditions—with us from LAF into the new firm. Our firm gave the legal services clients continuity of legal representation.[10]

In June 1997, Bob and I filed *Dupuy v. Samuels,* the first class action lawsuit we initiated after leaving LAF. *Dupuy* would eventually take over 13 years and five federal circuit court appeals before it formally closed in the federal court, following a well-orchestrated but ultimately unsuccessful petition to secure the U.S. Supreme Court to review Illinois' safety plan practices.

Bob and I didn't represent the plaintiffs by ourselves; all told, by the time the *Dupuy* case was finally closed on the federal court's docket in 2011, 14 lawyers, three law firms, two nonprofits, and more than a dozen law clerks had worked on behalf of the plaintiffs in the case. Another dozen lawyers got involved in our unsuccessful attempt at Supreme Court review in 2008. The plaintiffs' team, which I co-led, included distinguished lawyers and law professors, including law students who later became legal superstars.

One of our initial law clerks, Michele Landis Dauber, now holds an endowed chair at Stanford Law School; others are partners in law firms throughout the United States. Three pre-eminent lawyers led the Supreme Court review effort: Jeffrey Fisher, Stanford Supreme Court Clinic; Richard Epstein, formerly of the University of Chicago Law School, now at New York University Law School; and Carolyn Shapiro, codirector of the Institute on the Supreme Court at Chicago-Kent Law School and now also the former solicitor general for Illinois. Distinguished experts also got involved on the plaintiffs' side at the trial court level, including psychiatrist Dr. Robert Galatzer-Levy and psychologist Dr. Bryn Jessup.

When our team filed the *Dupuy* case, my older son was nine years old. I naturally hoped that the lawsuit could help to pay his eventual college tuition, through a hoped-for civil rights attorney's fee award to the plaintiffs' lawyers. Plaintiffs' civil rights lawyers first have to win significant relief to vindicate their clients' civil rights, and then they must file a petition with the court to award them attorneys' fees based on the time they put into the case.[11] By the time the case finally was over in 2011, my son had already graduated from college, and my younger son had just one year of college left. I should have known better than to hope for a fee award in less than a decade. The course of litigation is always unpredictable, and major litigation against State agencies can be notoriously slow to resolve.

Dupuy unfolded in two distinct parts. Initially, we sought and were granted the authority to represent a class composed of every person whose name had been placed and retained in the State child-abuse register following a CPS investigation that resulted in an "indicated" finding, determining that they were responsible for abuse or neglect. We provided, however, that individuals would not be class members if they had a criminal conviction for the same allegation. The claims of legal rights violations arose because these indicated findings could cause horrendous consequences for parents and other people who worked with children, impairing their ability to work in their chosen profession even before they had any opportunity to challenge the CPS decision against them on the merits. In the first phase of the case (*Dupuy I*), we focused on the investigations and registered indicated findings, but in 2000, we expanded the class of plaintiffs and began to focus on safety plans (*Dupuy II*).[12]

Initial discovery in *Dupuy I* showed there were an estimated 150,000 people in the plaintiff class—that was the number of people who had been registered as child abusers or child neglectors. Approximately 5,000 people were excluded due to their criminal convictions for child abuse. Just sorting out the class definition and other requirements to get a class action certified to proceed in litigation took considerable briefing and negotiation. With a class action of that magnitude, *Dupuy* quickly proved to be the largest scale case I ever worked on.

Dupuy I challenged the practices of registering people who work with children as child abusers without due process. By 2005, we had won a monumental victory in *Dupuy I*. As a school social worker and employee of an agency that worked on behalf of disabled children, Lynn clearly was among the group of people we had in mind who needed special protections before the State should be allowed to label them as child abusers in the register and disclose that listing to an employer, licensing authority, or educational institution.

The State's child-abuse register operated as an employment screening device. Many employers were required by law or practice to run a background check of the register. A "hit," showing an "indicated" finding for child abuse, would preclude many employers from hiring the registered person. Some categories of indicated findings posed absolute legal bars to employment for certain State-licensed child-care facilities. But even if not directly prohibited from hiring a registered person, employers who checked the child abuser register were unlikely to hire anyone with a hit for child abuse or child neglect. Having a child abuse finding operated as a serious impediment to pursuing a career—and rightly so, *if* the abuse findings were correct. The problem was that many, if not most, of the findings that got registered had no obvious validity, because the amount of evidence necessary to put someone's name in the register was next to nil.

CPS investigators—with review and approval by their supervisors, who are not lawyers or judges—were allowed by law to put determinations of child abuse or neglect directly into the register at the end of a CPS investigation. Parents, caregivers, and individuals who work with children (such as day-care workers, social workers, and pediatric nurses) had no right to challenge the register finding before it was finalized. It was as if police investigating a crime could decide that their investigation sufficed to declare a suspect guilty and level penalties before giving the suspect any chance to challenge the guilty verdict. Since there was no requirement of a court review first when indicated findings got registered, there was no way to stop an unjust guilt finding from ruining the career of an innocent person. Indeed, it sometimes was difficult for parents to find out what findings the CPS system had made, for the notices the system issued were confusing, misleading, incomplete, and sometimes not issued properly or in a timely manner.[13]

What made the *Dupuy* case especially hard to litigate or quickly win, however, was that there was little public understanding that the register operated as a CPS-controlled blacklist. We had to prove how it functioned with painstaking detail. Indeed, the register is *still* a mystery to most people, including many family lawyers and criminal defense lawyers who know of the sex offender register but not the child-abuse register.[14] When we litigated *Dupuy*, the shame and stigma against the parents we represented were so great and the sympathy for the presumed child victim so palpable that our legal team was sometimes seen as the bad guys for pointing out the gross legal defects in the registry, which had been set up to protect children.

Our arguments for due process for the accused were often met with claims that we, the lawyers for the class of people listed as child abusers and child neglectors in the register, were insufficiently attuned to the plight of child abuse victims. Instead of being viewed as champions of the innocent and those who had never had a change to defend themselves, we were treated as if we were defenders of the heinously guilty. We were made out to be child abuse deniers. As someone who sees herself as a protector of innocent families and as a child and family advocate, I have always been riled by being tarred with the label of "parent's rights advocate," as if that amounted to advocacy *for* child abuse and against children's real interests.

At first, it seemed that our two federal district court judges were skeptics, too—willing to give the CPS side, not the plaintiffs, every benefit of the doubt. Eventually, however, the strength of the families' resolve, the sheer number of similar stories of misplaced allegations, and the power of the plaintiffs' testimony convinced the federal court that something was "seriously and obviously flawed" with the CPS register system.[15] Those flaws were hurting children.

To counteract the assumption that our clients were abusive monsters, during the 18-day-long trial in *Dupuy I*, we brought many day-care owners, social workers, teachers' aides, and foster parents into federal court to testify.

Each person who testified in the federal court hearing had a more sympathetic story than the next; they had been railroaded, blindsided, caught in the middle of a complex set-up by a disgruntled employee, or they were victims of retaliation through misuse of the hotline by a soon-to-be ex-spouse or a client who didn't want to pay a fee for services. Some were blamed for actions that were not abuse at all. Others took the fall while another person with a lighter skin color got off the hook. Each of these child-care workers had been wrongly accused and blacklisted in their careers without a hearing, usually after an investigation that had presumed their guilt without any attempt to hear their side of the story.

After their names had been registered as perpetrators of abuse or neglect, a number of the plaintiffs who testified had lost their jobs. The Dupuys themselves had to close their day-care home. Eventually, they had to declare bankruptcy. The allegations in their case revolved around their 10-year-old daughter's diapering of a child entrusted to their day-care home.

When the registered-as-guilty plaintiffs tried to challenge their blacklisting through the CPS system's then-available administrative hearing system, it took, on average, 18 months to get a hearing before an administrative law judge. In one of the named plaintiffs' cases, it took over three years. Ironically, when these administrative hearings eventually were convened, the burden shifted back to the State to prove that the registered-as-guilty person actually had abused or neglected a child. By that time, however, the accused people long had been treated as if they were guilty of child abuse or neglect and had already suffered the consequences of the State's decision to put their names in the register.

By the time these plaintiffs came to federal court as witnesses, the CPS administrative hearing system had already cleared almost all of their names off the register. Eventually, every single named plaintiff or plaintiff witness who testified—over 30 individuals—won clearance through the

State's own administrative hearing system. One might have thought that a system of adjudicating guilt for child abuse would have caught at least one truly guilty person.

Without exception, all the people who testified had suffered months and years of agony and hardship while they had waited for relief from the false label of "child abuser" that had been affixed to them in the child-abuse register. Their families had suffered grievously too.

Financial hardship was not the worst consequence. Some plaintiffs had been treated as pariahs by other family members while they awaited exoneration. Others had been forced to separate from children who might be labeled "abuse perpetrators" themselves if they were older than six years old. Indeed, the Dupuy's 10-year-old daughter, as the accused perpetrator, was forced to live with relatives in another town; otherwise, the Dupuy's day-care home would have been shut down.[16] Having the State treat an accusation treated as true had devastating consequences for the self-esteem of anyone who worked with children. After all, the plaintiffs we represented derived both professional and personal satisfaction from caring for children; being accused of hurting a child seriously affected their sense of self and pride in their careers.

Federal Judge Rebecca R. Pallmeyer's landmark *Dupuy I* decision came down in 2001.[17] Judge Pallmeyer's 101-page opinion drew extensively from the 373-page findings of fact our legal team had proposed in summarizing the evidence. Judge Pallmeyer declared that the disclosure and use of registered findings, the notices, and the hearing process the State employed violated the plaintiffs' constitutional rights.

Critical to our team's success in the case was our case file analysis, which showed that the State itself overturned the registered findings 74.6 percent of the time. Judge Pallmeyer found the rate of error "staggering," as she connected the dots between these errors and the "practically nominal" burden of proof the caseworkers used to register guilt findings and then shift the burden to the child-care worker to appeal and get the findings reviewed by a neutral administrative law judge after the fact. The more-erroneous-than-not system was hurting the children of Illinois, Judge Pallmeyer declared.[18] That system hardly helped children whose parents lost their jobs or the children whose teachers, day-care providers, or therapists could no longer work with them due to a false and unfair label of guilt.

Clearly, Judge Pallmeyer appreciated the Kafkaesque nightmare that so many of our clients had been through. At the same time, however, the opinion cautioned that the CPS investigation system was so flawed that real child abuse likely was being missed; guilty people could be exonerated if the delays in hearing evidence went on too long and critical witnesses disappeared. This was a good point, although not one we had pressed on behalf of the plaintiffs. It was important for our legal team to recognize that the State's interests in protecting children required some of the same improvements to catch the guilty as were necessary to protect the innocent.

The 2001 opinion set the stage for orders to remedy the constitutional defects in the child-abuse registry system. After many meetings and cross proposals, the federal court in 2003 directed the State to do fuller and fairer child abuse and neglect investigations. It ordered the CPS agency to ensure that investigators gathered not just inculpatory evidence against the accused persons but also exculpatory evidence bearing on the accused person's innocence. It directed the State to provide people who worked with children much fairer and faster processes through which they could challenge decisions that the CPS investigators rendered against them, after Judge Pallmeyer referred to the delays they had experienced as "agonizing" and "frustrating."[19]

These new, expedited review processes would eventually help Lynn stop the State from ruining her exemplary social work career. But the *Dupuy* litigation had not provided any remedy for safety plans, despite a monumental effort our legal team had mounted. For in *Dupuy II,* the due process challenge to safety plans, we had a devastating legal defeat.

In 2000, after the 1999 trial in *Dupuy I* and while we awaited Judge Pallmeyer's ruling, the *Dupuy* legal team moved on to tackle the due process problems with safety plans. Many of the families we represented in *Dupuy I* had been separated during the CPS investigations, including during the time an indicated finding had been registered against them. CPS caseworkers had directed these separations without affording the families any opportunity to object and to obtain a decision from a neutral decision maker.

Sometimes the separations would continue for months, and the conditions under which families lived were extremely restrictive. Sometimes parents were forced to eject one child from their home indefinitely, under threats that all the children in the home could be taken if they refused to eject the alleged offender. Sometimes grandparents were told that they had to come care for their grandchildren and supervise their son or daughter round the clock; otherwise, their grandchildren would be taken into foster care. By examining hundreds of case files during *Dupuy I*, we saw many instances in which CPS investigators issued terrifying threats without having a shred of evidence to justify removing the children from their parents.

These safety plan practices were even more arbitrary than the register practices at issue in *Dupuy I*. If the CPS caseworkers truly believed the parents had seriously harmed their children, moreover, and if they had possessed solid evidence to support that conclusion, then why should the caseworkers believe that telling parents to leave their home under a safety plan would adequately protect the children? In cases of real child abuse, shouldn't CPS caseworkers be required to get a court order to stop accused perpetrators from abusing the child again?

After observing the rampant CPS practice of threatening the families first and then gathering evidence later, our legal team decided to mount a constitutional challenge to the manner in which CPS caseworkers were separating families under safety plans.

As we developed the evidence for a trial in *Dupuy II*, we examined the State's policies governing safety plans. Illinois' safety-assessment protocols commanded that children could be deemed "unsafe" based on mere allegations to the hotline. There was no requirement that CPS caseworkers gather any evidence to support the hotline call. These protocols liberally allowed—indeed, they compelled—CPS caseworkers to tell parents that their children would be removed even without evidence of any danger to the child by the parent. The State's policies authorized in black and white the baseless threats to the plaintiff families that preceded the CPS demand for safety plan separations.

As we worked on the *Dupuy II* safety plan challenge, our legal team came to view the due process violations as more blatant than those involved in *Dupuy I*. The fundamental rights of parents and children to live together as a family were at stake, and the restrictions on family life were extreme. The *Dupuy I* litigation had concerned rights to prevent employment blacklisting—important interests, to be sure, but not ones that the U.S. Supreme Court had labeled "fundamental" and hence worthy of the highest degree of constitutional protection. But what could be more important than the right of a family like Ben and Lynn's to live together in their own home?

As many as 10,000 Illinois families each year were being separated under these safety plans, according to the CPS deputy director's own estimate. To be sure, there was no hard data about safety plans—it just wasn't recorded or kept—so exactly how many families were affected was impossible to know. But safety plan separations frequently started upon the first contact between the caseworker and the family and then continued indefinitely for weeks or months. One father had a three-year-long safety plan that no one told him had ended. Something was very wrong with this picture, legally speaking.

The specifics of the safety plan terms varied according to the discretion of the CPS caseworker and supervisor. One plan we examined during the litigation required a mother to stay up and watch her sleeping teenage son all night. Another forbade a child accused of abusing his siblings from being with "other children," without clarifying if that meant he couldn't go to school. Usually, though, the terms were just like those in Ben and Lynn's safety plan. Oftentimes, the investigator and supervisor would draft a form safety plan agreement document before meeting with the parents.

When the CPS agency's attorneys tried to defend these safety plans as if they had been carefully crafted in collaboration with the family, our team could point to dozens of counterexamples: safety plans routinely presented as "take it or leave it" demands. In fact, some safety plans were never signed by either parent. It was common for CPS to omit getting a signature of one of the parents, just as Ben's signature was omitted. Sometimes, there was no written safety plan agreement at all but simply an oral directive by the CPS caseworker that the parents must leave their homes, transfer their children to another parent, or have a relative come into the home to supervise them round the clock. Parents were told that their children would be taken into foster care if they failed to abide by these demands.

Safety plans rarely included ending dates, but even in the rare cases that set time limits, many parents still feared a harsh response if they resumed unsupervised contact with their children without a CPS caseworker's express okay. To add insult to this injury, it often proved impossible to reach the caseworker to discuss lifting the safety plan. Sometimes, only formal exoneration after a register appeal hearing or an unfounded decision at the end of an investigation would convince parents that it was safe to go home.

No parent ever called the CPS caseworkers' bluff. None of them said to the child protection caseworkers, "Go ahead and take my child into foster care." Given the "choice" of having the children live with a grandparent for the time being—hoping for the best at the end of the investigation—or having the child go live with strangers in a foster home, every single parent we talked to and every case file we examined showed the same decision: families went along with the CPS safety plan demand. When the families were told they had to sign a safety plan "agreement" so that the children wouldn't be taken into foster care, they signed it. When they were orally instructed to leave, they left. All parents we talked to about their experience thought that they had "no choice" but to agree.

In August 2002, the 22-day *Dupuy II* trial began. Once again, we regaled Judge Pallmeyer with tale after tale of the ordeals that the plaintiffs had endured. Few made it through their testimony without tears, and oftentimes, one or more of our co-counsel needed Kleenex too. The testimony was heart wrenching.

One professor at a major Chicago university spoke of being forced to break his promise to his adopted daughter that he would never leave her. He was forced out of his house following an anonymous hotline call. The professor suspected the hotline caller might have had a racial motive against him, for his daughter was African American and both the professor and his wife were Caucasian. The caller claimed to have seen the professor perform a sex act on a small female. But his wife was small herself, and it was unclear how any caller could have seen into the window. After his traumatic banishment from his own home, which he struggled to hide from his daughter, the allegations against him were judged unfounded.

Another father had been unable to teach his six-year-old disabled son to ride his bicycle during the summer. The father was ejected from his home after an anonymous hotline caller had complained that he had inappropriately tickled his son on a train ride into Chicago to see dinosaurs. The caller was unaware, of course, that tactile contact with his son had been recommended by the child's doctor. The child's mother used a wheelchair and couldn't keep up with the active boy outside, but despite this, the safety plan required her to be constantly present whenever the child was with his dad. The safety plan restrictions lasted throughout the hot summer and caused hardship to the whole family, including developmental setbacks for the child.

A third family was separated after a preteen girl for whom the mother babysat accused the mother's husband of kissing her. But the preteen accuser was mentally unstable and had previously made false allegations against others. Even though the husband was exonerated after a three-week separation, the husband was so fearful as a result of the allegations that he no longer felt he could hug or kiss his own children.

In each of these cases, the allegations against the parents were eventually deemed to be unfounded. But terrible damage to the family was done in the days and weeks of separation. I later learned, to my dismay, that the first and third of the couples in these three stories divorced; they viewed the CPS action against them as a pivotal point that had eroded their sense of safety and stability in their own homes.

Each case we presented at the trial seemed more tragic than the last. By the end of the trial in 2002, following what we thought had proven pervasive violations of the families' constitutional rights, we asked the federal court to order an appropriate legal remedy that would afford the families due process. We sought clear standards governing when CPS caseworkers could demand safety plans in the first place and a system for affording some form of a legal review. The system we asked the judge to order would allow parents to show the lack of factual basis underlying the CPS investigators' demands that the parents separate from their children.

The State's sole defense of safety plans was that they were "voluntary" and that therefore no such review process was required. In the face of the evidence that the State demanded family separations under threats of seizing the children from the parents, the contention that safety plans were voluntary seemed to us exceedingly weak, almost frivolous.

On March 22, 2005, Judge Pallmeyer issued a lengthy ruling in the parents' favor on most of our constitutional claims concerning safety plans.[20] She soundly rejected CPS's "voluntariness" defense. She declared that the ultimatums given to parents that required them to separate from their children were plainly coercive. Because safety plans were not voluntary waivers of the family's fundamental constitutional right to live together, the CPS system needed to provide the families some due process protections.

To be sure, the form agreements the State used for its safety plans labeled these agreements as "voluntary," but Judge Pallmeyer looked beyond the forms and found that all of the parents who testified had been expressly threatened that their children would be taken into foster care if they didn't sign the safety plans. Because this express coercion was rampant, the CPS agency's safety plan policies and practices did not provide adequate protections to assure that parents' decisions to separate from their children under safety plans were voluntary.

While we won the central claim that safety plans were not voluntary, however, Judge Pallmeyer ruled against the plaintiffs on other important aspects of our due process challenge. She rejected our contention that a CPS caseworker must possess more than "mere suspicion" before issuing demands that the parent or child must leave the home involuntarily. When Judge Pallmeyer issued a second decision, in December 2005, purporting to establish remedies for the constitutional violations that she had found, she held that safety plans could remain in place for 14 days before any review was required. Furthermore, the eventual review did not have to be conducted by a neutral person; the reviewer could be an administrator who was involved in issuing the safety plan in the first place.

To our legal team, allowing 14-day separations based on "mere suspicion" seemed an almost pyrrhic victory. We had won a constitutional victory, but we had not solved the problem. If we did not appeal Judge Pallmeyer's December 2005 *Dupuy II* ruling, families would be subject to weeks of separation from their children without any evidence of wrongdoing and without meaningful recourse. The case law we examined permitted coerced family separations under emergency circumstances to last no more than five days before some form of a hearing was required.[21]

In retrospect, our legal team should have lived with Judge Pallmeyer's *Dupuy II* rulings, which offered some safety plan review process following the declaration of constitutional rights violations. We should have declared victory and worked to improve the due process remedies the court had directed. But we didn't make that decision, because we firmly believed the law required stronger due process remedies than Judge Pallmeyer had directed.

Our legal team decided to appeal Judge Pallmeyer's order that allowed CPS caseworkers to demand family separations based on "mere suspicion." We also appealed the decision that the reviewer did not need to be neutral. We sought a quicker, more objective review process. Perhaps aware that Judge Pallmeyer's order did not require very extensive changes in CPS practices, the CPS director, who was the named defendant in the case, did not appeal the constitutional ruling in the plaintiffs' favor.

When we got before the federal court of appeals—Robert Lehrer presented the oral argument on September 20, 2006—the argument did not go well. Judges Posner, Easterbrook, and Evans, for the U.S. Court of Appeals for the Seventh Circuit, heard the argument. This surprised us, for the *Dupuy I* case had been before the Seventh Circuit before. We had expected the same panel would hear the *Dupuy II* appeal. We were wrong.

At the argument, Judge Posner asked most of the questions. My partner, Robert Lehrer, a graduate of Harvard Law School with honors who had argued in the Supreme Court and had numerous appellate arguments to his credit, had never faced such a hostile panel. For most of the argument, Judge Posner's questions focused on whether Judge Pallmeyer had issued her December 2005 ruling in the proper "separate order" format. Neither side had complained about this deficiency. Nevertheless, Judge Posner's attention was sharply fixated on this technical point of federal appellate jurisdiction. The coercive practices of the State of Illinois in forcing parents to agree to separate from their children or otherwise have them taken into foster care seemed almost an afterthought at the oral argument.

The court's opinion came out quickly, on October 3, 2006.[22] We read it with dismay. It seemed, at least at first, that the case concerned an arcane point of federal appellate procedure rather than a question basic to family life in America. For the first three pages, the Posner-authored opinion focused on the technical question of whether Judge Pallmeyer's rulings were appealable. At the end of that technical legal analysis, however, Judge Posner declared "enough said about the procedural issue."[23] The opinion turned to the question of "what a 'safety plan' is."

The opinion went on to make mincemeat of the fundamental rights of families. The opinion's reasoning was stunningly broad, and it flew in the face of the extensive factual determinations Judge Pallmeyer had made, all without so much as a mention of a single finding of fact. Appellate judges are supposed to defer to trial judges' factual findings, based on the theory that the trial judge hears the witnesses and can best decide which witnesses are credible. In this instance, however, that basic rule was entirely ignored.

The Posner opinion described what was at stake with safety plans as "less extreme than removing the child from parental custody altogether and sticking him in foster care."[24] Nevertheless, such removals could "count as deprivations of liberty," "triggering the right to a hearing."[25] But then, the opinion announced that the "decision to agree to a safety plan is optional"; the parents could "reject the plan" and "thumb their nose at it."[26] This conclusion by the court of appeals ignored the fact that not one parent whose experience was recounted in the massive trial record had ever done so.

Acknowledging that rejecting a safety plan could leave a parent in a "worse pickle" than accepting it, the opinion labeled this problem as one that is "implicit in the settlement process."[27] Of course, this labeling of the safety plan agreement process as akin to a "settlement" ignored the extensive evidence showing that safety plan negotiations were nothing like settlement discussions in lawsuits. The parents were given no choices and virtually no information, and they almost never had counsel to guide their decisions. No case had been filed against them first, and they were usually confronted with safety plan demands of the very first day of contact with anyone from CPS, giving them no time thoughtfully to respond to the sudden demand that they separate from their children.

The Supreme Court had directed that assessments of voluntariness must turn on a "totality of the circumstances."[28] The plaintiffs had shown that none of the traditional voluntariness factors cut in favor of finding that safety plan agreements were voluntary. One of those factors was whether there was equal bargaining power between both sides; there was a great imbalance in power between the CPS investigators and the parents. Another factor was whether there was time pressure; the parents who testified had to decide about separating from their children on the spot.

Additional factors included their knowledge and understanding of their alternatives, but the parents testified that they were not given information that would help them make decisions. Moreover, many of the parents in the plaintiff class had limited education, and some had disabilities that would prevent them from making a reasoned decision about separating from their children. Finally, the conclusion that safety plans were uniformly voluntary ignored that the State had no process to assess whether one safety plan was voluntary and another was not. Safety plan policies and practices simply had no indicators of voluntariness, let alone a method to assure that every safety plan was voluntary in fact.

The Posner opinion ignored all of these factors. Instead, it zeroed in the preprinted safety plan agreement form, which told parents of the "possibility" their children would be removed if they did not agree to a plan—information that the opinion referred to a "truism."[29]

Judge Pallmeyer's detailed decision had rested on what the evidence showed happened in practice, not what a preprinted form said. Of course, many parents hadn't even been given or signed the safety plan form, as Judge Pallmeyer had found in one of her many findings of fact that the Posner opinion ignored.

In short, the Posner opinion made lawful the CPS use of ultimatums that were the equivalent of telling robbery victims that they had the "option" of "agreeing" to give up their money or their life and then, if the victims reasonably chose to protect their life, concluding that the victims had "voluntarily" donated their money to the robber. According to the Posner opinion, a reasonable parent given the "option" of a safety plan should tell the caseworker to go ahead take his or her child into foster care and see what would happen.

Furthermore, the Posner opinion ignored the real-life practical problem that no reasonable parent *could* know, in the heated moments when a CPS investigator first threatened them, whether the CPS investigator's threat of seizing the child and putting him or her into foster care was a baseless one or one supported by some evidence. How was any parent to know if the CPS investigator had a factual or legal basis to carry out the threat? Which parent could afford to take a chance and guess wrong?

The opinion's answer to these questions was that since it was lawful to threaten people in a settlement negotiation, the only legally problematic safety plan was one that directly misrepresented the evidence against the parent. In short, unless the CPS caseworker was directly lying to the parent, there was nothing unconstitutional about threatening a parent with the taking of his or her children based on mere suspicion. Suspicion could "ripen."[30]

To add insult to injury, even if there were a rare case in which a parent *did* know that the investigator had lied in order to get a safety plan, the court's decision still left such a parent with no due process remedy.

In rationalizing safety plans as constitutionally acceptable voluntary agreements, Judge Posner's opinion had offered up a pointed analogy: the choice parents faced as to whether to leave the home or have their children taken into foster care was comparable to a limited choice between cocktails given to a guest at a cocktail party—"an initial choice between a Martini vs. a Manhattan" that was amended by the host to offering a martini alone. How is one "worse off," Judge Posner's opinion asked rhetorically, for being offered "more rather than fewer options"?[31]

Our legal team had an obvious rejoinder. At a cocktail party, responding, "No, thank you," is always a reasonable option. No one is forced to accept a martini if he or she doesn't drink alcohol. But none of the families reasonably could say, "No, thank you," to the threat that CPS would take their kids.

After the court of appeals ruling in *Dupuy II*, I struggled repeatedly with the question of how to counsel clients like Ben and Lynn about the excruciating choices they faced between having to leave their homes or having their children taken. I could not bear to tell clients that our esteemed Seventh Circuit Court of Appeals had insensitively compared their situation to beverage choices at a cocktail party. I never came up with a satisfactory way to explain this aspect of the *Dupuy* decision to any client. Law students and new lawyers in our office also struggled to understand the paradoxical declaration that safety plans were voluntary when the plans were practically as coercive as a robber telling people at gunpoint that they had a choice between their money or their life.

Though we had won *Dupuy II* in the federal trial court, the appeal we had filed from the December 2005 order resulted in a devastating loss for the plaintiff class. Technically, the court of appeal *affirmed* Judge Pallmeyer's decision since the CPS director had not appealed it. This anomalous result made it necessary for us to return to Judge Pallmeyer's courtroom for her to dismiss our legal claims. Only then could we proceed to back up through the appeal process and eventually ask for U.S. Supreme Court review.

All this legal wrangling led to a second decision of the federal court of appeals in *Dupuy II* on July 31, 2007.[32] The decision ratified the first court of appeal in *Dupuy II* decision, affirming the trial court's compelled dismissal order. At that point, our only possible recourse was with the Supreme Court. But the Supreme Court reviews less than 1 percent of the petitions it receives. Getting a hearing in the highest court was a long shot.

Between the time of Judge Pallmeyer's March 2005 initial safety plan ruling in *Dupuy II* and the court of appeals ruling on October 3, 2006, I founded the Family Defense Center. I started to work in the center's offices 20 percent of the time as its new executive director. Besides me, the center had one law clerk and one part-time administrator. I had continued to work on the *Dupuy* case as an attorney in a solo public interest law practice until the Family Defense Center's legal status as an independent nonprofit was established. Once the center acquired its formal nonprofit status, *Dupuy* became my first major case in my capacity as the executive director of the Family Defense Center, starting in January 2007.

Our *Dupuy* legal team, led by Robert Lehrer and me, mounted a valiant attempt in the U.S. Supreme Court to overturn the court of appeals' astonishingly broad and dismissive opinion. Jeffrey Fisher from Stanford Law School and Richard Epstein from the University of Chicago, both leading constitutional lawyers, joined in our plea for U.S. Supreme Court review, as did Carolyn Shapiro, a Chicago-Kent Law School professor who previously had consulted on the case while she was a Skadden Fellow with the Shriver Center. Three friend-of-the-court briefs signed by a dozen different groups supported our request that the Supreme Court hear the case (technically, a petition for certiorari or "cert").

Our principal claim was a simple one: in order for a safety plan to be voluntary, the option of saying, "No, thank you," to the "offer" of a safety plan had to be a real option. Forced choices between two bad options or a limited choice that a person had no right to decline were inherently coercive. A coerced choice could not be the basis for claiming that parents had waived their fundamental rights to live together as a family.

National media and SCOTUS Blog, the well-known Supreme Court–watcher Web site, notified their readers to watch the action on our petition for Supreme Court review. But on June 16, 2008, the U.S. Supreme Court turned down the petition.[33] The eight-year-long fight to get some due process to enable families to resist demands for safety plans was over.

The denial of our petition in the U.S. Supreme Court was devastating. Our team of lawyers had put our hearts, minds, time, and no small amount of expense into the case over the course of eight long years. Now we were left with no remedies for the parents we represented who had been forced to separate from their children under coercive safety plans. The families would be stuck with safety plans. With *Dupuy II* over, we had hit the end of the road.

The litigation had been hard fought. Through the years in which the litigation had been pending, we had hoped to stem the abusive treatment of families that safety plan threats and family separations without due process had embodied. After we had won *Dupuy II* at the federal trial court level, even though we were not happy with the remedy the federal trial judge had ordered, we sensed that even the CPS director had started to question the voluntariness of safety plans as mere wishful thinking.

But when Judge Posner's opinion declared that safety plans represented universally voluntary agreements to reasonable options, the opinion fueled the State's broader embrace of safety plans and its resistance to any improvements. While the State's lawyers had told us that the State would maintain the fledgling safety plan review system that Judge Pallmeyer had directed, that offer was effectively withdrawn after the Seventh Circuit ruling. No system of accountability for safety plans that banished parents or children from their homes was developed.

Just before I started working on Ben and Lynn's case, I worked on proposed legislation for the 2009 Illinois legislative session that would have provided some due process for safety plans. But that measure didn't even get called for hearing by the first legislative committee to which it was assigned, even though the Chicago Bar Association's board of managers had voted unanimously to support it.

The situation for families facing safety plan demands would start to improve in 2011. But for the time being, families like Ben and Lynn's were stuck with separating from their children for as long as CPS caseworkers demanded. Parents continued to be coerced into accepting safety plan restrictions on their family life in order to prevent CPS from putting their kids into a foster home with strangers.

FIVE

A Night to Remember

It was the middle of the afternoon on Thursday, October 1, 2009. Lynn could not shake her fear that Dr. Felix had made up her mind that Robert was abused without considering any of the information in her favor.

Some welcome news had come that morning, however. The pediatric orthopedist Mary Broderick had recommended and who had examined Robert on September 30, Dr. Carl Sheridan, told Ben and Lynn that he considered child abuse an "unlikely" explanation for Robert's fracture. Dr. Sheridan was willing to submit a report for the CPS team to consider although he warned it might take a few days to type it up.

Ben called to tell me that Caseworker Janelle Green had asked him to come to her office the next morning with the children. She said she wanted to discuss the "status of the investigation." My legal antennae instantly got engaged. I knew what these words meant, even if Ben didn't fully understand yet. The CPS investigators were finishing up their investigation. Dr. Felix must have finished her MPEEC report, and Janelle Green was getting ready to act on it.

I had just received Dr. Sheridan's oral opinion myself, stating that abuse was unlikely as an explanation for Robert's fracture. Dr. Sheridan had relied on his extensive medical experience in treating fractures, including ones that parents could not explain. Child abuse doctors had told Caseworker Green that Robert would have cried inconsolably the moment his leg was fractured. But Dr. Sheridan knew this assertion was simply untrue.

It was possible, for example, to have a partial or nondisplaced fracture first and then to have a further break later so that each break would be less painful than if the fracture occurred all at once. Children's pain thresholds are different, too, and there is no such thing as a distinctive fracture cry that any conscientious parent would know. A cry for another reason could mask the pain of a fracture. Dr. Sheridan knew some doctors who had fractures themselves and didn't realize it. Finding healing fractures on children was commonplace, and some children had never showed any obvious signs of any pain at all.

A parent's character and past conduct mattered to Dr. Sheridan, although these factors seemed to have no apparent sway with Dr. Felix or the CPS caseworkers. Ben and Lynn's conscientiousness as parents had been apparent to Dr. Sheridan, who cited Lynn's history of working with children as a social worker as further reason to believe her statements that she didn't know what caused Robert's fracture.

I decided to confer about next steps with Melissa Staas, who was the Family Defense Center's most senior staff attorney although she was just two years out of law school. Despite her relative inexperience, Melissa had the makings of an excellent lawyer from the start. She worked on the *Dupuy II* petition for Supreme Court review right out of the gate. A *magna cum laude* graduate of Loyola Law School and the editor-in-chief of its *Children's Legal Rights Journal,* Melissa soaked up complex legal and medical questions and delivered first-draft memoranda of law with unusual polish. I wanted Melissa to dive into Ben and Lynn's case with me. She could provide a sounding board for the tricky decisions we would have to make.

As soon as we heard of Dr. Sheridan's favorable medical expert opinion, we wondered how best to intercede with the CPS investigative team to provide this opinion to them. It would be best if the team would *actually* consider it. After all, Judge Pallmeyer in *Dupuy I*, affirmed in the first appellate ruling of the Seventh Circuit, had ordered CPS caseworkers to do exactly that: consider all the evidence, both pro and con, before deciding the outcome of an investigation.[1] What could be more exculpatory than a pediatric orthopedist's opinion saying that child abuse wasn't a likely cause of Robert's fracture?

By the time Ben told us that he had been "invited" to come into the CPS office with the kids the next day, however, we had little hope of changing the CPS caseworkers' minds. So far, none of Ben and Lynn's support letters or explanations had made any difference. The investigative team seemed bent on listening only to the child abuse fellow, Dr. Felix.

Moreover, Ben and Lynn still had no explanation for how the fracture occurred. We hoped, nevertheless, that having a second medical opinion could slow down the CPS team's final decision. It might cause someone a step or two above Janelle Green's supervisor to take a closer look at the case against Ben and Lynn. Knowledge of a contrary second opinion might lead the CPS team to seek out a neutral third medical opinion in an effort to discover where the truth lay.

These legal-strategy ideas weren't just far-fetched hopes. Getting a third opinion in such cases was what CPS's written policies required, backed up by what the federal court in *Dupuy I* had directed. If the CPS investigative team had followed CPS's own rules, then maybe Ben and Lynn would be exonerated after all—before a lengthy and costly court battle. I had occasionally succeeded in getting a CPS agency deputy director to stop a planned removal of children from their parents. While it was a long shot, perhaps Dr. Sheridan's opinion in the hands of higher-level CPS administrators could make a difference.

We would have to act fast. After all, Dr. Felix's report was all that Janelle Green had needed to complete the investigation. She would very soon make a decision about the next steps, including whether she would label Robert an abused child, put Lynn or Ben's names into the State register as child abusers, or proceed to take protective custody of the children. Now she had invited Ben to come in tomorrow to talk about the team's decisions.

Ben and Lynn had remained in the dark as to the CPS team's deliberations since the hotline call. They had received nothing in writing about information Dr. Felix had given to CPS. This was galling; it was Ben and Lynn's own concern about treatment for Robert's unexplained fracture that had brought Robert to Dr. Felix's hospital. They had never been told that the hospital worked under a contract with the State of Illinois CPS system. Yet, the CPS caseworkers now treated Ben and Lynn's chosen medical providers as the State's agents and insisted on keeping Dr. Felix's medical opinion and report confidential from Ben and Lynn.

There was no time for raising concerns about the hospital's child abuse fellowship program or the MPEEC contract between the hospital and CPS. The best possibility at the moment was to try to slow down any action against Ben and Lynn's family by getting someone farther up the CPS chain of command to consider the evidence with fresh eyes.

On Ben and Lynn's behalf, I picked up the phone. I got through to Janelle Green, who quickly got her supervisor, Kirby Long, to join the call with Melissa and me. We needed to work up the chain of command, starting by telling Caseworker Green about Dr. Sheridan's opinion. We would follow up the call with a notice to the administrators above Long.

Melissa and I introduced ourselves. We immediately told Green and Long that we had a second opinion from Dr. Carl Sheridan, a chair of pediatric orthopedics at one of Chicago's leading hospitals, stating that abuse was not the likely cause of Robert's fracture. We asked the CPS team to "hold off on the meeting" with Ben, Lynn, and the children so that they could receive and review Dr. Sheridan's written opinion. We explained that while Dr. Sheridan had reached a favorable conclusion, his written report was being prepared from dictation and would be available in a few days.

Their answer was a quick and firm no. Tomorrow's meeting could not wait. Even though they had waited three weeks for Dr. Felix's opinion, they would not wait until Monday for another doctor's opinion, even if that doctor was someone who had specialized knowledge of fractures. Melissa and I told the caseworkers that we would advise Ben and Lynn accordingly. We immediate called Ben and Lynn. We told them the bad news that the CPS investigative team had refused to consider Dr. Sheridan's opinion.

We alerted Ben and Lynn to expect that protective custody of the children would be directed soon, though it was still possible that the CPS caseworkers would let the kids stay in the home with their grandparents. We expected that Green would instruct the grandparents the next day to take the children for medical checkups with a CPS doctor. That sort of notification often was the sole way a parent (or the parent's lawyer) could discern that the State had assumed legal protective custody of a child. A prompt medical exam for children coming into the State's protective custody was CPS policy. The signs were ominous that a case involving the three children would be heading for juvenile court soon.

Of course, there was no emergency basis for a legal seizure of the children into State protective custody, as the due process clause of the Constitution required (and as the court of appeals would directly hold in the *Hernandez v. Foster* case in 2011).[2] But the State's CPS system generally paid no heed to this particular prong of the constitutional requirement for taking children from their parents without a court order. The constitutional logic required that if there was time to get a court order *before* taking the children, then a judge had to authorize the removal; the State could not just act on its own. Once the State initiated a request to take custody of the children, an orderly process, all with judicial sanction, could then occur.

Seizing a child without a court order is an extraordinary power that should never be used if there is time for a court to review the evidence first. Because the hotline call had been made on September 10 and it was now October 1, the State easily could have gotten a court order *before* it took Ben and Lynn's kids. But the caseworkers were used to taking protective custody first and getting court orders afterward. It had been all but impossible to stop this entrenched practice.

At the same time as we were discussing next steps with Ben and Lynn, Janelle Green; her supervisor, Kirby Long; and his supervisor, Kim Ford were meeting. Green's CPS file note, written on October 1 at 4:51 p.m., recounts Dr. Felix's opinion, including her "concerns" about Lynn's mental health status—Lynn's reported "symptoms of depression." The note fails to acknowledge that Dr. Felix's account was an arm chair mental health diagnosis of Lynn based on Dr. Felix's own mistaken note about Lynn's grandmother's mental health, not her own. The CPS file entry ends by reciting that Green "will take protective custody of all three children and inform the parents of the upcoming hearing date and time."

It would take several days before Melissa and I saw these file notes. When we finally got the full CPS investigation file, the message was crystal clear: news that the parents had obtained legal counsel and a second medical opinion had been unwelcome. As soon as the CPS team sensed that Ben and Lynn were fighting back with lawyers and doctors of their own, the team decided that the CPS system should no longer follow the polite and easy course of having the children come into the office. Now was the time to take the kids. The time to consider the exculpatory evidence in the parents' favor had passed, federal court orders or not.

Caseworker Green didn't call Ben or Lynn to tell them to get the kids ready for their encounter with the State's foster care system. But she did call the police for backup to assist in removing the children from their home. The family's worst nightmare was unfolding outside their home.

Our assumption that the CPS investigative team would leave the children with their grandmother had been too optimistic. We had failed to reckon with the fact that in the eyes of the CPS caseworkers, Ben and Lynn were child abusers who had committed the mortal sin of getting their own medical opinion as well as independent legal counsel. Since Ben and Lynn didn't have any relatives in Illinois, the protective custody placement would have to be in an emergency shelter or with a stranger who was a licensed foster parent.

Now that the CPS caseworkers knew that Ben and Lynn did not plan to go gently into signing over their children to become wards of the State of Illinois, they decided that the State didn't have to go gently, either. There was no more time for talking about the evidence or working out alternative supervision for the children in their own home. CPS directives were issued to take the children from their parents and their grandmother. Evidence could be looked at later, when the case came before a judge. By then, decisions about the children's fate would be out of the CPS caseworkers' hands.

Lynn's next call to me came at 6:30 p.m. Janelle Green had just knocked on her front door and demanded to come in. Lynn's mother-in-law and her three children were just finishing dinner. Three police officers, coming from two different squad cars with flashers blazing, flanked Green near the door. As Janelle Green waited outside, I advised Lynn to stand her legal ground. It was time to refuse to let Green come into the home. I said, "Tell her she needs a warrant to enter. You have the right to refuse to let her into your home right now, and she has no right to come in without a warrant. If she gets a warrant, then you have to cooperate, but right now you can tell her that, on advice of your lawyer, she needs to get a warrant."

It was lucky that I still was at the office when Lynn called. It was lucky, too, that she had gotten through to me immediately. The CPS team's decision to initiate a full-blown siege of the family home, its refusal to consider Dr. Sheridan's report, and its unwillingness to postpone the requested next day's meeting made it clear that the CPS team had no intention of letting the children stay in the home. Lynn's choice was clear. Unless she wanted to give up her legal right to keep her children, she needed to stand up to Green's demand now. She needed to use the words I gave her to say.

Lynn was ready to do exactly what I said. She demanded that Green get a warrant in order to enter her home to take her kids.

While I had more than 25 years of experience as a family defender, I had never been on the phone with a client just as the State, complete with police escort, was attempting to take protective custody of children. To be sure, I sometimes had gotten calls from a distraught parent who had a CPS caseworker at his or her door, wondering if the caseworker should be allowed inside. Usually I'm able to read the situation accurately, advising the parent it was safe to allow the home inspection but still letting the parent know of some steps to take if things went badly. Occasionally, I was able to speak to a caseworker directly who had come inside the home, and I had talked the caseworker out of taking the kids by presenting some other options.

And at other times, it wasn't just the caseworker who needed to be walked back from the cliff. My own client sometimes would be escalating an argument with the caseworker, and a decision to take the kids could occur if the client herself didn't change his or her tone. At other times, I simply couldn't give *any* advice or help to the people who had CPS at their doorstep, because our office had not processed their request for legal services in time. If I or the lawyers who worked with me had no information about the basis for the CPS system's action against them, we had to steer clear of intervening in the matter until we had more information.

CPS caseworkers often reacted defensively to any form of legal intervention, so the last thing we wanted was to escalate a parent's legal woes before we were ready to handle potential fallout. So it was especially rare to find myself on the phone during the taking of protective custody in a case like Ben and Lynn's, where I had already been advising them for nine days. A solid medical opinion from a leading pediatric orthopedist also wasn't something most parents had already lined up at the time the State was attempting a seizure of their children.

With my steadiest voice, I advised Lynn. I tried my best to mask my own anxiety as to how this in-progress seizure of the children might end up.

It was unusual for parents to stand on their rights, as I had instructed Lynn to do. Parents almost never insisted that a CPS caseworker get a warrant in order to remove children. If Ben and Lynn hadn't already been getting legal advice, however, they, too, might have believed—as many parents do—that they had no choice but to let CPS caseworkers inside the house. They then would have been powerless as the caseworkers proceeded with police backup to take their children.

Janelle Green left as she was told to do, noting in her case record that she had managed to get a peek in the window at the twins being comforted by their grandmother. One of the twins had come toward the door, but the grandmother stopped him. Both twins looked "fine," Green's note says. So did Robert.

Ben hadn't gotten home yet, but as soon as he learned of the attempt to take the kids, he called me, urgent concern in his voice. Now he wanted a new kind of help from me: media attention. He had a contact at Channel 7 ABC News. He decided to head over to the TV station to try to stop the in-progress child seizure at his home.

I didn't rule out Ben's idea. Media attention was often the only way to get the attention of CPS system higher-ups. A well-placed call to the CPS director or top administrator from a journalist occasionally had slowed an in-progress child seizure. I thought to myself that the CPS director might be unhappy to see headlines about CPS taking children from a federal judge's daughter. Nor would the CPS director be happy to learn that his staff took this action after refusing to look at the medical report from a pediatric orthopedist at one of Chicago's top hospitals. I decided to call a journalist at the *Chicago Tribune* myself, someone I knew who covered CPS issues.

Though my main goal was to stop the State from taking Ben and Lynn's kids, I had another reason for trying to reach a *Tribune* reporter. I wanted the public to know what was happening to families. The overreaching of the CPS system usually hurt the underprivileged and minority families, but a wake-up call was needed to reach a broader audience.

News media focus on cases where the children are horribly abused. The public is justly concerned about children's well-being and recoils from the terrible stories of child abuse that populate the news. While parents abuse children, they deserve punishment and restrictions in their ability to cause further harm. They also rightly can be compelled to undergo rehabilitative services before being allowed to resume full care of their children outside the watchful eye of authorities.

At the same time, media reporting on horrendously abused children skews the public attitudes; accusations quickly are presumed to equal guilt. Finger-pointing turns immediately against parents, including innocent ones. The public desire to hold someone responsible for child maltreatment means that the public is primed to believe that whenever there is smoke, there is also fire.

Stories like Ben and Lynn's, involving CPS overreactions where children were wrongfully seized from loving homes, rarely get any headlines. For every family in Ben and Lynn's demographic, moreover, there were hundreds of less advantaged mothers and fathers who similarly had done nothing wrong but were losing their kids to the State on evidence just as one-sided as the evidence against Ben and Lynn.

I knew that the news media gravitated to telling compelling stories involving white middle-class suburban families. The police stakeout-in-progress involving this near-picture-perfect family seemed like a chance to tell how the CPS system overzealously removes children at the same time as it misses children who are genuinely abused. With a client like Ben game to talk about what was happening to his own family, I was willing to try to help Ben reach a reporter.

Although it was already close to 7:00 p.m., I got through to the *Tribune* reporter. Hoping to whet her interest in covering the case, I told her the facts I knew, mentioning how exemplary the parents were and how the mother's own mother was a federal judge. The reporter was polite; she took some notes. But there was a big obstacle that stopped her from taking any immediate action on Ben and Lynn's story.

The hang-up was that no one could prove Ben and Lynn's innocence right then and there. The reporter asked me, point-blank, "What if Ben or Lynn caused Robert's fracture after all?" She pressed me to assure her that neither of them had abused their child. We had no conclusive proof of innocence. How could we? We were still awaiting Dr. Sheridan's written report. Moreover, we had to acknowledge that a doctor (albeit one who was still in training to be a child abuse pediatrician) at the children's hospital believed that Robert had been abused.

The reporter's questions demonstrate one reason why it was so hard to draw media attention to stories like Ben and Lynn's, including dramatic ones with a stakeout-in-progress. If Ben and Lynn really were child abusers, the newspaper would be taking a risk if it wrote about the case before the facts had been aired in court. The reporter politely expressed interest in a possible future story, but she gave no commitment. She told me to call back if the family was exonerated in the court case. But by the time that happened, of course, the stakeout at the family home would be old news.

No one wants to take a chance on being on the wrong side of a child abuse story. One of the stories waiting to be told is how child abuse accusations silence innocent parents.

The media never did tell Ben and Lynn's story. By the time their ordeal had passed, it wasn't news.

Disheartened at striking out with the *Tribune* reporter, I left my office for the evening. Ben got no response, either. He raced home after his unsuccessful attempt to speak to a reporter at ABC Channel 7 News.

I called Ben from my car. After consulting with me about their legal rights, he and Lynn decided that they should leave the house with Ben's mom and the kids. It was likely that CPS caseworkers soon would return, demanding to take the kids. If the caseworkers got a warrant, that would leave Ben and Lynn no choice but to turn the children over to the authorities for a hellish overnight experience with the Illinois emergency-shelter system. Once there was a warrant, refusing to turn over the kids would cause serious legal repercussions that no parent would want to face. But there was no requirement that Ben or Lynn must stay home in order to greet the CPS or police again. They had every right to come and go from their home with their children as they pleased.

The case would come into court very soon. Now that the CPS team knew it needed a warrant, it was certain that Janelle Green or her supervisor would take steps to start the judicial ball rolling. If Ben and Lynn, together with Ben's mom, could keep the kids in the family until the court date, a judge still might allow the kids to stay with their grandparents. Judges tend not to like to change the status quo. Judges tend to be more willing to ratify CPS child removal decisions after the fact. It is another matter for a judge, on his or her own authority, to direct that children should be taken from their grandparents. If Ben and Lynn could keep the kids with the grandparents overnight, it was possible we would be able to persuade a judge to allow them to remain in the home with family.

The family stayed with neighbors overnight. They were lucky. They were able to vacate their home while Janelle Green and company regrouped for the evening.

At 7:40 p.m., Supervisor Kirby Long put out an all-shift alert to the CPS investigations division of the State of Illinois, noting that Lynn and Ben's mother had refused to turn over the children without a warrant. The note added, "The family has obtained legal counsel," as if that note explained the alert's urgency. The note repeated that the decision to take the children into State protective custody was based on Dr. Felix's conclusion that abuse was the likely explanation for Robert's fracture and that the parents had "no explanation" for how the fracture occurred. It concluded, "Protective custody of the other two children is due to risk." The term "risk" was not clarified.

By 9:02 p.m., additional caseworkers were assigned to try to execute the protective custody command. At 11:15 p.m., Caseworker John Allen came to the home. He rang the doorbell. No one answered, so he was unable to enter. The all-shift alert passed to a CPS overnight team.

At 12:35 a.m., yet another caseworker got the request for assistance to take the children into State protective custody. At 3:30 a.m., a CPS manager went to the home himself and rang the bell. He recorded his "good faith attempt" after calling for police backup once again. Three squad cars went to the home. This effort failed, too, so the manager dutifully wrote to his own supervisor that a warrant to seize the children was needed.

And so the night ended. The next phase of Ben and Lynn's struggle to prevent their children from becoming wards of the Illinois foster care system was about to start. It was time for the juvenile court to intervene.

SIX

Planning for a Court Date to Keep the Kids

It was the morning of October 2. The family was still together, for the CPS and police had not located them overnight. The children had been able to sleep through the night, but the grown-ups' anxiety levels prevented them from getting much rest. Ben's mom had been terrified to see the police cars and sirens, with the CPS caseworkers knocking on the door demanding that her grandchildren be turned over to the investigator.

In my last call with Ben, I had suggested that Ben's whole family minus the children should come to my office in the morning to plan for a now-inevitable court hearing. So shortly after I got to my office, Ben and Lynn and Ben's parents arrived. After they filled Melissa and me in on the further details of their terrifying experience the previous evening, we started to discuss next steps.

It was a matter of hours, a day at most, before a court action would begin. To start a juvenile court case, the State's Attorney first would have to file a Petition for Adjudication of Wardship as to each child. The State most likely would also file motions (i.e., written requests) asking the judge to order that temporary legal custody of children be given the CPS guardianship administrator. Such an order would authorize the CPS agency to control the decisions concerning the children, including decisions as to where the children would be placed.

It was conceivable, though, that the CPS caseworkers could place the children with relatives, including with Ben's parents as relative foster parents. When legal custodial decision-making powers were taken from the parents and transferred to the State CPS Guardianship Administrator, CPS caseworkers also had the power to place the children with foster parents who are strangers to the children or into emergency shelters or group homes.

Exactly where the children would go depended on the juvenile court's decisions and the recommendations of various parties to the juvenile court case. If the CPS agency decided to put the children with relatives, the temporary custody power allowed the CPS agency to remove children from a relative's care without coming back to court. Once children were placed with relatives, however, the CPS agency usually didn't exercise its power to remove the children unless an incident that seemed dangerous or inappropriate occurred (though arbitrary and unfair removals certainly occurred, especially if the foster parents became demanding). Usually, however, removal from relative foster homes provoked conflicts that the CPS caseworkers would try to avoid. It wasn't as if there were other foster homes begging to have these children.

The events of the previous night made it extremely unlikely that the State's Attorney's office and the CPS agency would be satisfied with any order allowing Ben and Lynn to retain legal custody of their children. It was likely we were heading for a temporary custody hearing very soon. Occasionally, the State asked for orders allowing caseworkers merely to monitor a family, providing social services to correct any conditions that had caused the CPS agency to believe the children were abused or neglected. Such orders left the parents' custodial rights intact. But such orders at the beginning of a case were not the norm. Moreover, that sort of order was almost never granted in a case involving an unexplained fracture in a young infant.

Melissa and I knew what was coming, but Ben and Lynn and their parents did not. If the CPS agency was granted temporary custody, placement of the children with Ben's parents as foster parents was not a certainty. Regardless of where the children were placed, they would remain under CPS legal custody, subject to the CPS agency's direction as to their care. That status would continue through an eventual trial on the merits of the State's contention that Robert had been abused. Under Illinois law, that trial would have to occur within 90 days unless Ben and Lynn allowed that trial deadline to be extended.

By demanding a warrant, Ben and Lynn had prevented the children from being seized and placed outside the family, but they had not stopped the inevitable progress of the CPS investigation toward a juvenile court proceeding. The legal self-defense of the family would become expensive.

Juvenile court cases are never quick or simple. Especially because of the medical issues in Robert's case, hundreds of hours of legal work would likely be necessary before Ben and Lynn's legal ordeal would be over.

Ben's father was experienced in working with lawyers. He appreciated his son and daughter-in-law's need for knowledgeable legal counsel in this new and unfamiliar legal forum. We quickly worked out an initial retainer agreement, allowing us to prepare legal authorizations and forms needed to represent Ben and Lynn in the ensuing court proceedings.

Ben and Lynn wanted us to represent both of them; a unified defense was in their mutual interest. Representing each parent separately would magnify the costs and suggest a conflict between them in the eyes of the judge and other parties. In some cases, however, including if parents had different versions of significant events or if they did not live together, Melissa and I would have insisted that the parents should secure separate counsel. But we had no reason to believe that Ben or Lynn were likely to develop a conflict between their legal positions later on. We warned them, however, that if a conflict did emerge, we wouldn't be able to represent either of them. Ben and Lynn understood and agreed to joint representation.

Ben and Lynn stayed strong and united. It took a special sort of marriage to weather the sort of accusations they were facing. I later could see that Ben and Lynn did not always view the experience through exactly the same focus. Even so, they worked through their differences. They had many family matters to concentrate on. They would need to remain strong together for many years after my involvement as their lawyer had receded into the past.

A sad fact of child protective services intervention was that it often created family instability and tension between family members. State child protection agencies all profess the goal of preserving and reuniting families. But the families are always changed by the CPS hotline call, which brings outside scrutiny by governmental officials into the family's most intimate relationships. Joyce McMillan, whom I met through her leadership at the Child Welfare Organizing Project in New York City, uses the mantra "surveillance is not support" in critiquing the role of CPS involved with families for whom she advocates. When CPS intervention and restrictions are applied to a family wrongly accused of abuse, it is especially hard for the family to pick up all the pieces and move back to a normal familial relationship, even if they are exonerated in the courts.

It helped Ben and Lynn's prospects that neither of them had been specifically identified as Robert's abuser. If one parent were more clearly blameless, there could be pressure on the parents to formally separate so that the nonaccused parent could continue to care for the children. CPS caseworkers would sometimes foment suspicion of one parent against the other. In effect, separations and divorces could be forced upon families so that children could be returned to one parent.

If a nonaccused parent agreed not to let the accused parent be alone with the children, the State would oftentimes agree that the kids could stay with the parent believed to be innocent. But setting up one parent as the monitor of the other could challenge the parents' relationship beyond the breaking point. While Lynn had been with Robert the most on the day the injury was noticed, no one could say that the injury happened while Robert was with her and not Ben. The fact that they vouched for each other and that their accounts were remarkably consistent helped reassure Melissa and me that they did not need separate legal counsel.

After we dealt with the terms of our retainer, the discussion focused on Ben's and Lynn's goals in the ensuing court case and strategies for avoiding the children's removal from the home.

When parents are accused of abusing a newborn baby, judges in the Cook County Juvenile Court naturally are cautious. Lacking independent knowledge of the case, they rely on the lawyers who regularly appear in their courtrooms, assigned by various state and county agencies. Lynn was the primary target of the CPS investigation, but Ben was hardly exonerated. We thought there was a low likelihood that the children would be allowed to go home with Ben, and we didn't want to press that result at Lynn's expense.

It was critical that a decent juvenile court judge—one willing to listen to the parents' story with an open mind—got assigned to hear the family's case. Viewing the parents who appeared in their courtrooms with jaded eyes, some judges were more prone to credit CPS investigators and the State's Attorney. Illinois provides the right for each party to request one change of judge without needing to provide a reason. We would exercise that right on Ben and Lynn's behalf if necessary.

Soon, there would be new parties entering the case. The State's Attorney's office would prosecute the case, so I had already left a message with the office to let them know that Melissa and I would be representing Ben and Lynn. I asked that we be contacted as soon as any petitions against them were filed.

Once the court petitions were filed and assigned to a judge in one of a dozen courtrooms hearing abuse and neglect cases in Cook County, a dual purpose guardian ad litem/attorney (GAL) for the children also would be appointed. This individual was responsible for advocating the children's legal interests and objectives (in their attorney role) and, at the same time, for advocating what they saw as the children's "best interests" (in their guardian ad litem role).

Playing that dual role is no easy feat; serious conflicts could develop between what a client's objectives were and what their guardian ad litem considered best for the client.[1] This is especially true when children want to go home to parents who have mistreated them. At initial stages of the case, when infants were involved, the attorney/guardian ad litem's role usually devolved into a position that allied with the State. This was true even though the vast majority of the children taken from their parents, if able to voice their wishes, would say they wanted to live with their parents.

But in Cook County, the guardian ad litem usually took a hardline position that the best interests of the client required removal from the parents' care. In practice, this meant that the parents had to defend themselves against two attorney offices—the State's Attorney and the Office of Public Guardian (the guardian ad litem's office)—with the added disadvantage that whatever position the guardian ad litem took was proclaimed as the children's "best interests."

Protracted proceedings made it hard for parents to get their children home. Illinois currently leads the nation in delays in returning children to their parents, with delays averaging four years. Even when parents did everything asked of them and the CPS agency itself was ready to return children home, guardians ad litem sometimes pressed for children's continued placement in foster care. Parents would face the all-but-impossible task of dispelling all fears of what might happen to their children if they were returned home, no matter how speculative those fears might be. Securing orders that allowed parents to regain custody of their children could take many months, sometimes years. And judges tended to listen to the guardian ad litem, the party who purported to speak for the children.

These realities reinforced the necessity of pressing to keep Ben and Lynn's children with their grandparents at all costs. Fortunately, neither the State's Attorney nor the guardian ad litem had any ax to grind against grandparents in general or against these children's grandparents in particular. Ben's parents were community leaders and devoted caregivers. By now, they had been caring full-time for Robert and the twins for three weeks without any incidents of concern. Sadly, many children in the foster care system in

Illinois did not have grandparents able to travel hundreds of miles at a moment's notice to care for their grandchildren, while putting their own lives on hold.

While grandparents and other relatives bear a tremendous burden in the foster care system, many children have relatives who don't come forward. Sometimes the relatives are never notified that a child they would be happy to care for has been placed with strangers. Sometimes relatives simply can't accommodate a child who has been removed from parents—because of their own careers or if they are already caring for other children. Some relatives are unwilling to come forward due to conflictual relationships with the parents. Given the challenges of finding good homes for children removed from their parents, the State, the judges, and guardians ad litem often appreciated relatives who stepped in, knowing that this was the best alternative when parents were unable or unfit to care for their children.

While we prepared Ben and Lynn for what to expect in court, they were acutely aware that any wrong turn could mean a potentially permanent loss of their children to the State of Illinois. Melissa and I had to be careful not to alarm them even more, so we kept our own horror stories to a minimum. It was a delicate balancing act: encouraging Ben and Lynn to hope that their children would be returned to them so that they stayed positive with all the players in the court system while providing them a realistic assessment of what might happen over the next several weeks or months. Of course, we didn't know exactly what to expect ourselves, but we knew the possibilities.

Many parents who face State petitions to take their children from them become understandably angry. They may take out their frustrations on the opposing attorneys, even venting before the judge. Such conduct, though understandable, reinforces CPS's negative narrative the judge has already heard about them. Lawyers play a very important role in reframing that narrative, legitimizing the parents' just complaints, and calming the parents' frayed nerves in the process. Much of this positive lawyer's role is played just by listening.

While the law on the books allowed parents to get petitions dismissed right away when there was little or no evidence of wrongdoing, there was no realistic chance of that occurring for Ben and Lynn. The medical opinion of a child abuse pediatrician made dismissal at the first court date extremely unlikely. Most juvenile court judges ratified the requests of CPS investigators to take temporary custody of the children whose cases came to their courtrooms.

In fact, it was rare for judges in the child protection courtrooms to be asked to hear contested evidence at the outset of a case. If the State could not establish probable cause to believe that the children were abused or neglected, the case could be dismissed right away and the children released to their parents' care. But the number of cases in which the State's petitions were dismissed for lack of probable cause at this beginning stage was close to zero. Usually the parties stipulated that the State possessed probable cause and set the case on a course toward trial months later.

There were some practical reasons why the judges in the juvenile court heard few claims of lack of probable cause from parents' attorneys early in the case. Most cases started with the seizure of children into protective custody; it was this seizure that started the 48-hour judicial clock running, during which time (excluding weekends) a petition in Illinois had to be filed and presented to the judge. But at the time most children are seized, very few of the parents have access to legal counsel to explain what to expect at the end of the 48-hour mark. Few families have anyone gathering evidence and preparing arguments on their behalf for the first scheduled court date. Most parents in the juvenile court are indigent, and even those who are not indigent likely have difficulty finding a knowledgeable and experienced lawyer to help them within the short time before the first court date.

For indigent parents entitled to have counsel appointed for them,[2] the first chance to meet their court-appointed counsel usually comes right as the 48-hour mark expires. Parents arrive in court, if they know where to come, utterly unprepared to challenge the State's petitions. Their newly appointed counsel knows nothing about the case. This lack of preparation effectively forces the parents to enter into agreements they wouldn't neces-sarily want if they had more time to respond to the State's claims at the start of the case. Of course, parents often don't make it to court at the first court date, sometimes because they haven't been told of the action against them, so temporary custody of their children is taken by default.

The State has significant advantages at the 48-hour initial hearing before the judge. Over the prior weeks and months, CPS caseworkers had already pulled together the information that supported the State's petitions. They reviewed the records prepared by State-paid experts. When the petitions are filed, a State's Attorney meets right away with the CPS investigator to prepare the essential information for the initial court hearing. Hearsay testimony is liberally allowed at the first hearing, so the caseworker can simply recount evidence gathered during the investigation to support taking the kids from their parents under a temporary custody order. Moreover, most of the caseworkers had some experience presenting information to a judge, while most parents had no comparable experience.

The net effect of these practical considerations is that if the parents wanted to demand an initial probable cause hearing, the State's Attorney usually would be ready to put on the necessary evidence against the parents, and the parents, with their newly appointed counsel, barely would be ready at all.

At the 48-hour hearing, parents' attorneys would have only a few minutes to review the lengthy packet of notes and reports that the CPS investigator had assembled. This was true for us in representing Ben and Lynn, too.[3] After we filed our appearance forms, we would be handed the CPS investigation packet, which might run hundreds of pages and would contain the notes of all the contacts made during the CPS investigation. While the packets provided enormous grist for cross-examination, the hurried meeting and immediate court call at the outset of a case was the worst possible setting in which to prepare for an effective cross-examination of the State's potential witnesses against the parents.

Unprepared to fight for the parents' continued custody of the children and presented with a flood of information that needed to be digested carefully, parents' attorneys of every stripe naturally felt pressure to enter into agreements that allowed the State to assume temporary custody of the children—especially if these agreements were presented as "just temporary." Once these interim agreements were reached, the newly filed court case could be set over to future court dates for fact gathering, preparation of witnesses and exhibits, and an eventual trial on merits of the State's abuse or neglect claims against the parents.

It was easy to get sucked into this logic. As a practical matter, resisting it could be impossible. As a result, attorneys for parents often counseled parents that opposing the State's request for temporary custody was against the parents' own interests. Frequently, there was no upside to fighting the State right off the bat. Attorneys for parents could reasonably conclude that the parents would inevitably lose an initial fight. If they fought with the State too soon and without sufficient preparation, they could damage their credibility. Strategically speaking, demanding a hearing right away could help the State make the case against the parents by providing a gratuitous opportunity to sway the judge against them.

All of these considerations led Melissa and me to carefully weigh the question of whether we should try to mount a case against the State's initial 48-hour-mark request to take the children into the State's temporary custody. We had to be cautious as we were aware that putting on State witnesses and demanding court time in a crowded court call might only harden minds against the parents in the longer run. It wasn't exactly payback, but no one appreciated parents' attorneys who fought fruitless battles that consumed excessive court time.

In theory, we could agree that there was probable cause to believe the children were abused but still argue that the children should not be taken from their parents because the State could not show an "urgent and immediate necessity" to remove them, as the law required. But this was tricky, because if the judge believed there was a sufficient likelihood (i.e., probable cause to believe) that the child was abused, the judge usually would find sufficient "urgent and immediate necessity" for removal.

Sometimes the suspicion against the parents was not especially strong, so one or both parents might convince a reasonable judge to allow them to keep their children and maintain their custodial rights intact. The children could be returned home to one or both parents, and the child protection case would still proceed to trial while the children remained home. In such cases, the judge typically would enter an order requiring the parents to engage in services, like counseling and drug treatment, to demonstrate that they had addressed the concerns that led to allegations against them. Agreeing to such services and allowing CPS workers to have regular access to their home to monitor their care of the children were the usual costs of getting children returned home under such orders. But orders returning the children under these conditions would rarely be entered if the State and guardian ad litem did not agree.

We doubted that the State or guardian ad litem, let alone both of them, would agree to Ben and Lynn keeping custody. At a minimum, they would want a lot more information about their ability to protect the children— information that needed to come from service providers who worked with the parents over several months.

In short, however much Melissa and I believed in Ben and Lynn's worthiness as parents, we doubted that we could convince either the judge or the to-be-assigned attorneys to allow the children to remain in Ben and Lynn's custody. Then, if the judge ruled against them at the temporary custody phase, Ben and Lynn were facing a likely two-to-three-month delay before the State would be required to come to trial on the petitions against them.

At the eventual trial, the judge would finally decide, based on all the evidence, whether Robert really had been abused. The State's Attorney bore the burden of proving the abuse, under a burden of proof that was typical for any civil case: a "preponderance of the evidence." This meant the State had only to prove that abuse was "more likely than not." The State didn't even have to prove *who* abused the child, as long as it established that a parent was responsible for the abuse or allowed it to occur. At the eventual trial, if the judge found Robert was not abused, the case would be dismissed, and the three children would go home right away. If the judge found that Robert was abused, however, then the case would be set over for a dispositional decision, which could include giving permanent legal guardianship of the children to the State of Illinois.

The procedural steps were complicated to explain, a true hybrid that seemed neither fish nor fol. Though considered civil cases, the stages in a child protection case mirror those of criminal cases. A criminal case starts with an initial arraignment/bond hearing, then proceeds to trial as to the accused person's guilt or innocence, and finally concludes with sentencing if the judge or jury finds the accused guilty.

Similarly, child protection cases start with an initial hearing on whether to hold the child in State custody pending trial and are followed by the adjudicatory trial as to the underlying facts regarding abuse or neglect and then a dispositional hearing, at which reports from social service agencies function like probation reports in criminal cases and are used to fashion the long-term plans for children.

Traditional family court proceedings involving custody disputes are very different. They start with a complaint, an answer, and a discovery period. In the meantime, orders are entered only at the parties' request, and the burden of proof is upon the party asking for a specific order.

Parents can prevail in a child protection case at any one of the three primary stages of the case. As in a criminal case, however, an appeal of an unfavorable decision to a higher reviewing court must wait for the final dispositional order. Altogether, Ben and Lynn were facing a juvenile court process that was likely to take three to six months to resolve, even if they demanded a speedy trial. If they lost the temporary custody hearing, the trial, and the dispositional hearing, the chance of getting to appellate court was half a year away, at a minimum.

All of this information was overwhelming to contemplate. As Ben and Lynn's lawyers, we had a duty to explain the juvenile court process as best we could, answer their questions, and then come up with a plan as to when and how we should address the State's claims.

We concluded that it would be address but not impossible to put up a fight to oppose the State's initial request for temporary custody of the three children. While Illinois law liberally allowed a full hearing of the evidence at the 48-hour mark, even if temporary custody was taken at the outset, there was a provision under Illinois law for a full temporary custody rehearing within 10 days. In Ben and Lynn's case, asking for such a rehearing made a lot of sense; within 10 days, Dr. Sheridan's report would be ready, and Dr. Sheridan himself might be available to testify.

I knew the Illinois law on temporary custody rehearing procedures well, as I had written it. I worked on due process revisions to the temporary custody sections of the Juvenile Court Act in the 1990s. The need for clear rights to written notification of the State's claims against parents and clear provisions for parents to get hearings in the absence of notice had been a pressing issue when I first started working on behalf of families in the juvenile court. Oftentimes, hearings concerning the custody of children who had been taken from their parents would commence, and parents wouldn't be told about the court date. Other times, they got garbled messages from caseworkers telling them to come to court but without information as to *which* court was hearing the case.

When I was a supervising attorney at the Legal Assistance Foundation (from 1984 until 1996), I worked as part of a team on an active legislative project regarding proposed revisions to state law, including the Juvenile Court Act. That freedom to work on legislative reforms ended in 1996, when restrictions on federally funded legal services programs took effect.[4] Legal services programs for the poor often advocated for stronger social programs for poor clients at public expense, along with fair processes to implement these programs. These processes sometimes cost states money, though they also saved money by preventing unfair decisions, including the decisions that caused children to go into foster care unnecessarily. After the federal funding restrictions took hold, I was unable to dedicate any of my time to legislative projects until 2009.

Seeing the need for a center for family advocacy that could do it all—fight for individual clients, bring class action suits, work on legislative and regulatory policy reforms, and educate the legal, professional, and client communities about the rights of families—had motivated me to create the Family Defense Center in 2005.[5]

In 2009, the center's budget had grown enough that we were able to hire a legislative affairs consultant to help us present proposed changes to Illinois law for the benefit of the families we represented. Melissa and I started to work on some legislative projects, including ones that would have helped Ben and Lynn. But of the many provisions we proposed that year, only one legislative change was adopted: a requirement for certified mail notice of indicated findings in the child-abuse register. Though it passed into law, that change was never implemented, due to lack of funding for the added mailing costs. It was more than a little frustrating to see our hard work on good proposals get whittled down and then stymied. The temporary custody rehearing provisions I had drafted in the mid-1990s had been a more satisfying project. It was gratifying to use the fruits of my work over a decade later to help Ben and Lynn fight for their children.

SEVEN

"Without Prejudice" Means You Lose the Kids for Now

On October 2, 2009, when the petitions were filed against Ben and Lynn, Melissa and I already had been working on Ben and Lynn's behalf for 10 days. For once, we had a real advantage over the State's Attorney's office, though the assistant State's Attorneys assigned to prosecute didn't realize it. These attorneys were used to winning their cases in the juvenile court, so they could appear dismissive of anyone who suggested that they might not have so strong a hand. While the State's Attorneys and guardians ad litem had the advantage of knowing the juvenile court folklore and the predilections of the specific judge before whom Ben and Lynn would have to appear, Ben and Lynn had an advantage of having lawyers who were zealous family defenders, who knew most of the essential facts of their case before the courtroom drama began, and who were willing to fight assertively with the State to keep their kids home.

While we met with Ben and Lynn and Ben's parents, Caseworker Green was meeting with the screener at the Cook County State's Attorney's office to get a case filed against Ben and Lynn in the juvenile court. State's Attorney's office screeners convened every morning with CPS caseworkers to review cases in which petitions needed to be filed within 48 hours after children had been seized from their parents. The CPS caseworkers prepared most of the standard-form court papers. They explained to the screeners the evidence they had gathered that pointed toward child abuse or neglect.

Sometimes the screeners rejected cases, directing the caseworkers to get more information before a petition could be filed. If that occurred, children who were already in State protective custody should be released to their parents (although we had seen violations of that requirement aplenty and even sued about such violations in the *Hernandez v. Foster* case, as discussed in chapter 14).

However, if CPS investigators had medical evidence from a trusted source, like the hospital's child protection team, the State's Attorney's screener was very likely to accept the request to file the case. It didn't matter much if the parents had their own medical experts. It was the judge's job, after all, to decide which doctor's opinion to credit. So even though the screener knew that Ben and Lynn had a medical opinion from Dr. Sheridan, the screener approved Green's request to file three Petitions for Adjudication of Wardship, one for each of Ben and Lynn's three children.

Janelle Green's sworn affidavit was attached to each child's petition. That affidavit proclaimed that the State had made "reasonable efforts" to keep the children with their parents. The specific reasonable efforts, however, were not detailed.

The three petitions were filed at 12:52 p.m., on October 2, 2009, along with motions for temporary custody for each child. It was now official; the State of Illinois was asking a judge to make Ben and Lynn's three children "wards of the court" whose care would be the legal responsibility of the State CPS agency. The State's Guardianship Administrator would become the temporary legal parent of the children. Ben and Lynn's rights to make decisions about their children were about to be suspended indefinitely.

Two assistant State's Attorneys were assigned to prosecute the petitions against Ben and Lynn. The less experienced of the two, State's Attorney Candace O'Neill, had gone to law school with my co-counsel, Melissa Staas. Assignments to the State's Attorney's Juvenile Court's Child Protection Division often functioned as steps in a ladder to the office's criminal divisions, though the division had taken steps to keep experienced attorneys in its Child Protection Division. Many assistant State's Attorneys wanted to prosecute criminals, not butt heads with parents charged with abuse or neglect.

Most of the families in the juvenile court found themselves in child protection court because of substance abuse or domestic violence. Mental health issues and other family instability often added to the grounds for the State's stepping in. Contrary to the public image, sexually abused and severely battered children were not the most common alleged victims in child protection court caseloads. Nevertheless, the Child Protective Division heard a number of cases involving serious child abuse and neglect issues, with medical, law enforcement, and CPS witnesses testifying against the alleged abusers and neglectors.

An assignment to a child protection courtroom could provide good legal practice for assistant State's Attorneys' future criminal prosecutions of murderers and rapists. In some cases pending in the juvenile court, moreover, there were criminal cases pending against the parents, so the State's Attorney's office sometimes had to coordinate its prosecutions.

After Janelle Green screened the case against Ben and Lynn, the court files with the three petitions for each of the children passed to State's Attorney O'Neill and her supervisor, State's Attorney Gary Bailey. Fortunately, Janelle Green told them that I would be appearing on Ben and Lynn's behalf. I also left a message with the screener.

The State's Attorneys were eager to have the parents show up in court. They wanted Ben and Lynn to turn over the children to the CPS caseworker in an orderly manner. Having a family on the run was to be avoided, for it didn't make the State look good if suspected child abusers were allowed to flee with their children before they could be served with court papers.

State's Attorney O'Neill's call to me in the middle of the morning was polite and professional. She let me know that the petitions had been filed and assigned to Judge Rodney Sanders. She asked if we would come to court for a temporary custody hearing. I asked her to fax the petitions to me, and I offered to be in court at 2:00 p.m. Since the children had not been taken into state custody as the CPS team had planned, Ben's and Lynn's court case did not have to adhere to the typical 48-hour clock.

The fact that the children hadn't been taken into protective custody seemed to irritate State's Attorney O'Neill. She quickly accused the parents of evading the court process by refusing to turn the children over on demand. But Ben and Lynn hadn't violated any order. I politely informed State's Attorney O'Neill that Ben and Lynn had a constitutional right to refuse to let the CPS investigator into their home without a warrant, unless the children had been in immediate danger. I may have goaded her a bit, too, asking her what danger the children faced at the time they were home with their grandmother.

State's Attorney O'Neill had trouble responding, for she hadn't yet read through the thick CPS investigation file herself. Nevertheless, I offered to discuss the legal issues with her at 2:00 p.m. State's Attorney O'Neill dutifully informed the judge that the family had private attorneys (i.e., attorneys not appointed by the court) who would be in court that afternoon.

Melissa and I arrived before the scheduled court time in order to file our attorney appearance forms with the court clerk and meet both the State's Attorney and the guardian ad litem before the case got called for hearing. We had decided that it was neither safe nor necessary for Ben and Lynn to come to court or for the children to be brought there, although we wanted the grandparents to be present in case anyone had questions about their ability to serve as the children's primary child-care providers. We could call Ben and Lynn to come to court quickly if necessary.

Melissa and I wanted the State's Attorneys to know about the extensive evidence in Ben and Lynn's favor, including Dr. Sheridan's medical opinion, for it wasn't clear to us that they knew of his disagreement with the child abuse pediatrician. Had they filed the petitions without considering his opinion? If so, that might constitute a potential legal ethics violation, for State's Attorneys are supposed to conduct an investigation of reasonably available facts before they sign and file court petitions.

As soon as we arrived in the assigned courtroom, we met with a senior supervisor in the State's Attorney's office. He acknowledged awareness of Dr. Sheridan's opinion, but no one on the prosecution side, including the CPS team, had talked to the doctor. However, the supervisor considered it the court's job to sort out the competing opinions; it wasn't his office's job to decide which doctor, Dr. Felix or Dr. Sheridan, was correct.

We complained that there had been no reason for the fabricated emergency attempt to take the children into State custody the night before. The mere fact that the CPS team had finally gotten a child abuse opinion in writing from Dr. Felix didn't make the case an emergency. That opinion provided nothing new. In fact, when we were given a chance to look at the CPS investigation file, we soon saw that Dr. Felix had held the same child abuse opinion since September 11.

None of the assistant State's Attorneys wanted to debate constitutional due process or the Fourth Amendment's provisions on unreasonable seizures with us. They were used to CPS's taking protective custody whenever the CPS team was good and ready. It wasn't their job to second-guess the case-workers on the timing of their actions. While the senior supervisor knew me and knew that I had won some important constitutional cases involving child protection and family rights, he expressed confidence in the State's case against Ben and Lynn, while admitting that he, too, had questions about all the medical opinions in the case.

As we defended the parents' decisions not to let Janelle Green snatch the children from our clients, we quickly tried to shift the discussion from blaming the parents to the topic we cared about most: keeping the children with their grandparents. Fortunately, the State's Attorneys and the guardian ad litem did not object to the children staying in their own home with their grandparents.

Needing to cooperate with the caseworkers to present their testimony, they were not quick to question the actions of the CPS team, but the State's Attorneys had no need to defend the CPS team, either. Illinois had an unusual system of child protection prosecution that helped us in this instance. An independent, county-based State's Attorney's office files and prosecutes child abuse cases, reviewing and passing on the merits of the investigations conducted by the State CPS agency. It is a bit like the relationship of police to prosecutors in criminal cases. In many other states, however, the CPS agency's own attorney acts as the prosecutor. One advantage of the Illinois system was that State's Attorneys sometimes openly disagreed with CPS positions in cases.

The CPS caseworkers had their own CPS attorneys, however, and sometimes that only added an extra State-paid prosecutor-side attorney to the case. In addition, the children's appointed attorney/guardian ad litem rarely bucked the State's Attorney at the outset. This odd and costly multiplication of the number of attorneys involved in juvenile court cases in the child protection division had many disadvantages for parents. With three government-funded lawyers on every case (a State's Attorney, a CPS agency attorney, and an attorney/guardian ad litem for the children) arrayed against them, the legal deck already was heavily stacked against parents. But in a case in which the CPS investigators seemed to have a vendetta against a client of ours, as it had begun to seem for Ben and Lynn after the attempted seizure of the children the night before, it could be helpful that the State's Attorney's office was not wedded to the CPS team's position that the children needed to be removed from their home.

Not having Dr. Sheridan's report in writing put the State at an advantage if we were forced to go to an immediate hearing. If Caseworker Green were called to testify—she was already at the courthouse—she could present hearsay information about Dr. Felix's opinion. Moreover, the judge could read that opinion for himself. The judge could decide that he had enough evidence to order the children into State custody. Since it was urgent for the family to remain together, we faced a choice between starting a hearing we would likely lose in the short term or agreeing to a temporary custody order conditioned on the children staying with their grandparents in the hopes that we could also get the judge to set the case over for rehearing when we had Dr. Sheridan's report.

In Cook County Juvenile Court parlance, however, to accomplish this goal we were forced to accept an order of "temporary custody without prejudice." Under this order, the State agreed to allow the children to stay with their grandparents in Ben and Lynn's home. Ben and Lynn understood that the option of having the State withdraw or dismiss its petitions was a nonstarter. While nothing sounded more prejudicial to parents than the news that a judge had ordered their children into State temporary custody, the "without prejudice" caveat protected Ben and Lynn from any claim that the judge already had ruled against them on the facts and the law. In short, the deal Ben and Lynn were forced to make caused their children to become temporary wards of the State of Illinois on October 2, 2009. It was a terrible and an ugly deal, but it was all we could do to keep the children in the home with their grandparents that day.

After discussing these terms with the State's Attorney and the guardian ad litem, Judge Sanders called the case to be heard in order to accept the agreement. He announced that he was finding probable cause for purposes of the case as it stood. It was painful to hear, given the State's willful failure to gather or consider the evidence that would show abuse was not a reasonable likelihood. But the judge added that the order was "without prejudice" and would be subject to a rehearing as if there had never been any determination against the parents. It was all an elaborate dance to create a new status quo in favor of the State, taking away the parents' legal control of their children.

Still, the family had done well, by child protection court standards. The judge was sensitive to Ben and Lynn's interests in being as involved as they could be in every aspect of their children's care. He expressly directed that they should get notice of any medical appointments the CPS agency arranged for the children, since the children's medical care was now the responsibility of the CPS agency. He adamantly stated that "the children are not moving anywhere." He directed the State agency to prepare a service plan so that in the event the case proceeded to a full trial after the temporary custody rehearing, the case could move forward quickly. And he directed production of all the medical records from the two hospitals involved in treating Robert and from Dr. Sheridan's office so that all the lawyers could get ready for the first day of the temporary custody rehearing in 12 days, a date we confirmed would work for Dr. Sheridan.

Finally, a neutral judge would decide if there was reason to believe that Robert had been abused.

Ben and Lynn's luck during the month of September had been awful, but by October 2, they started to catch a few breaks: the favorable opinion of Dr. Sheridan on October 1 and good luck in their draw of a judge on October 2. Judge Sanders was a singularly pleasant judge. He had a fine judicial demeanor, a calm and thoughtful presence on the bench. Judge Sanders had a sufficiently good reputation among our family defense lawyer colleagues that it would be foolish to ask to change judges. Neither the State's Attorney nor the guardian ad litem had opposed the plan to allow the grandparents to continue as the children's caregivers, becoming their relative foster parents. Looking forward, Melissa and I thought that Ben and Lynn's case might have turned a corner. We could now focus on what we knew how to do best, which was to aggressively litigate cases for parents whose kids were taken into state custody.

Frankly, though, we couldn't imagine how Ben and Lynn maintained their composure. Now, although no one had welcomed juvenile court action, it was a relief to find a more orderly and predictable process starting to take place, even if that process meant that Ben and Lynn no longer had legal custody of their kids.

Another very lucky break—one that not every parent in a child protection court case is allowed—was that Judge Sanders agreed that Ben and Lynn could continue to have as much supervised contact with their children as the grandparents would afford them. Allowing Ben and Lynn to see their kids as long as a grandparent or another supervisor was present, their safety plan had been more liberal than some plans I have seen over the years. By the time the case came before Judge Sanders, Ben and Lynn had a track record of compliance with the CPS safety plan that gave reassurance that this relatively liberal contact should continue. Of course, the grandparents were not about to limit Ben and Lynn's time with their children.

Judge Sanders gave a brief endorsement of the placement with grandparents and the supervised visiting arrangement as "ideal for the kids." It probably helped matters that the State didn't claim to know who had abused Robert, even though it firmly believed Dr. Felix's opinion that abuse by someone was the likely cause of Robert's fracture.

Once the case entered juvenile court arena and the children became temporary wards of the State, the CPS agency's staffing of the case shifted.

The family's CPS case became a "placement case." Responsibilities for monitoring the children's safety and well-being moved to a private child welfare agency that held a placement service contract with the CPS agency. This new assignment meant that a new caseworker would provide services to the family and make recommendations to the juvenile court.

This shift provided some relief to the family. They no longer needed to let Green see their children on a weekly basis or whenever she decided to make an unannounced visit. If the family never had to see Green or her supervisor again, that would be fine with each of them. Moreover, the newly assigned caseworkers immediately took to Ben and Lynn and the grandparents. For the family, working with the new private child welfare agency was a relief.

Still, the CPS investigation against Ben and Lynn was not over. In fact, Ben and Lynn's decision to resist the protective custody demand on October 1 seemed to delay the CPS team's wrapping up the investigation. When we looked at the CPS file provided to us on October 2, it was troubling how little real investigation the CPS team had done. It appeared that none of the support letters for Ben and Lynn had been read or reviewed. None of the witnesses who had been with Lynn on September 10 had been interviewed, either. It began to seem that the CPS investigators had studiously refused to make the contacts that they ordinarily should make and had responded with passive aggression to all of the parents' efforts to provide them with exculpatory evidence to contradict the opinion of the child abuse doctor.

As the hearing of evidence unfolded, the investigation that should have been done in September started occurring in the courtroom under our watch.

The court hearing resumed on October 14. Between October 2 and October 14, Melissa and I combed through the CPS investigation file. We also prepared witness testimony and exhibits.

When the case was called for hearing, the three children came into the courtroom with their parents to stand before the judge's bench. Lynn held Robert in her arms while Ben held the twins' hands. Each child was cuter than the next. Robert still had his cast on, but otherwise the children were the picture of health. We wanted the judge to see the children for himself. These were the allegedly abused children who had been taken from their parents. We wanted the judge to see the whole family as it was before the hotline call had torn them apart, forcing Ben and Lynn to live away from their children. Even though the juvenile court proceedings are supposed to be all about the children, children are rarely seen in these courtrooms. The guardian ad litem seemed to be a bit miffed that we had asked the grandmother to bring the children to court. She announced that her office staff had already been to the home and that it wasn't necessary for the children to be there.

As lawyers for the parents, our focus for the hearing was to show the judge what kind of parents Ben and Lynn were. It was important to show the judge just how absurd the allegation of abuse against them was. Ben and Lynn's personal character and their character as parents had been utterly ignored by the CPS agency. By filing petitions accusing them of abusing Robert, the CPS agency and the State were denying Ben and Lynn's truthfulness, disbelieving their denials of hurting their son. In effect calling them liars, the State treated them with grievous disrespect. But no one on the State's side of the case seemed to understand how deep an insult they had caused or how the "child abuser" label contradicted everything true about Ben and Lynn.

At the heart of the child abuse pediatrician's opinion was the belief, expressed in the text of the opinion she had written, that either Ben or Lynn, or both, must have known when and how Robert leg was fractured because he would have cried inconsolably at the moment the fracture occurred. The pain of the fracture would have been so great that no reasonable parent could have missed it. Therefore, Ben or Lynn's denials of abuse were not to be believed. One or both of them was a child abuser, and one or both of them had to be lying.

The assumption that one of them was lying struck us as a fundamental and obvious error. The medical evidence of abuse was hardly airtight. The strong pediatric orthopedic opinion we had obtained from Dr. Sheridan showed that, at a minimum, there was a genuine medical dispute in the case. Given that the abuse claim was debatable, the fact that both parents had never injured another human being and had stellar reputations should have counted for something. Their character should certainly have been considered. By the same token, we believed that the State had to have some factual basis to label them liars before the judge should credit its accusations of the most awful of actions against their newborn child.

One obvious way to impress the judge with Ben and Lynn's exemplary character was to offer testimony from other excellent judges of character who made credibility judgments for a living: two federal judges who both knew Ben and Lynn well. It was unprecedented for me to have two federal judges vouching for a client. Lynn's mother, Natalie, was an obvious witness to impress Judge Sanders. A second federal judge in Chicago was a close family friend; his wife had been one of the first people to sign up to be an additional safety plan supervisor.

These judges' testimony would provide strong character evidence for Ben and Lynn and simultaneously send a signal to the judge that the case wasn't going to go quietly into the archives of the juvenile court. The underlying message was that this family had some clout and that the State should beware of repercussions when mislabeling Ben and Lynn as child abusers. At a minimum, the judge should not accept the cavalier assumption that the parents were hiding something.

When we announced our intention to call two federal judges to testify, however, the State's Attorney's office wanted no part of this parade. It seemed that Judge Sanders also considered the plan to call federal judges as witnesses heavy handed. Understandably, he was reluctant to turn his courtroom into a circus. Perhaps we were overplaying our hand, but nothing seemed to stop the child protection system from churning in the direction of family destruction. Ben and Lynn's character and parenting abilities didn't seem to matter to anyone. It didn't matter that their children were healthy, happy, and thriving in their care. All that seemed to matter was that a child abuse pediatric fellow considered them to be child abusers.

While the State ordinarily presented its witnesses first, we agreed to call Dr. Sheridan to testify first, out of the usual order, due to his busy schedule. But as soon as the case was called to commence the hearing, it became apparent that completing Dr. Sheridan's testimony that day would be a challenge. A routine fire drill interrupted us right when we were about to start. Once again, it seemed that Ben and Lynn couldn't catch a break.

As soon as we came back in front of Judge Sanders from the drill, the State's Attorneys announced that they wanted to call two new doctors besides Dr. Felix as witnesses. The guardian ad litem wanted time to secure a medical consultant, too. The court day was already overbooked. The hearing had not yet commenced, but it was getting longer as each new item of scheduling came up.

Ben's mother had come from out of state to care for the children. The prospect of a multiple-month-long hearing was becoming a frightening possibility. While I had no doubt that Ben's mother would tough it out as long as necessary, it wasn't fair to force her to remain in Illinois for weeks on end just so that the State could put on a new parade of witnesses that the CPS caseworkers had never talked to during the investigation.

Temporary custody hearings are supposed to be expedited and preliminary. They are not supposed to be dragged-out trials. The low probable cause threshold to proceed to trial on a petition applies precisely for that reason. That's the reason, too, that hearsay testimony is allowed at the first hearing; it helps to expedite the decision as to whether there are enough grounds to continue the case for trial.

It was quickly becoming clear, however, that temporary custody hearings are expedited only because parents don't usually fight back. As soon as it was the parents rather than the State who wanted to put on detailed evidence, in order to show that the State's case was erroneous from the start, a quick hearing became nearly impossible. Although placed with their grandparents, the children were in State custody, so the State was effectively winning its plea for a temporary custody order by default. By adding new witnesses to the list, the State seemed to be trying to prolong its advantage as long as possible, at the family's expense.

EIGHT

Bringing on the Witnesses

I prepared Dr. Sheridan to testify, and I knew he would be clear and engaging. Dr. Sheridan was a gifted teacher—a quality that generally translates well into the courtroom. He could explain complex areas of orthopedics in a concise and dynamic manner. Direct examination provided an opportunity for Dr. Sheridan to provide readily digestible answers to questions that naturally arose about Robert's fracture.

We saw some advantage in putting our strong case for the parents' exoneration first, before the State's Attorney presented their witnesses against the parents. We expected, however, that the State would try to paint him as biased in favor of parents and "soft" on child abuse. That's what the State genuinely seemed to believe. It was hard to shake such a fixed view of an expert witness, no matter how wrong it might be. If only the State had viewed its own experts with half as critical an eye as they applied to Dr. Sheridan.

As I started questioning Dr. Sheridan, State's Attorney Bailey quickly agreed that he should be recognized as an expert in pediatric orthopedics, saving considerable time in preliminary questions. But I still wanted to highlight a few points: his editorial board positions on academic journals, his research in the field of child abuse, and his training of residents on the orthopedic evaluation of child abuse.

Expert witnesses, like Dr. Sheridan, are central to child protection litigation in physical abuse cases. Judges and attorneys are laypeople when it comes to the assessment of the causes of injuries to children. For better or for worse, medical opinion matters enormously to the outcome of child abuse cases. Discerning whether a fracture is accidental, due to a medical condition, or due to abuse turns on understanding bones, the way they fracture, bone diseases, and conditions that weaken bones and, ultimately, on divining human intent from physical evidence. How does any doctor know what caused a fracture, especially if there were no verbal witnesses? What factors go into the medical assessment? Why would a doctor who is considered a child abuse expert know more or less than an orthopedist about what happened to cause a newborn to have a broken leg?

According to Dr. Sheridan, the answers were quite simple: no one has a crystal ball, although science has a lot to say. Bones don't tell doctors the cause of their breaking. There is no such thing as a unique "abusive force" in the physical world; there is only force. Since human intent cannot be discerned from the manner in which bones present themselves in X-rays, a doctor can't claim to know if abuse caused a fracture just from reading bone scans. Virtually all fractures can be caused by either accidental injuries or abuse, and underlying medical conditions can contribute to the fragility of bones. While some fractures are more commonly accidental and others may be considered more commonly occurring in abuse, looking at the bone and the way it fractured doesn't give an answer to what specific source of force caused it to break. Nor can any bone fracture, no matter how severe, tell a doctor whether a human being with a particular state of mind acted in such a way that the end result was a broken bone.

To be sure, there are many factors to consider in concluding whether any fracture is due to an accident, a medical condition, or abuse: the presence of other injuries, including bruising and burns; the history the parents or other witnesses provided; and the environment in which the child was placed at the time of the injury. Some fractures are more suggestive of abuse than others, including multiple fractures in different stages of healing and unusual fractures in locations not usually seen in accidental injuries, such as the spine.

Femur fractures like Robert's can be suggestive of abuse, because as a newborn, he couldn't cause the fracture on his own power, since he couldn't even roll over by himself. However, the location and type of his fracture was common in accidental femur breaks, too. The mere presence of a femur fracture, regardless of its form being a spiral or straight and linear, does not determine whether the cause of the break was an abusive force as opposed to an accidental force. The same fracture pattern could occur both accidentally and through abuse.

Dr. Sheridan described his own examination of Robert and his review of the X-rays other hospitals had taken. He saw no other injuries besides

Robert's broken leg, which was healing. He had talked to both Ben and Lynn and had learned that Robert had been a little irritable in the few days before they noticed his swollen leg and that they were perplexed about how the injury occurred. Because Robert had two older siblings, an accidental injury during play with them was possible. Dr. Sheridan noted that "we wouldn't have to be telling two-year-olds to be careful around their little brother" if they always were as careful as they needed to be and if they couldn't cause damage.

To show how Robert's fracture appeared on X-rays, Dr. Sheridan gave a slide show demonstration in the courtroom, using a projector and a pointer as if he were lecturing to first-year medical students in an anatomy class. This demonstration showed off Dr. Sheridan's superior expertise in evaluating fractures. Dr. Sheridan explained that orthopedic surgeons don't generally rely on radiologists to read X-rays for them. Orthopedists need to have a sophisticated understanding of X-rays. They might need to make quick treatment decisions during surgery based on what they were seeing in the patient and on films. They generally consulted radiologists with harder questions, not for basic X-ray reading.

Viewed laterally, Robert's fracture was a long oblique fracture, not a spiral as Dr. Felix had asserted. An oblique fracture is a straight, cut-across fracture at an angle, typically caused by a bending force. Usually fractures are caused by some degree of bending and some degree of torsion, or twisting, and Robert's fracture followed that pattern. A spiral fracture, caused by more twisting than bending forces, would curve up the bone "like stripes on a barber pole." At the end of the spiral would be a line from the top to the bottom of the fracture, though that line was not always easy to visualize.

Robert's fracture was displaced, meaning that the two sides of the bone had separated. A nondisplaced fracture would be more like a crack in china, which would show the fracture line while the bone as a whole would be "still one structure." If the bone fully separated, then the fracture was classified as displaced. The degree of separation determined whether the fracture should be classified as minimally, mildly, moderately, or severely displaced. Robert's fracture would be considered minimally displaced. Swelling would increase with the amount of displacement.

Dr. Sheridan had prepared three simple clear-plastic tubes with red marker lines showing fracture patterns. The oval pattern of an oblique fracture plainly appeared as a straight line when viewed from the side, with an abrupt break and line up at a certain point on the tubing. The spiral twisted all the way up, with no straight line down from the top, no matter the angle of view. Anyone in the courtroom could plainly see what an oblique fracture versus a spiral fracture looked like. Robert's fracture didn't have the pattern of a spiral.

The third tube showed what a displaced fracture looked like. Dr. Sheridan had cut another tube along the red oval line around the tube. This was exactly what Robert's fracture had looked like on the X-ray—a classic oblique fracture.

Fracture dating is approximate, based on whether the bone shows signs of healing. Robert's fracture at first had no signs of healing. It therefore had to be less than seven days old when it was discovered. But X-rays can't go back in time to show if the fracture first had been nondisplaced and later became displaced. Robert's September 24 skeletal survey showed real signs of healing. Marks looking like fluffy white clouds appeared on both sides of the femur bone. It takes 7 to 10 days for signs of healing like these to appear; after 14 days, there was "fairly abundant healing." A September 18 X-ray narrowed the window of when the fracture occurred, for there was only slight healing then. So the likelihood was that the fracture occurred within the few days before Lynn and Ben first saw Robert's swollen leg.

Fractures, especially in children, usually heal easily. Orthopedists say that the bones will heal as long as they are "in the same room." The healing would be 100 percent; eventually—in a year or two—no one would be able to see that Robert ever had a fracture.

Robert's fracture was not severe. It was not difficult to treat, and it posed no short-term or long-term danger to him. Some fractures could be life-threatening, but Robert's fracture was not going to affect his overall health.

As for the amount of force necessary to cause Robert's femur fracture, Dr. Sheridan first noted that the femur of a newborn is not very strong. Bones become stronger as loads are put on them. Children who walk have much stronger femur bones than immobile infants do. Still, it was impossible to give a specific measurement in units of foot-pounds as to how much force was necessary to break the femur of a four-week-old infant. In any event, no specific amount of force differentiates an abusive injury from a nonabusive one.

Dr. Sheridan had asked Lynn if she knew how Robert's femur break had occurred. She told him she had no idea. In children and adults who are able to walk, Dr. Sheridan's experience taught that unexplained fractures happen "all the time." Dr. Sheridan knew doctors as well as many patients who had fractures themselves and didn't realize it. A parent's lack of an explanation for the cause of a child's fracture, even in a newborn, does not establish child abuse, although it certainly provided reason for concern and reasonable grounds for an investigation.

Dr. Sheridan had seen other newborn patients with unexplained fractures. One of Dr. Sheridan's patients had gotten a fracture in utero, which was difficult to explain. It was important to both rule in and rule out possible explanations for the fracture before reaching a conclusion. Dr. Sheridan had no reason to rule in abuse as the cause of Robert's fracture, for there was no affirmative evidence of an abusive action directed at Robert. While the concern that caused the investigation of Robert's fracture was his parents' lack of an explanation for it, there was nothing specifically pointing to abuse as the cause. Most fractures are not due to abuse, even if they aren't explained and even for newborns.

Many daily activities could have the potential to cause a fracture, including dressing a child and a sibling pulling or hitting the leg while in play or otherwise pulling on the baby while he was in a baby seat or another fixed position. Two-year-old siblings are "absolutely" strong enough to fracture a newborn brother's leg. Many actions could create sufficient force exerted on Robert's leg without the parents noticing.

Fractures do ordinarily cause pain, and a child would be likely to cry from a fracture. But such cries would not necessarily be inconsolable or distinctive. An unrecognized event could have occurred as much as five days before detection of the fracture. If the child had been crying for another reason, an event that caused the child to sustain a fracture could go unnoticed.

Fracture can initially be nondisplaced and asymptomatic at the time of the break but later become displaced through another minor force. Fractures do not cause swelling, however, unless they become displaced. Routine activities can cause an initially nondisplaced fracture to become displaced, and the displacement would lead to the swelling due to bleeding from the bone marrow under the muscle by the bone.

In supporting these medical opinions, Dr. Sheridan cited his 25 years of experience as a pediatric orthopedist and, before his orthopedics training, his education in physics. Dr. Sheridan had graduated at the top of his college class at the U.S. Naval Academy with a physics major. The notion that forces acting on objects like bones had something to do with physics was logical.

Dr. Sheridan concluded that Robert's fracture was much more likely to be accidental than due to abuse. With that conclusion to the direct examination, the judge called for a break. The State's cross-examination would have to await Dr. Sheridan's return to court as soon as we could arrange another date for his testimony.

In civil cases heard by judges and not juries (there is no right to a jury trial in most juvenile courts, including in Illinois), witnesses were often shuffled into time slots that worked with for them and fit the court's own calendar. Sometimes the hearing recessed for days and weeks, with witnesses going out of order when they were available.

After Dr. Sheridan left the witness stand, the case resumed its usual order of presentation. The State began its case by calling Caseworker Green to testify first. State's Attorney O'Neill went through a litany of questions about her investigative interviews. The judge ruled in our favor to stop Green from giving hearsay testimony about what the suburban hospital nurse told her, for the nurse would be coming to testify in person. But State's Attorney O'Neill insisted on being allowed to ask the questions anyway, because the parents had been trying "to put the CPS system on trial." O'Neill claimed to need to defend the credibility of the CPS agency and the CPS investigators from the parents' mounted attack. Our aggressive advocacy for Ben and Lynn plainly had put the State on the defensive.

The nurse had told Investigator Green that Robert's leg was "floppy," but Robert had only cried a bit when the leg was repositioned. This testimony suggested there had been no extreme pain response that would have alerted Ben and Lynn to the fracture when it occurred. After all, if the fracture had been extremely painful to Robert, the nurse who first examined him would have noted Robert's crying inconsolably.

Suddenly the State's Attorney started to ask Janelle Green to describe "issues" she encountered in trying to take protective custody of the three children. I objected. The judge stopped her answer, for this question called for legal conclusions the investigator was not qualified to give.

The State's Attorney asked Green why she hadn't taken protective custody upon Robert's discharge from the hospital on September 11. This answer played into our hand. Green didn't take protective custody of the children right away because they "were waiting for the final report from our child abuse doctor." No one on the State's side seemed to realize that Green had just confessed to a lack of any emergency when the CPS team attempted to seize the children on October 1.

The State's Attorney pressed on: "Still you determined it was safe for the child to return to a home where the paternal grandmother would supervise?" These questions moved the State into no-win territory; no matter how Green answered, it couldn't possibly help to convince the judge that there had been an emergency need to remove the children on October 1. Janelle Green explained that the CPS team considered the children to be safe under the safety plan; otherwise, the children wouldn't have gone back home with their grandmother.

Janelle Green recounted that Dr. Felix had told her that "anyone would notice" the fracture. Dr. Felix, Janelle Green added, had said that a fracture was something you would hear. Now her testimony was heading off script. None of the notes said that the fracture itself would have been *audible*. Maybe she meant the baby's crying would have been audible. I would have to clarify, but the more outlandish she made Dr. Felix's opinion out to be, the better for Ben and Lynn.

Then the State asked if Investigator Green knew about Dr. Sheridan's opinion. She did. But that opinion didn't matter.

"We decided to go with our child abuse doctor's report. That was the report we had," she said.

The admission was stunning. The entire CPS team, including the CPS manager, had deliberately ignored the family's second medical opinion, all without even trying to contact Dr. Sheridan. Moreover, they hadn't tried to talk to their own expert, Dr. Felix, to see how she would respond to the proffered opinion of a pediatric orthopedist at another leading hospital in Chicago. Perhaps Dr. Felix might have agreed that a third opinion was needed, or she might have wanted to talk to an orthopedist at her own institution.

"Why didn't you wait for Dr. Sheridan's report?" the State's Attorney asked. Soon the judge wanted to know, too, asking the investigator to clarify the timing of her discussions with her superiors on October 1.

The answer was that the team had already decided to take protective custody after getting Dr. Felix's report earlier that afternoon. When they learned of Dr. Sheridan's report, they had met and decided to stick with the plan to take protective custody of the children.

This testimony confirmed the chronology of protective-custody decision making when Janelle Green had invited Ben to bring the kids to the CPS office on October 1. That "invitation" *did* reflect that the protective custody decision had already been made. We had been right when we had told Ben that the signs had become ominous.

My gut was telling me the judge was not happy to learn that the CPS team decided so precipitously to take the kids from Ben and Lynn when they knew there was contrary opinion from the parents' medical expert. The judge wasn't playing any cards, but this testimony seemed to be going our way. Judges don't tend to like it when important information isn't considered by the offices that are supposed to investigate cases. And the judge had seemed to respond well to Dr. Sheridan's testimony earlier that morning. He was taking it all in.

The State's Attorney kept digging, though, wanting to know why she didn't wait for Dr. Sheridan's report. Green's response was revealing: "That's what we have the child abuse doctors, the MPEEC doctors, for. We had said [to Ben and Lynn] that we were waiting for the final MPEEC report, and that's what we did. When we got the opinion, the decision was made."

She added, "Even though we had another opinion that was coming in, we decided that it was a necessity to go ahead and take protective custody of the children at that point."

This was distressing to hear. Years of federal litigation since 1997 to establish the CPS investigators' duty to gather and consider exculpatory evidence seemed to all have been for naught. Nothing seemed to have changed about the way CPS caseworkers conducted their investigations. While there were now good rules on paper—rules that instructed CPS teams to consider the opinions of orthopedists—those rules were roundly ignored.

Before I got to cross-examine Green, the State's Attorney returned to questions related to the CPS team's efforts to take the three children from their home on the night of October 1. Green's description of the stakeout at the home perfectly matched Lynn's description of what had happened that night.

I started my cross-examination with some basics.

"When did you review your notes?" I asked and followed it with, "You gave us new notes this morning, didn't you? Your investigation isn't over, is it?"

She had gone over her notes with the State's Attorney earlier that morning. And no, the investigation wasn't over yet.

It was typical for the State's Attorneys in juvenile court cases to prepare witnesses the same day as they testify. This litigation was on the fly; all the people working in the juvenile court building were doing the best they could without much advance preparation time.

It wasn't that way for Melissa and me, however. The case was an opportunity to demonstrate critical defects in the CPS training and in caseworkers' understanding of the rules. Some of my questions and their answers would bring to the juvenile court judge's attention specific CPS rules on the appropriate investigation of cases that might not have been brought to his attention before. Even though the CPS rules set forth detailed requirements for the full consideration of evidence in each type of abuse or neglect allegation, the rules on paper were being willfully ignored.

"You followed the CPS rule defining the bone fracture allegation, correct?" I asked Green.

"That's correct," she replied. Nothing she did in the case was out of the ordinary, she explained.

It was important for me to set her up as following the rules before I demonstrated how Green's investigation contradicted the CPS system's own requirements.

She had tried to be as thorough as possible in her notes, but "some things" might be missing, she admitted.

"You did interviews after October 1, didn't you?" I asked.

She had, so I asked, "Did you give those additional notes to the State's Attorney?"

She said she had done so.

"Do you have those notes with you?" I asked.

"No," she replied.

A break was needed to find the missing notes. Still, notes of the conversation with Ben and Lynn's family friend whom Janelle Green claimed to have interviewed were missing. She had no idea where those notes would be. She did recall, however, that Robert seemed fine.

Janelle Green had interviewed the detective, but she admitted that she hadn't talked to anyone at Lynn's hair salon, where Lynn had gone on the afternoon before the fracture was discovered. Nor had she contacted any of the doctors, lawyers, and family friends who had written support letters on the family's behalf.

The CPS team was starting to look like the Keystone Cops.

"You didn't do an alcohol screen when you first met with Lynn, did you? Or a domestic violence screen?" I asked.

"No, I didn't," she acknowledged.

"It's CPS policy to do those screens on parents, isn't it?" I pressed.

"Yes."

The investigator's claim to have followed all the CPS rules was starting to unravel. Clearly, she had skipped a few steps.

A note on a CPS form dated September 22 had the statement that "Lynn had, other than accidentally, caused moderate to severe injury" to her child. Janelle Green denied that this note meant what it said.

"I really hadn't made a conclusion. I just have to pick a safety factor," she explained.

Janelle Green admitted that she considered the children safe with their grandmother. Receipt of the faxed report from the child abuse fellow, Dr. Felix, triggered the CPS team's decision to take protective custody of the children.

These preliminary questions had already yielded some significant admissions. But I still hadn't established all the ways the investigation was faulty. I pressed on.

Caseworker Green acknowledged that she never contacted Robert's regular treating pediatrician, contrary to a clear requirement in the CPS bone fracture investigation rule.

"You knew there was a police report in the case, didn't you? But you didn't have it on October 1, did you?" I asked.

Again the answer was no.

It was becoming clearer that any person, police included, who supported the parent's innocence had been ignored, regardless of the CPS investigation rule—or the constitutional case law—as to the duty to gather and consider all available exculpatory evidence.

I asked, "Was the information about Lynn's claimed mental health problem included in the information you provided to the State's Attorney when you requested the filing of this case?"

Green acknowledged she had given the State's Attorney that information and also admitted she had never asked Dr. Felix to back up her arm chair diagnosis of Lynn.

Then I started to hone in on October 1, when Janelle Green had invited Ben to bring the children to her office the next day. She explained she made that request because it would be a "less traumatic" and "neutral setting."

"You were basically asking the father to come in and surrender his children to the department?" I tried to keep my tone of voice as flat and nonjudgmental as I could.

The investigator admitted it. And she didn't fight me on the follow-up question: "But you didn't tell him that was the purpose of why you were asking him to come in, did you?"

No, she didn't.

What had just been described in the courtroom was a well-conceived plan to make it easy for the State to seize children from their unwitting parent who had done nothing wrong. Indeed, Green's seizure plan had been a calculated ambush to take children from a parent whom Janelle Green herself didn't truly suspect of hurting his kids, as soon became clear.

But for Lynn's holding firm and insisting on a warrant on October 1, the three children likely would have been living in a shelter or a foster home with strangers by now. Their family life would have changed forever. By now, we could have been picking up the pieces of an entirely broken family whose children would have experienced untold trauma that they would never be able to explain or understand themselves.

It was time to discuss Dr. Felix's opinion. I asked, "Did Dr. Felix tell you how certain she was of her opinion?"

Green answered simply, repeating that the doctor had said abuse was most likely.

"Did she tell you which doctors she consulted with?"

Green thought that she had consulted an orthopedic surgeon but didn't know that doctor's name.

"You were supposed to talk to an orthopedist yourself?" I asked, as that's what the CPS rule said, although consulting a radiologist was also permissible.

She admitted she didn't know.

"You didn't try to confirm Dr. Sheridan's opinion yourself when I told you about it, did you?" I followed up.

She acknowledged that she hadn't.

"Did you call Dr. Felix to discuss it?"

Yes, she *had* tried to call Dr. Felix. Notes of that call were missing from the file. Green hadn't gotten through to Dr. Felix, however.

"Did you ask Dr. Felix if she thought the children were unsafe with their grandparents?"

"No," Janelle Green answered. I expected that answer, for child removal and placement decisions were left to the CPS team. No one expected doctors to investigate caregivers' backgrounds. Even though doctors gave the critical opinions about whether the child was abused, they usually weren't asked to weigh in on what action CPS should take in light of their opinions. After all, their opinions were just one piece of the fuller investigation that was the CPS responsibility.

I took out the CPS rule and showed it to the CPS investigator. It directed the caseworkers to consider the opinion of doctors with the "relevant specialization" to be more credible than those without such specialization.[1] Given Robert had a bone fracture, orthopedics was the relevant specialization that should be consulted.

Now Green was becoming cagey, trying have it both ways. For a bone fracture case, the relevant specialty was orthopedics, she acknowledged. But for "my case," the relevant specialty would be child abuse. Of course, that answer was conclusory; child abuse was not the relevant specialty if Robert's fracture had nothing to do with abuse.

It was circular reasoning to say that child abuse doctors have the greater expertise than other doctors whenever they found child abuse existed but not when they didn't. It was also wrong to say that that orthopedist had superior knowledge of all fractures *except* those caused by child abuse. Both of these views begged the questions of what a child abuse assessment actually involved. To what degree was medical knowledge essential, and to what degree was social history or psychology or forensic science in other areas besides medicine necessary to make a child abuse assessment?

Following the *Dupuy I* decision,[2] the State had wanted leeway in creating CPS policies governing the fair consideration of evidence, both inculpatory and exculpatory. But a lot of basic questions, such as which type of doctor to consult, were fudged a bit. There were practical limits on how prescriptive rules on investigations should be. As it was, the CPS rule adopted in 2003 was helpful. But investigators like Janelle Green ignored the rules. Unfortunately, too often, so did their supervisors.

Janelle Green didn't know what training, if any, Dr. Felix had in the field of radiology. While she knew that Dr. Felix had consulted with other specialists, she did not know who they were or what they had said. The total number of doctors anyone from CPS had spoken to was exactly one: Dr. Felix.

In fact, two supervisory notes in the CPS case file specifically directed Janelle Green to contact the attending radiologist and an orthopedist. Janelle Green now claimed that she hadn't seen those notes although she had testified to reviewing the whole file before she testified in court. So I asked her who the attending radiologist was. She didn't know.

Getting defensive, she reiterated that "We work with MPEEC doctors when our children go to MPEEC hospitals." She added that her investigation wasn't over yet; she might still make her own contacts with these doctors if necessary.

Necessary for what? I wondered to myself. The most intense litigation in this family's life was underway. What would a future contact with a radiologist at this late date add?

Janelle Green admitted that the children all looked healthy when she saw them in the doorway on October 1. Indeed, she never saw the parents act inappropriately with the children. No reports said anything except that they were model parents. The fracture was all she relied on to suggest that Ben and Lynn had any blemishes as parents.

She also knew that Lynn was a social worker. My questions about Lynn's work history, however, drew objections from the guardian ad litem, who claimed that Lynn's career was irrelevant to the abuse claims. But the judge allowed Lynn to answer. Green hadn't considered Lynn's work history. All she cared about, she declared, was "what happened" to Robert.

Naturally, I inquired about her attempts to verify where Lynn had been with Robert on September 10. She answered that since Lynn had said she first noticed swelling at 5:00 p.m., she didn't consider it necessary to double-check Lynn's account about earlier in the day. Apparently, the investigator had been willing to take Lynn's word for everything she had done, except for her denial of child abuse.

Green testified, "I didn't doubt what Lynn told me."

That was a stunning statement. If the assigned caseworker didn't doubt Lynn's credibility about what had happened on September 10, then why was the family in court fighting for their children? The follow-up question was obvious: "But you doubted her denial of the abuse, correct?"

Janelle Green answered that she hadn't doubted Lynn in that regard, either. "I just took a note of what she said," she reported. "I didn't have an opinion at this point either way."

It apparently wasn't the caseworker's job to think about what she was doing to the family.

"So at this point you are not sure when, if ever, Lynn abused her son?" I asked her. I wanted to be sure that I understood what she was saying about why we were in court now and what the State's case against the parents rested on.

Caseworker Green answered honestly, "I don't know who did it. They can't tell me. That's what I'm going on."

She, too, didn't know what happened to cause Robert's fracture. She didn't know who was present when the fracture occurred. What she had to go on was that Lynn was Robert's primary caregiver.

The case was looking more and more mindless. We had moved from Kafka's absurd and inaccessible justice, to Orwell's oppressive State surveillance and doublespeak, to Hannah Arendt's banality of evil, all in quick succession. Now Janelle Green was the good soldier, just following orders from above. No one suspected Ben or Lynn of actually abusing Robert. They just took the kids anyway.

That was a good time to end Green's cross-examination. It was clear that the CPS team had no good reason to take the kids on the night of October 1. Nothing more I could ask would make the point any clearer.

Now the judge had a few questions of his own. He wanted to know how the CPS agency arranged the MPEEC consult with Dr. Felix. Had Janelle Green requested it?

"No," she answered. When a child is seen at one of the MPEEC hospitals, the consult was "automatic."

The judge asked what other hospitals had MPEEC contracts and why those other hospitals hadn't done the consult. The investigator couldn't answer. The common practice was that the hospital that had seen the child did the consult with the CPS agency, no matter that this practice intruded on the family's trust in its chosen medical providers and created a direct conflict between the hospital and the family. Use of an independent hospital to provide second opinions would have caused no such problems, but that wasn't the practice.

Now the State's Attorney got a chance to try to rehabilitate Janelle Green. First, however, State's Attorney O'Neill requested a break so that she could read the CPS rule on bone fractures. She didn't know these rules before my cross-examination, although I had sent her a courtesy copy in advance of the court date. It seemed likely that she had never seen a thorough cross-examination of a CPS investigator about her duties under the CPS bone fracture rule before.

Juvenile court proceedings are governed in Illinois by the Juvenile Court Act, and the caseworkers investigate child abuse under a different law, the Abused and Neglected Child Reporting Act. As a result, even though this combined body of law is not terribly voluminous, lawyers who work in the juvenile court oftentimes were not well versed in the CPS rules adopted under the Reporting Act.

After the break, O'Neill's examination of Green continued. That's how it went—back and forth, from side to side, until there were no more questions based on the questions that had been asked in the last round.

O'Neill's rehabilitation effort was quite brief. She first got Green to say the failure to do an alcohol or domestic violence screen on Lynn had been an oversight. Next, she highlighted a CPS rule cautioning that information from a person with "something to gain" from the outcome of the investigation is "less credible" than the information of someone without such an interest. This question foreshadowed a planned line of attack on Dr. Sheridan, since the State's Attorney's office, quite unfairly, viewed him as a hired gun who would stop at nothing to defend child abusers. In fact, Dr. Sheridan selflessly undercharged parents for his work on their cases. Many orthopedists would charge well over $600 an hour. His bills were always a fraction of what others, though less qualified, might charge. Sometimes he had waived all his charges, viewing his role as a public service.

"Was Dr. Sheridan the family's retained expert, paid by the parents for his testimony?" State's Attorney O'Neill wanted to know.

I objected. How would Janelle Green know how Dr. Sheridan was being paid? Janelle Green had never talked to him; she pointedly had refused to consider his report. She hadn't asked Ben or Lynn anything about how they obtained his opinion, either. The judge stopped these questions but said he would allow her to ask the same questions of Dr. Sheridan directly.

In my re-cross-examination, I wanted to know what Janelle Green had heard about Dr. Sheridan. She answered that the "hired gun" reputation was something she had gleaned from child protection manager Kim Ford, Kirby Long's supervisor. Janelle Green also didn't realize that Dr. Sheridan was providing follow-up care to Robert as his treating orthopedist, even though she had seen notes about his putting a new splint on Robert's leg.

When Green was finished at nearly 4:00 p.m., time was still available for another witness. The State had no witnesses ready to take the stand, so we asked to present testimony from Lynn's mother, Natalie, the federal judge. But it took 20 minutes of argument before she was allowed to take the stand.

The guardian ad litem insisted on an "offer of proof"—a synopsis of what Natalie would say. This was an unusual request in regard to a grandparent; extended family members commonly testified at temporary custody hearings, and there was no basis to bar a grandmother from testifying. Melissa eloquently described how Natalie would refute the inferences of abuse that the State was trying to draw. But the guardian ad litem wasn't satisfied, pointing out that Natalie hadn't been at the home when the fracture allegedly occurred.

The judge wanted to hear Natalie. He pointed to the State's claims about Lynn's mental health—claims that Natalie, Lynn's mother, could address. The fact that Natalie was also a federal judge didn't make her testimony in her role as grandmother less relevant.

Now State's Attorney O'Neill jumped in to object. The opposing parties had started to protest too much. It was unseemly for the children's appointed lawyer to try to stop a grandmother from testifying in juvenile court.

In arguing that this federal judge should not be allowed to testify, State's Attorney O'Neill made a startling statement. Since Natalie was being offered as a character witness, State's Attorney O'Neill declared, "The parents' character is not in question. They are merely bolstering their reputation before it's really been put in question. They haven't testified yet. She can testify after they do *if it is alleged that the parents are, in fact, lying.*"

Now the judge was as surprised as we were. He responded bluntly, "If the parents' character is not in question, I don't know why we're here."

It suddenly became apparent that no one at the CPS agency or in the State's Attorney's office had realized that by calling the parents child abusers, by disbelieving their claim not to know how the fracture happened, and by disputing their claims not to have heard Robert cry inconsolably, the State *had* called the parents liars. To be sure, the words "you're lying" had never been said to Ben or Lynn to their faces.

It probably would have been better for everyone if the State had directly accused Ben and Lynn of lying. That accusation would provide clarity about why their children had been taken and why they needed to defend themselves. The State's representatives hadn't figured out that proving Ben and Lynn were liars was central to their case. Indeed, believing the logic that the proceedings were just about the euphemism "best interests of the child," the State proceeded as if the parents' integrity, truthfulness, and character didn't matter. Since all that mattered was what a child abuse doctor said, the prosecution had become a runaway train, let loose on the tracks by a hotline call and a single doctor who couldn't explain the fracture any better than the parents could.

The State had not presented a shred of evidence that either Ben or Lynn had lied about anything. Now it was apparent that the State actually had believed them both, too, until a mysterious point in time when Robert must have "cried inconsolably" and the parents had denied hearing it.

Natalie's testimony was brief but to the point. She and Richard, Lynn's dad, had been married for 45 years. They had two children: a son, who was 39, and Lynn, who was 34. Natalie had known Ben for over 10 years.

But when Melissa asked the standard question, "Where do you work?" State's Attorney Bailey objected. The guardian ad litem joined in. The judge was having none of this nonsense, though.

"Overruled," the judge tersely announced.

After Natalie described the courtroom in which she presided, the judge allowed her briefly to describe Lynn's family life growing up.

"We have a very close family," Natalie said. Even though she had worked full-time since Lynn was two weeks old, there were loads of family vacations. Education was a priority at home.

When each grandchild was born, Natalie came to stay with Lynn. Lynn's first words to her about Robert were, "Isn't he beautiful, Mom?" While Lynn took care of Robert, Natalie viewed her job as taking care of Lynn. She had to tell Lynn to put Robert into his bassinet and rest. Lynn would answer, "No, this is giving me so much joy." Since the twins were born, Natalie tried to visit every two months, for three days to a week at a time.

As for whether Lynn had ever had any mental health issues, Natalie was adamant, "Absolutely not." Lynn never needed a therapist, and she had never behaved in a way that suggested she might be depressed. Nor had Lynn ever been inappropriately angry with her children. Moreover, Lynn was an "extremely organized woman," adept at juggling tasks. She established an "absolutely wonderful schedule" so that they "get up at the same time, eat at the same time, and they're always clean and well dressed." Natalie took some credit for teaching Lynn these skills.

Lynn had told Natalie, "It's all about the babies now." Lynn had nursed the twins for six months, which wasn't easy. They were "very much loved." The twins would run to Lynn when she entered the room, and they would run to their dad, too. The children got a lot of affection, and they meant everything to Lynn and Ben. It was inconceivable to Natalie that they would intentionally harm their children. They were "incapable of it."

Ben was "one of the most loving fathers" Natalie knew. When Natalie had offered to let Ben and Lynn go out, Ben had refused, telling her that he wanted to spend more of his precious time with the kids. Ben was a hands-on father, diapering them, carrying them, and taking them to the park whenever he could.

Both parents were gentle disciplinarians, merely correcting the twins or giving brief time-outs when they needed redirection. Their home had been thoroughly safety proofed. Natalie had never seen any bruises or blemishes on the children—not even a diaper rash. Natalie considered both Ben and Lynn more patient than she was. They had considered caring for Robert "a breeze," since he was sweet, quiet, and gentle. The home was surprisingly organized and calm after Robert's birth.

The contrast between the care the children got with Lynn and the care they might have gotten at a shelter or foster home with strangers couldn't have been clearer.

The judge had not allowed us to question Natalie about her October 5 letter to Janelle Green, since it was written after the CPS decision to take the children into temporary custody on October 2. But when State's Attorney Bailey started to cross-examine Natalie, he went straight to that letter, where Natalie had referred to Lynn as her "best friend." Bailey apparently considered that statement odd. He turned to question the family's move to the western suburbs. Then he probed for details about her child-care knowledge, even asking whether Lynn unsnapped Robert's onesie in a particular way, trying to trip Natalie up if she answered wrong or didn't know how to answer.

Though more experienced in the courtroom than O'Neill, State's Attorney Bailey seemed no better at asking questions. The answers he elicited reinforced how careful and attentive a mother Lynn was.

The final line of questions challenged Natalie about when Ben and Lynn had moved to the western suburbs and when *Ben's* parents had visited. Natalie couldn't give precise information. Getting testy, Natalie shot back at Gary Bailey, "Are you listening to me?"

Natalie's judicial "I'm the boss" attitude was coming out. The next question was worse; it provoked Natalie's retort, "You can't ask the question that way." Never a demure person, Natalie was moving out of her "just answer the questions" role as a witness, acting as if she were the judge in the case. It was impossible to stop the line of questions that were making Natalie look defensive.

Things got better quickly, though. Testing Natalie's knowledge of the allegations against Ben and Lynn, Bailey asked Natalie to relate the entire conversation she had with Lynn right after the first safety plan had been set up. Cross-examiners shouldn't ask for this sort of narrative.

Natalie related that Lynn had said, "We will go to our grave not knowing exactly what caused Robert's fracture." Natalie testified that Lynn expressed shock about the injury. Natalie was shocked, too, offering to help any way she could. Natalie used her judicial experience to advise Lynn not to try to come up with possible explanations for the injury. "Tell the truth," was her motherly and judicious advice to her daughter.

Soon the questions were over for the day. Natalie was tearful, more stressed than she had anticipated. Judge Sanders handed her some Kleenex. She smiled, commenting, "I'm always offering Kleenex myself." Her brief stint as a witness, sitting on the other side of the bench, was over.

The hearing would resume in two days for the testimony of the State's star witness, Dr. Felix.

There wasn't a lot of time for postmortems, but the two grandfathers had patiently waited outside the courtroom to hear the details of our day. Dr. Sheridan's testimony had been very strong. The judge's comment, "Why are we here if the parents' credibility wasn't in question?" stood out as a signal that judge seemed to be viewing the State's case critically.

We started to hope that the family's ordeal might end soon. We were half-right; the ordeal would come to an end, but we were only halfway through. The State's effort to fish for evidence against Ben and Lynn had just begun.

NINE

The State's Star Witness and Someone the Investigation Missed

Back in court two days later, we decided to call a witness who might be able to answer how and when Robert's leg was broken: Lynn's hairstylist, Susan. Janelle Green had never talked to Susan, even though Lynn had been at the hair salon just shortly before the fracture was discovered. When we investigated the case for ourselves in preparation for the hearing, Susan's information about Robert's fracture surprised us. She could pinpoint a plausible time when Robert's fracture first might have appeared, for Susan remembered a brief comment about Robert's leg that Lynn had forgotten.

Susan recalled Lynn's arrival with Robert at the salon on the afternoon of September 10. Lynn first had her hair colored by another stylist. Susan could see Lynn and Robert during that time. Robert did not cry; he stayed in his car-seat carrier. Then, when Lynn had her hair color rinsed out, Susan held Robert for a few minutes. He was "pretty much sleeping," she reported. When she was ready to cut Lynn's hair, Susan handed him back to Lynn, and Lynn settled him back down into his car seat. At that point, Robert started to fuss, so Lynn picked him up again, putting him under her cape during her haircut.

When Lynn put Robert back into his car seat, Lynn pointed to Robert's leg and asked Susan if it looked a bit swollen to her. Susan recalled looking. She saw that it *did* look just a bit bigger than the other leg. Robert wasn't crying at all. Susan hadn't given any definitive response one way or the other. She wasn't sure Lynn was right. She simply had responded, "Maybe."

Lynn had used the restroom just before her hair color was done. She had taken Robert in with her. But no one heard any crying coming from the restroom.

Was that when Robert was injured? If Lynn had deliberately hurt him, of course, she wouldn't have been likely to ask her stylist afterward if she noticed anything wrong with Robert's leg. Perhaps it had been the stylist herself who had banged Robert's leg inadvertently against a salon chair. It was impossible to know. No one at the salon noticed Robert seriously crying, so there was no red flag that his leg might have been injured while he was at the salon. If he had cried inconsolably, someone who was at the crowded salon certainly would have noticed. Lynn and the stylist both would have remembered that, too. Still, the fact that Lynn noticed something might be different about his left leg provided the closest thing so far to a time and a place where an injury may have happened.

Susan's account also provided a timing explanation consistent with Dr. Sheridan's theory that Robert may have had a nondisplaced fracture first, maybe for days, that later got displaced, like a crack in china. Perhaps it was simple displacement, not a first break, that had occurred at the salon when Lynn changed him in the bathroom or when Susan held him. It wouldn't have taken much force to cause the displacement of an already-cracked bone. This would make sense of the very minor swelling Lynn thought she saw then, and it would explain the increase in the swelling that became alarming by 7:00 p.m.

Of course, this possible explanation completely exonerated Lynn, unless someone really wanted to believe that she had snapped while in the salon's bathroom, viciously attacking Robert there, all while no one in the entire salon noticed. That would be far-fetched at best.

As Susan testified, the CPS team, the State's Attorneys, and the guardian ad litem were first learning this information, 37 days after the hotline call and 15 days after the CPS team had tried to seize the three children from their home. Susan was the last person who had been with Robert, other than the immediate family members, before Lynn and Ben decided that there was something clearly wrong with Robert's leg.

The CPS rules clearly state that all persons who had been with the child before they were injured should be contacted during the investigation. But no one on the CPS team had talked to Susan. Now, the investigation was occurring while Susan was in the witness chair.

The State's medical expert, Dr. Felix, was up next to testify. State's Attorney O'Neill questioned her first about her work on the hospital's child protection team, where she had been working for 14 months before Robert became a patient of the hospital's emergency room. She was a child abuse fellow and a physician in the pediatrics and urgent care departments, covering inpatient and outpatient services. She supervised nine residents, three interns, and two to four medical students. She was busy; her service required her to be on call 50 percent of the time. Twelve-hour days were routine. She had to deal with calls from the emergency department, urgent care center, and outpatient services as well as general questions about children believed to be physically or sexually abused or neglected.

Dr. Felix was one of six MPEEC doctors at the hospital who consulted with the CPS caseworkers. In the 14 months of her child abuse fellowship so far, she had been involved in an estimated 1,000 child abuse evaluations, playing a lead role in approximately one-quarter of them. Though she was still in training to specialize in child abuse, she was a licensed physician and had completed her residency in pediatrics in June 2008.

While any licensed doctor can testify as a medical expert, it mattered whether Dr. Felix should be recognized as a *child abuse* expert. Opposing parties are allowed to question the expert preliminarily about their credentials and their field (doing what was known as a "voir dire" exam) before they decide the scope of Dr. Felix's expertise.

My preliminary questions confirmed that Dr. Felix hadn't yet taken her board exams in pediatrics. She also wasn't eligible yet to take board exams in child abuse pediatrics, which were just starting up in November 2009. Her child abuse fellowship program did not include any rotations in orthopedics. Her orthopedics training was basic, what all pediatricians receive in their pediatric residencies. Whatever on-the-job training she had in orthopedics came through discussions of fracture cases with orthopedists at her hospital. I asked Dr. Felix which orthopedic journals she read. She couldn't name one.

I asked her about the field of child abuse pediatrics. Did she consider child abuse to be a clinical diagnosis? She did. But when I asked her if child abuse was one diagnosis or more than one, she answered curtly, "It's a diagnosis."

I think Dr. Felix is wrong. To my way of thinking, the subspecialty of child abuse pediatrics is misnamed. It should be called "pediatric forensic medicine," which is how some other doctors refer to it. If these doctors were simply forensic pediatricians—doctors whose role is to testify in court proceedings involving children, particularly in child protection cases—then it would be clearer and more neutral, not a specialty stacked in favor of finding child abuse.

Child abuse isn't a single diagnosis, I would argue. It isn't just one set of symptoms that add up to a child's medical condition of being "abused." There are no agreed-upon diagnostic criteria for child abuse, as there are for just about every other injury or condition. There are just judgment calls, often based on credibility assessments of the sort judges, not doctors, are trained to make, and an elaborate court system is available for review when they get their judgment calls wrong.

If "child abuse" were a diagnosis, then what kind of diagnosis would it be? It seems to be a *legal* diagnosis, not a medical one. Child abuse isn't just one thing; it is many types of actions lumped together into a single conclusion about an injury's cause. When one hears the label "child abuse," it conjures no specific injury—except a stereotypical image of a battered child, with telltale marks all over his or her body.

The limitations of that image are obvious, since child abuse encompasses a wide array of injuries, ranging from bruises, burns, head injuries, or fractures; to forms of sexual abuse showing no outward signs or symptoms; and to emotional abuse. Each type of physical abuse affects different systems of the body—the skin and vascular systems; the skull, brain, and neurological system; and the bones, sometimes singly, sometimes together.

The subject area of physical child abuse injuries alone (to say nothing of the areas of sexual abuse and psychological abuse) covers so many disparate areas of anatomy, physiology, and development that it would seem foolhardy for a so-called child abuse expert to claim advanced knowledge of all these areas of medicine. Yet I have heard several child abuse doctors, including Dr. Felix's supervisor (who signed the MPEEC reports in Ben and Lynn's case), claim to know more about the mechanism of fractures than orthopedists do. That's pure hubris.

Unfortunately, the consumers of child abuse pediatric opinions—judges, State's Attorneys, and CPS investigators—too often believe some child abuse pediatricians' hype about their superior abilities to discern child abuse over that of orthopedists, radiologists, and neurosurgeons. Judges may rely on child abuse pediatricians who confidently testify that they know child abuse when they see it over doctors who present their nonabuse conclusions less confidently but more correctly.

Even if a single doctor could synthesize all the medical opinions about a child's condition, as a truly multidisciplinary evaluation team discussing child abuse should do, that still wouldn't answer the question of whether the child was abused. It still wouldn't provide a diagnosis. What distinguishes child abuse from accidents isn't a medical or physical difference between the injuries caused by abuse versus those caused by accidents; it is a difference in the intent of the person alleged to have caused the child's injury.

How can divining the intent of an unidentified person provide a medical diagnosis? It isn't like cancer or heart disease. That was part of the point Dr. Sheridan made about bones. They don't tell the cause of their breaking. It takes judgment about who is telling the truth and an assessment of the full story. Those are the sort of conclusions we expect judges, not doctors, to make when all the evidence is in.

Of course, medicine provides important pieces in any child abuse puzzle; some conditions are more likely to be caused by abuse, and some are very unlikely to be the result of any intent to injure a child. There are medical conditions that look like burns. There are genetic conditions that cause bones to break with minor impact. These conditions are widely acknowledged as explanations for multiple fractures that otherwise would be highly suspicious.[1]

For any injured child with more than a playground scrape, a simple cut, or first degree burn, medical assessment about the extent of the child's injuries requires that medical opinion be gathered and synthesized. Describing the injuries can require sophisticated medical knowledge. Certain medical findings taken together are considered highly suspicious; for example, multiple rib fractures in different locations and in different stages of healing are considered, reasonably enough, to be more suspicious of abuse than tibia fractures in toddlers, which are so common that they are called "toddler fractures." Regardless of prevalence, however, freak accidents happen, and unusual medical conditions can account for the same injuries that are attributed to abuse.

After all the descriptive medical work is done, child abuse doctors have no crystal ball. They are making judgments about people they may not know and circumstances that they haven't fully investigated. Their perceived medical superiority over other medical specialists may lie in their power to get CPS caseworkers to listen to them.

In our system of justice, it should be the job of the judge, not the child abuse doctor, to pull the facts together and make a decision as to whether these facts add up to child abuse. Deferring to the child abuse doctor as the person who knows best when a child is abused is a judicial and CPS system cop out.

If doctors diagnose child abuse and are wrong, it can make children's medical matters worse; they can send a genuine medical mystery off in the wrong direction. A child's true medical condition can be missed. The risk of misdiagnosis is especially dangerous when child abuse doctors rely on flawed investigations, interrogations of parents after sleepless nights, and arm chair psychological assessment of parents based on mistaken notes.

Could the abuse claims against Ben and Lynn have been an example of a team of child abuse doctors rushing to an abuse judgment and not seeing the real medical story? I wondered if medical doctors had missed something about Robert that would have shed light on his unexplained fracture.

It was time for Judge Sanders to rule on Dr. Felix's qualification as an expert. I asked the judge to recognize her simply as a medical doctor. Since she was a licensed physician, the judge was required to allow her to provide medical opinion testimony. Beyond that, it was not clear she had sufficient demonstrated expertise in child abuse.

Judge Sanders granted that request, leaving out any further endorsement of her credentials. The State's Attorneys weren't happy that their star witness was seen as just a doctor, not a child abuse expert.

State's Attorney O'Neill started by asking Dr. Felix to describe her examination of Robert. Robert was groggy, but he awoke, wanting to feed. He was "happy, moving around" and moved his leg in the split. He didn't like having the splint removed, and he fussed.

Next, Dr. Felix interviewed Lynn alone in a room away from Robert's room for about an hour. When Lynn recounted how she spent September 10 with Robert, she did not mention an inconsolable cry. Lynn had mentioned stresses in their family life due to the move, her C-section four weeks before, and its complications. Lynn got up slowly, Dr. Felix noted. Lynn had not yet fully recovered from Robert's delivery.

Following that exam, her discussion with Lynn, and her review of the medical chart and radiographic images, Dr. Felix concluded that it was likely that Robert had been abused. She claimed to have made that diagnosis to a reasonable degree of medical certainty—that abuse was "more likely than not."

In a civil case like this one, the "more likely than not" standard was all that the State had to meet. Still, an expert is supposed to have a "reasonable degree of medical certainty," and I wonder if a near 50/50 opinion like hers would qualify as reasonable certainty in the child abuse field.

State's Attorney O'Neill turned to Dr. Felix's methodology in assessing physical child abuse cases. Dr. Felix considered four factors: the biomechanics of the injury, its severity, its symptoms, and its history.

This was odd. None of the factors Dr. Felix listed were what one would commonly associate with a child abuse assessment. Dr. Felix hadn't mentioned family or social history; a criminal, substance abuse, or domestic violence history; or dangerous conditions in the children's home. She mentioned nothing that would be considered a risk factor pointing in the direction of crediting or discrediting a parent's explanation for a child's injury. It was all about mechanisms and the specific injury itself—the stuff that orthopedists know and the child abuse doctors don't have much specialized training in. These factors didn't distinguish abusive injuries from accidental ones. The child abuse diagnostic process was starting to look like it had little to do with what physical child abuse actually is—a violent attack on a child by a human with malevolent intent.

Even though her knowledge was clearly inferior to Dr. Sheridan's, State's Attorney O'Neill began to puff up Dr. Felix's expertise. "Did you look at X-rays?" she asked.

Dr. Felix described the X-rays she reviewed and then described "biomechanics" as the "kind of force" necessary to cause the injury. She labeled the force needed to break Robert's leg as "significant" but gave no more detail than that.

The femur was the largest and strongest bone in the body, Dr. Felix noted. At less than one month old, Robert couldn't move himself to produce enough force to cause a fracture. Children start to roll at three to four months. Normal baby handling—changing clothes, picking a baby up, and putting him in a carrier—wouldn't cause a fracture. These activities provided "just not enough force." There were no police reports of healthy children getting fractures from these activities, Dr. Felix noted.

"Was Robert healthy?" State's Attorney O'Neill inquired.

Dr. Felix said, "Yes."

But how did she know? No genetic tests had been run on Robert. He was only four weeks old. The course of his development had yet to be charted. She was making assumptions from a very summary exam, plus a couple lab tests and X-rays. She had ruled out bone disease by doing a "thorough history, family history, diet history, baseline labs, and radiographic imaging." Robert's bones were no more fragile than any other baby's, she concluded. But even if Robert had an undetected bone disease, Dr. Felix still held the opinion there would have be "some force" greater than "regular baby handling."

Under Dr. Felix's second factor, severity, she classified Robert's displaced femur fracture as a "very severe injury" because the bone was completely separated into two parts. Robert's age contributed to the severity of the injury, in her view.

Symptoms of the injury, the third factor, included one critical symptom: pain. Robert would have cried out in pain, Dr. Felix announced with certainty. Even a nondisplaced fracture would cause severe pain. Robert would have cried whenever his leg was moved or manipulated. The pain from a fracture occurs because it disrupts a fibrous membrane, known as the periosteum, which contains blood vessels. Swelling occurs from bleeding from the broken blood vessels in the periosteum, which combines with an inflammatory response. The amount of swelling depends on the severity of the injury.

Dr. Felix acknowledged that the fracture could have been nondisplaced at first and become displaced later, but she considered this possible explanation unlikely. That explanation required two traumatic events, not one. Lynn hadn't reported any trauma. Dr. Felix later allowed that a nondisplaced fracture might not have much swelling, though.

It was apparent that Dr. Felix didn't think she needed to explain what made abuse a likely explanation for Robert's injury. In fact, her theory that Robert had been abused didn't need to have details at all. It didn't need a "when," a "where," a "how," a "who," or a "why"—all the elements that allow someone to tell if an account is believable or not. All the abuse explanation needed to do was supply a conclusory label: "child abuse."

It is almost always possible that nonverbal children's injuries from unknown causes are due to abuse. Then, because the public has come to believe that "any parent can snap," abuse explanations appear plausible without further elaboration. It seemed that child abuse had become a default explanation for any otherwise unexplained injury. It didn't need to be specifically ruled *in* with solid support, and it could almost never be ruled *out*.

Was it now so easy to accuse otherwise obviously good parents of child abuse? That was the "heads, I win; tails, you lose" logic behind the State's case and the medical opinion upon which it rested.

The final factor in Dr. Felix's assessment, the history of the trauma (i.e., the injury), was simple to describe. Neither parent had any history to account for the fracture, nor had they noted any unusual or inconsolable crying. There were no accidents, no incidents, no signs of severe discomfort. Dr. Felix considered this reason to believe abuse occurred.

It was odd, though, that a lack of an explanation had come to be viewed as a positive reason to believe child abuse occurred. A lack of a history was quite different from an inconsistent or an implausible history—the sort of fabricated account that doesn't fit the injuries doctors find. Parents who have mistreated a child may give these sorts of inconsistent or implausible accounts. They also tend to stay *away* from doctors until the last moment, when they cannot avoid medical attention for the child any longer. By contrast, parents' lack of an explanation usually sends them *to* doctors seeking answers as soon as they notice something wrong. That's what happened in Ben and Lynn's case.

Dr. Felix conflated parents' inconsistent stories with the accounts of parents who simply didn't know how their child got hurt. Ben and Lynn's inability to offer any explanation should have been read in their favor that the parents were honest and not trying to make up a story. Yet, in cases I have handled, child abuse pediatricians frequently conflated a parent's genuine lack of an explanation with inconsistency and turned that against them to support a child abuse conclusion.

State's Attorney O'Neill moved on to clarify the oblique versus spiral classification. Dr. Felix explained that the two types of fractures could look similar on X-rays. She was right about that, for Dr. Sheridan had waffled a bit himself when looking at one of the X-rays. From certain views, the distinction between the two fracture types wasn't visible.

The dispute as to whether the fracture was spiral or oblique was a bit of inside baseball, created by child abuse doctors' history of associating spiral fractures with child abuse. But research had shown that spiral fractures were less commonly due to abuse than had been believed.[2] Perhaps the characterization of Robert's fracture as spiral contributed to Dr. Felix's early conclusion that abuse was its likely cause.

Next, the State's Attorney asked Dr. Felix about her consultations with other doctors. She had attended weekly staff meetings with the other child protective services team members, including three other doctors, and they had discussed Robert's case on September 16. Social workers, nurses, and the chaplain had also been there. Reportedly, they had all agreed that abuse was "more likely" than an accidental injury.

But I wondered how it was that more than a half dozen people at a meeting, none of whom had met Lynn or Ben, could decide that they had lied about abuse? And what abuse story did these other doctors have in mind? Did all of these team members rely on any evidence that newborns with injuries that parents can't explain turn out to be abused most of the time? How was it possible for these professionals to assume that abuse occurred if they didn't know who did it? This team opinion was cited to bolster Dr. Felix's opinion, but it introduced more questions about whether groupthink rather than science was at work.

State's Attorney O'Neill inquired next about Dr. Felix's conclusion that Lynn "seemed depressed." Dr. Felix said that Lynn had seemed "just tired and overwhelmed." Lynn was "rubbing her eyes"; she had "a lot going on." Dr. Felix herself appeared oblivious to Lynn having been kept up all night after she became the target of a child abuse allegation and forbidden from feeding her famished child until early that morning. When Dr. Felix told Janelle Green that Lynn had "seemed depressed" and that she was "concerned" about it, she claimed her motivation was that she "just wanted to make sure that Lynn was OK."

Ben's call to Dr. Felix on October 1 was the next topic for O'Neill. According to Dr. Felix, Ben had been "very upset, very angry" about Dr. Felix's conclusion in her MPEEC report. Ben had said he would "take the case to the top—that he would and he could." He let her know he "had the means to do that." All Dr. Felix did was listen. Ben had also asked her how he slept at night.

State's Attorney O'Neill sat down, content to end the direct examination of Dr. Felix on the note that highlighted that Ben, the father whose children were being taken from him, had been angry at Dr. Felix.

Perhaps State's Attorney O'Neill got the answers she wanted, answers that showed Ben capable of an angry tirade against a defenseless and well-meaning doctor. But Ben sounded pretty reasonable under the circumstances. How *did* this doctor sleep at night? How *could* she justify her work in this case as protecting children and helping families? Did she realize that her actions had let loose the runaway train that had moved so fast in the direction of family destruction?

The guardian ad litem's inquiry, up next, delved into two areas: cause of injury and extent of pain. Could the twins have caused the injury? Dr. Felix answered evasively, claiming that there was no report in the medical literature showing a toddler had caused a fracture "without a significant amount of force." It remained unclear what she meant by "significant." She added that even if an older sibling did cause the fracture, the injured infant would still have been in pain. Toddlers can jump off something high and injure a baby sibling, though, she admitted.

The guardian ad litem also asked Dr. Felix to elaborate on the pain Robert would have experienced. The doctor explained that when the bone is broken all the way through, the blood vessels and nerves around it are also broken, causing a significant amount of bleeding and leading to swelling, both immediately and over the ensuing hours. This would have been obvious to caregivers, she said, for the baby would have cried whenever his leg was moved.

It was my turn to question Dr. Felix. I started with her experience with fractures. It was pretty rudimentary. She had done the usual medical student rotation, but she had never put a cast on a child by herself. She relied on radiologists to read X-rays of fractures and then read their reports. I asked her *when* had she reached the conclusion that Robert had likely been abused. The sooner it was, the more that would show she hadn't considered new information during the investigation. She acknowledged that she "had the feeling it was more likely abuse" on September 11, when she looked at the medical records and images. She finally completed her written report on September 30, typing it herself.

Next, Dr. Felix confirmed that she had not given Lynn any information in writing about her role in evaluating Robert's injury. Nor had she disclosed the MPEEC contract between her team and the CPS agency. Also, no notes of the staffing meetings on child abuse cases with the other team members were kept in the hospital files for the children involved.

"Did you know Lynn had been up all night?" I inquired.

Yes, she did know that. Lynn hadn't wanted to go get anything to eat, although Dr. Felix had offered to wait while she got some food.

"Did Lynn tell you she hadn't been allowed to feed Robert?"

"No, she didn't."

My questions were aimed at the judge, not intended to score any points with Dr. Felix or the State's Attorney. The target audience is always the judge—or a reviewing court if the trial judge is making a bad ruling. It rarely pays to argue with someone like Dr. Felix. Quarreling with a witness can enhance their standing at a client's expense. But bringing out facts that paint the doctor as insensitive would help to undermine her conclusions. If Lynn had forgotten something important or come across as stressed, who could blame her if she'd had virtually no sleep and had been caring for a famished baby all night?

Dr. Felix had no specific notes of her conversation with Ben at the September 24 clinic visit; she had just written that the parents "denied" any history of trauma, falls, or accidents. Nevertheless, she considered the account she got from both parents to be a "complete history." She had discussed with Ben the lack of any evidence showing Robert had brittle bone disease, the sole genetic condition she recognized that could have explained Robert's fracture as an accident or the result of disease.

I pushed for specifics. Without details, it is difficult to expose the defects in a child abuse theory. "When did the fracture happen?" I asked her.

She answered honestly, "I don't know exactly. Likely one to three days before presentation. Less than seven."

I pressed, "Is it more likely one-to-three than four, five, or six days?"

She started to sound more tentative. "All I can say is it's less than seven definitively."

So I asked, "Did you do an exhaustive interview of Lynn's whereabouts for the prior seven days?"

"No."

"What about with Ben? Did you exhaustively interview him about that?"

"No."

"Who do you believe abused Robert?" I asked.

This question drew an immediate objection from the State's Attorney. The peculiarity of Illinois law is that it doesn't require the State to name an abuse perpetrator at this stage of proceedings or even at trial.[3] Many other states, though not all, have similar provisions. But there still has to be some connection to parental responsibility at the time of the child's injury; otherwise, parents could not have their children taken from them. To meet the legal "abuse" definition, the child has to be one whose caregiver (or other person responsible for their care) had inflicted an injury or allowed the injury to occur.

The judge allowed the question.

"I don't know," was her honest response. Dr. Felix didn't consider it her job to find the perpetrator or to confirm any parts of the parent's account. "That's the CPS investigation team's job," she added. "My job is to evaluate and assess."

So I asked her if "contacting eyewitnesses is the investigator's job?"

She answered, "Yes."

Turning to the same four factors that she had used in her evaluation, I probed for "mechanism of this fracture."

"Significant bending and twisting," she answered.

"Did it make a difference if the leg were in a fixed position?"

She didn't think so. But Dr. Sheridan had said that fixing the leg in position *does* create a counterforce that makes a leg break with less force.

"Does the amount of twisting matter?" I asked.

Again, the answer was no, which seemed to be another answer contrary to the laws of physics. Soon she was elaborating in ways that weren't responsive to my questions. Different fractures require different amounts of force, but "they are all excessive," she proclaimed.

Under the second of her factors, severity, I asked, "Would the fracture be severe if it weren't displaced?"

According to her, the child's age was a factor that made Robert's fracture "severe." But infants' fractures generally heal fast and fully, and it was not obvious how their age correlated with how serious their fracture was, medically speaking. If Robert's fracture *had* been severe, he would have seen an orthopedist and been given more than a splint and Tylenol as treatment.

Wondering how she actually differentiated fractures in infants by severity, I asked her, "Isn't it a policy of your hospital that *all* fractures in children under one year in age are reported to the child abuse team?"

"Yes," she acknowledged. Such fractures would always be reported to the State's child abuse hotline, too, if the parents had no explanation.

I asked, "Was there ever a case of an unexplained fracture in a child under one year that you concluded wasn't due to abuse?"

No, she always found abuse.

Dr. Felix had just admitted that nothing about a parents' character mattered. She also had just admitted that nothing the parents might say would sway her. If they couldn't explain the fracture, they were doomed. With severity determined solely by the age of the child, all that mattered was the fracture itself. Any parents would be labeled a child abuser if their newborn appeared with an unexplained fracture.

"Did you believe Lynn's account of how she spent her day?" I asked.

Dr. Felix said she did. She also believed Lynn's statement that she hadn't noticed any particular problem. But soon Dr. Felix parted company with Lynn's account: "But a reasonable parent would have noticed pain in a child when there was a manipulation of the leg."

The doctor's assumptions were starting to come out in full bloom, as she said, "I'm saying someone had to have noticed, so someone is not telling the truth."

I wanted to pinpoint when exactly the doctor thought Lynn's account deviated from what actually had occurred. "Are you saying Robert had a fracture in the morning of September 10?" I wondered.

No, she wasn't saying that. The doctor pointed to the evening of September 10 as the time of the fracture. Robert was "symptomatic" then. Ironically, it seemed that Lynn must have lied about Robert's fracture right at the time that she reported noticing it. It was an odd theory, to say the least: Lynn was accused of lying about the observations that she had reported to everyone.

I probed for more inconsistencies. "Robert didn't cry inconsolably when you moved his leg to examine him, did he?"

"No, he didn't," Dr. Felix admitted.

Do different children have different pain thresholds? I asked her. She said no, which seemed to me to defy common experience. This didn't seem like a scientifically based answer, either. Dr. Felix conceded that she had not reviewed the medical literature on children's pain levels recently. There were reports in the medical literature, she claimed, of fractures from children getting their legs caught in carriers but no reports of fractures occurring without the parent noticing the child's pain. On this point, Dr. Felix's testimony was diametrically contrary to Dr. Sheridan's. He had acknowledged that fractures were generally associated with pain but also that children sometimes got fractures that parents didn't notice.

I wondered how Dr. Felix had so much knowledge about how babies cried when their legs were fractured. So I asked her if this information was part of her medical school training.

It wasn't. Dr. Felix admitted that her opinion that Robert would have cried inconsolably at the time of the fracture was based on her *personal* experience "dealing with babies my whole life." It was based on her experience being around family members, friends with children, and infants who had fractures. It was based on her babysitting experience.

It had taken a long cross-examination to demonstrate that Dr. Felix's opinion rested on nothing more than the experience that a babysitter or an older child in a large family might have. Her claim that Robert was abused relied on no studies, no research, no direct clinical observations of how fractures occur, and no experience in treating fractures. Her central opinion was one she provided as a layperson who had seen a lot of babies.

She wasn't even a parent herself. If she were, she might have known better.

TEN

The Baby's at Risk If Breastfed in Private

If only the judge could have decided the case right then, the family might have been restored. The evidence was coming in our way. But the State had more witnesses to present, and so did we.

Lynn was the State's next witness. The State had the right to call the parents to testify. We could call Lynn to testify again in her defense. Probably the State's Attorneys thought they would show that Lynn was depressed, stressed, or angry and that she must have snapped and then lied about it. Whatever they thought, it didn't work.

Lynn became tearful as soon as she was asked to state her name. She seemed too emotionally drained to testify, but how could anyone blame her? She was fighting to remain the mother of her children. After some preliminary questions about her social work career, State's Attorney Bailey established that Lynn hadn't been working as a social worker since the twins were born, apparently to show that the State's actions would not impair her career. These questions missed the point that Lynn had kept her social work license current. If she was labeled a child abuser, she could kiss goodbye her ability to go back to work. The child-abuse registry would last 20 years—into Lynn's fifties.

The State's Attorney questioned Lynn about a note in her 2006 medical records. Lynn had seen an obstetrician/gynecologist when she started trying to get pregnant with the twins. The word "depression" appeared in those notes, though the context was unclear, a mere word on a page in a file. Lynn told the State's Attorney she had never been diagnosed with depression. The State's Attorney could have cleared the note up by calling Lynn's obstetrician to testify. But that same doctor had cared for Lynn through her two pregnancies. He had written a glowing letter about Lynn to the CPS team, saying it was "inconceivable" that Lynn would have abused any of her children. The State's Attorney must have concluded calling the doctor to explain his note wouldn't help their case.

Next, the State's Attorney focused on why Lynn hadn't mentioned seeing swelling on Robert's leg at the hair salon. The truth was that Lynn had forgotten about her comment to Susan, the stylist. Lynn had been reminded of the hairdresser's independent recollection when she had called Susan at the very end of September, giving Susan a heads-up that Janelle Green might call her. I wished myself that Lynn had remembered that comment sooner. I'm sure she wished it, too. That recollection obviously could have helped her and Ben's claim of innocence. It might even have pushed the investigation into a different direction. At a minimum, mentioning the conversation to Dr. Felix or Janelle Green might have led to a serious inquiry of the salon staff on duty on September 10. Now the State's Attorney seemed to be trying to blame Lynn for not remembering every conversation on September 10.

The State's Attorney was trying to pin all responsibility for Robert's care from September 7 through September 10 onto Lynn. Lynn usually changed Robert's diapers, but Ben did some of the diaper changes. State's Attorney Bailey pressed her to describe the minute details of how she changed Robert's diapers, wanting to know the order in which she moved Robert's limbs, took the old diaper away, cleaned him, and then put the new diaper in place. The level of detail Bailey was demanding Lynn to recall was absurd (or perhaps the State's Attorney truly did not know how to change a diaper). Lynn answered matter-of-factly. She usually would lift Robert by his torso, though she couldn't attest that she did it exactly that way every single time. Robert would usually kick when his diaper was being changed.

"Did you sometimes grab his leg?" State's Attorney Bailey asked. It was becoming clear that he pictured a very abusive diaper change. He was trying mightily to get Lynn to admit to his vision. But all Lynn said was that it was "possible that I had to manipulate his legs at times to get the diaper through."

"Could you recognize different types of baby cries?" the State's Attorney wanted to know. Lynn guessed that she could tell the difference between a cry of hunger and a cry of pain, repeating that while Robert had cried on September 10, he was never inconsolable.

He then tried to get Lynn to admit she had told police that she had heard Robert's leg pop during the evening diaper change on September 10. The police report includes an odd claim that Lynn reported hearing such a "pop." But Lynn flatly refused to admit that was what she had said. She had told the police she was scared to manipulate the leg, out of concern that something "would pop." By now, it seemed like the State's Attorney was just throwing out innuendos against Lynn, based on notes in records she had never seen before. He was hoping some of those innuendos would stick.

Lynn couldn't say more than that Robert was crying when she changed his diaper in the late afternoon. He wasn't screaming. She was always able to calm him down pretty quickly, even after the leg had gotten very swollen. She never noticed anything that would have caused the fracture. She never saw the twins roughhouse with Robert or pull on his leg. They were as well behaved, Lynn believed, as any toddlers could be.

The State was finished questioning Lynn for the time being. All he had managed to do, I believed, was reinforce that Lynn never heard the distinctive and inconsolable crying that Dr. Felix had insisted was a hallmark of any child fracture.

If Lynn or Ben *had* been liars about child abuse, they could have easily made up a story about the twins pulling on Robert's leg just a bit too hard during play. That simple story could have exonerated them both. But Lynn wouldn't lie, and neither would Ben. They would never blame another person, including one of their own children, for something they didn't see happen.

Short witnesses and a long argument about what was coming next finished off the second day of the hearing.

The police officer who interviewed both Ben and Lynn reported that they were very cooperative, answering all of his questions. The couple said they had nothing to hide, but they were very emotional. Both of them were crying; they hadn't slept, and they looked worn out. He had no reason to disbelieve anything either of them told him. Robert hadn't been dropped. He hadn't fallen. Neither parent noticed anything the twins did to injure him.

According to the officer, Lynn told him she heard a "pop" while changing Robert's diaper on the evening of September 10. This comment explained why the State decided to call this officer to testify, for nothing else said seemed to help the State's side. To put the word "pop" clearly into Lynn's mouth, the officer's in-person testimony had been necessary.

When it was our side's turn to question the officer, Melissa brought out that the officer's notes were not a verbatim account. Moreover, the CPS investigative team had not contacted him during the entire investigation.

It was already 3:45 p.m. on a Friday afternoon. The nurse from the suburban hospital was supposed to testify next, but he hadn't arrived. I argued that if the State had no more witnesses available, it should rest its case. Temporary custody hearings were supposed to be preliminary hearings, not a full airing of all the evidence to be presented at a full trial months later.

In response to my plea, State's Attorney Bailey announced that, besides the nurse, a radiologist under subpoena also had not appeared. Then Bailey launched into a litany of complaints in support of his request for more hearing dates on which to put on more witnesses for the State. The case was complicated. He couldn't be expected to track down every single witness and find dates for them in the short time he had been given. Judge Sanders noted, however, that at a temporary custody hearing, the State rarely called every doctor who had treated the child. He wanted to know why another continuance was necessary.

The State's Attorney's account of his efforts to get the radiologist to come to court sounded like a comedy of errors. Bailey had argued with the hospital's risk managers for 30 minutes about whether the doctor would come to court. The hospital had no one to cover for the radiologist on such short notice. While Bailey had made it appear that he expected the radiologist to arrive any minute, it now became clear he knew she wasn't on her way.

Then the State's Attorney shifted gears, announcing he needed other dates for Dr. Miller's testimony. Judge Sanders stopped him: "Who is Dr. Miller?" Dr. Miller was the hospital's orthopedist who had briefly examined Robert on September 11. Newly essential witnesses for the State were proliferating. It was news to us that the State intended to call Dr. Miller. She had never weighed in on whether Robert's fracture was due to abuse. The State's Attorney acknowledged he had not spoken to Dr. Miller. No one had, despite her status as the sole orthopedist who had been involved with Robert's care for the fracture prior to Dr. Sheridan's getting involved.

It would be hard for us to stop the State from calling the sole orthopedist who cared for Robert on September 10 or 11. The actual in-person testimony of another treating orthopedist could be potentially weighty. If

Dr. Miller agreed with Dr. Sheridan, it would strengthen our case. If she disagreed, it could be devastating. But Dr. Sheridan knew her, and he viewed her as a straight shooter. He didn't expect her to disagree with his assessment of the fracture. We were modestly hopeful that if the State called her to testify, it wouldn't hurt Ben and Lynn's case.

It was remarkable, though, that the State's Attorney planned to present a witness when he had no idea what she would say. We didn't know, either; if we tried calling doctors at the hospital, they would immediately secure legal counsel who would prevent the doctor from talking to us without a formal deposition. Clearly, the State also hadn't had an easy time getting through to the doctors. But the parents' side was at an immediate disadvantage. The State's Attorney had direct access to the MPEEC doctors under the subcontract with the CPS agency. For a full trial, we could ask to take Dr. Miller's deposition in order to learn her opinion before she testified before the judge. But now, we were trying to complete a preliminary, expedited temporary custody hearing. Finding time to talk to her in advance of her testimony, even by subpoena, would be a real challenge. Even so, the State was taking a big risk by calling her to testify without speaking to her first.

I complained to the judge that since the CPS team had not spoken to either of the doctors the State planned to call, how could the State claim that their testimony was essential? The State was prolonging the hearing at the family's expense. Though the initial order said temporary custody of the children was ordered "without prejudice," the delay had become extremely prejudicial. The parents hadn't been living in their own home for five weeks. There now seemed to be no end in sight as to when this long hearing would end.

When I finished speaking, the guardian ad litem raised another complication: her office had identified a medical consultant who was about to leave the country and would not return until October 26. She could not say what this doctor's opinion would be. He was available to testify on November 6 or on November 20—over a month away.

The poor children! The poor parents! The poor grandparents! Their lives would be put on hold for another month in order to wait for an unidentified doctor—or maybe two or three more doctors—to voice opinions that no one yet knew.

After I complained about the delay, the judge revealed that he had not realized that Ben and Lynn still were not living in their own home since September 11. That was odd. There was a visiting order, signed by Judge

Sanders on October 2, providing that the parents could visit their children at their home from 5:15 a.m. until 10:00 p.m. each day. This order wouldn't make sense if the parents already had been living at home. But the visiting order by now was one of many orders in the file, and Judge Sanders simply hadn't focused on it.

Sensing that Judge Sanders might be heading in a direction the State did not welcome, the State's Attorney quickly jumped in. The newly assigned private child welfare agency caseworker had no objection to allowing Ben and Lynn back into their own home as long as the grandparents remained there to supervise. But the State's Attorney was not about to agree. Nor would the CPS agency's counsel. Now, the State's legal representatives were at odds with the State's now-assigned caseworkers, who were the ones who worked directly with the family.

Judge Sanders saw the question of where the parents were living as a question that directly affected the children's well-being. He also understood that granting the State and guardian ad litem requests for more time for potential medical expert testimony would necessitate a continuance for several weeks at a minimum. Judge Sanders highlighted that there had been no evidence showing that either parent had abused Robert "other than circumstantial evidence that the parents were supervising the child and should have known if the child had received that injury."

Judge Sanders suggested that he could allow the parents overnight supervised visits in their home while the hearing continued. In other words, they could live at home while calling it "visiting." He noted that, as of a few weeks ago, there had been a policy change in the juvenile court to liberalize visitation whenever possible. He viewed his proposal as consistent with the newly announced courtwide policy. Judge Patricia Martin, the presiding judge of the juvenile court, herself a national leader,[1] had been working hard to make the court practices more supportive of children's relationships with their parents. While Judge Sanders knew the State wouldn't agree to this proposal, he indicated that he believed this was the fairest and best course of action.

At the same time, Judge Sanders was not going to force the State to rest its case. This was unsurprising. If the judge had refused to let the State make its case, an appeal might reverse that ruling. That was the last thing that would help the family.

Prior to ordering these overnight visits for Ben and Lynn, Judge Sanders wanted to hear evidence from the private agency caseworker in support of the recommendation to allow Ben and Lynn back into their home.

The caseworker's testimony was short and sweet. But what was odd under the circumstances was how that testimony was presented. Even though the State's Attorney opposed allowing Ben and Lynn back into their own home, the judge turned to the State's Attorney to present the testimony of the caseworker who recommended the parents' return into the home.

Deference to the State's Attorney as the prosecutor was part of the juvenile court's culture and decorum. The judge had requested this testimony in his role of judicial overseer of the well-being of the children. The requested testimony was akin to a progress report on the parents' cooperation since the case had come to the court.

Progress reports are commonplace throughout pending cases in juvenile court. Even as we were in the midst of a temporary custody hearing, a parallel track of services and monitoring of the family was occurring simultaneously. The CPS Guardianship Administrator's office had been assigned to take care of the children. CPS field offices throughout the State handled foster care placements, including relative foster placements. A large division of the State CPS system managed and oversaw the State's contracts with private child welfare agencies. These contract agencies provided rehabilitative services for parents and financial, medical, and social supports for children assigned to the State's custody and placed into foster care. Much of the CPS agency's work, and a lot of its budget,[2] went to supporting foster care placements and providing case management and services for children for whom the State had legal custody.

When grandparents become relative foster parents, they are entitled to receive a State stipend to care for their grandchildren's care, whether they ask for the financial assistance or not. Most families need the support, of course, including the medical coverage the State provided for the children. The assigned caseworkers also are expected to visit the home weekly, at least initially, make recommendations about the parents' visits with the children (including whether visits could safely increase) and to determine whether the family has unsatisfied concerns to address before the court can return the children to the care and custody of their parents. The caseworkers prepare service plans and make sure that the children receive timely medical care. The caseworkers are expected to report to the court on the parents' progress toward the goal of returning the children home.

On this parallel track, Ben and Lynn could win the return of their children just by being good sports, cooperating with the services and visits, and ultimately getting favorable caseworker and service provider reports. Cooperation with services thus provided an alternative route for parents to end the juvenile court and CPS's involvement with their family. Indeed, this "cooperation with services" route was the much more frequently used vehicle for returning children to their families, because over 90 percent of the cases in the juvenile court ended up with some finding of abuse or neglect.

This track to get children returned was filled with pitfalls of its own, but even if the judge believed one or both of the parents had abused the children, there still was a strong likelihood that the children could eventually be returned home.[3] Return-home rates for middle-class white children were significantly higher and faster than for African Americans, but for all families, the parallel track was terribly slow. Return of children under the "progress in services" track usually required the juvenile court process to run its full course. There would be trial or agreed finding of abuse or neglect, then a final disposition order committing the children to the guardianship of the State, and then a series of permanency hearings, where the parents' progress would be assessed.

The process could also be arbitrary. If the services the parents needed weren't readily available, if they got negative reports from service providers, or if their progress was deemed not "fast enough," they might face a change in the goal of returning their children home. If that occurred, the State might terminate their rights permanently. Parents had little or no control over these systemic barriers to family reunification.

On this second progress-in-services track, the State's Attorney wasn't the parents' adversary, per se, at least not unless and until the parents failed to cooperate with the services requested of them. In reporting on the parents' progress in the services track, the State's Attorney functioned more as an aid to the judge, bringing useful information to the court's attention.

This alternative track was less adversarial, generally speaking, because it was crystal clear where the power lay—with the State. Once the court had adjudicated their child abused or neglected, parents had no cards of their own to play to avoid the demands for services. The alternative track— earning the return of children through good behavior and compliance with services—gave the State's Attorneys and the guardians ad litem (who doubled-teamed with the State most of the time) a way to seem to be on the family's side while keeping to themselves the power to judge parents worthy or unworthy of regaining custody of their children.

In the progress-in-services track, parents had only one choice: they had to go along with the State's services demands. So even though Ben and

Lynn were in the battle of their lives over whether there was a legal basis to take the children from them, they were effectively compelled to work with the assigned caseworker. If that caseworker had been anything like Janelle Green or Kirby Long, it wouldn't have worked well. But the newly assigned caseworkers were friendly and kind, eager to help the family. They made no unreasonable demands.

Ben and Lynn and their family fully understood the necessity of cooperating with the assigned caseworkers. Fortunately, the newly assigned casework team had already come to like and respect them and had privately expressed doubt that either Ben or Lynn had abused Robert. It was unusual, but these caseworkers made no demands for social services for the family, perhaps because the case was unusual in that it hadn't yet passed the preliminary temporary custody litigation phase. But Lynn was a social worker, and she was well steeped in parenting techniques. Ben and Lynn already demonstrated mastery of the child discipline techniques that the parent education programs taught, so there was no need to train them further. It was easy for any caseworker to observe that they had mastered the basics of parenting.

My view of juvenile court and of the State's Attorney's too-powerful role in that court is affected by years of experience fighting for families who were struggling to reunify. For all its lofty rhetoric to the contrary, the juvenile court functions as a power and control system over families. Not all families are equally vulnerable, of course. Families of relative privilege, like Ben and Lynn's, had never experienced anything remotely like juvenile court before. Few families who look like them have the experience that is all too common for minorities, poor families, immigrants, and disabled parents. These already disadvantaged families are especially vulnerable to the State's use of its authority to remove children and have many fewer resources to fight back.[4]

Ben and Lynn, as a white, middle-class, suburban married couple with two lawyers in the family, stood out as exceptions to the typical powerlessness and vulnerability of the parents who ordinarily appear before the juvenile court. They were not poor; they weren't black, brown, or Native American; and they weren't recent immigrants or disabled. They were well educated and looked like the parents in *Ozzie and Harriet*. They had two privately retained lawyers who came to court with them on the first day of the proceedings. They were armed with medical experts ready to vouch for them even before the case was filed. All of this was extremely unusual, maybe unprecedented, in the Cook County Juvenile Court. That's why Lynn and Ben stood out so sharply as challengers to the usual expectations of the players in the system. It might explain why, when the State's basis for its demands upon Ben and Lynn was challenged, the State's Attorneys became defensive and anxious to prove abuse could occur even in a family like theirs.

Making middle-class white parents like Ben and Lynn out to be child abusers would establish the State's evenhandedness. If parents who looked like them abused their kids, they certainly deserved no special favors. The motivation to prove evenhandedness explains, I believe, why our highlighting that Lynn's mother was a federal judge and our mention of Ben and Lynn's standing in their community met with such vigorous objections. Implicit in our pleas for fairness was the recognition that since none of the families who usually came to the court got the truly fair treatment we were arguing that Ben and Lynn deserved, why should they? Our pleas came off as seeking special favors based on privilege. We had thought we were just mounting a strong defense—one every parent should get, but not all do.

Since the State's Attorneys and guardians ad litem generally saw themselves as serving the best interests of children, it was natural that they would bristle if anyone questioned their bona fides when it came to protecting the true interests of children, which are antithetical to being removed from their families. But many family defenders are seen as disturbing the applecart when they vigorously represent their clients. State's Attorneys and guardians ad litem do not like to see their role characterized as enforcers of power relationships, including patriarchal authority over mothers, who are the most frequent targets of the court system's intervention. They don't like to see themselves as destroying families, either. When a case comes into their courtroom where it becomes clear that they have got the wrong target for their zealous child advocacy, it's not unusual for the State's representatives to become defensive. Their advocacy against parents takes on a harder edge. Compromise becomes increasingly difficult.

It is the fate of a family defender to be viewed with skepticism tinged with a grain of hostility from the lawyers and advocates who side with the State when children are taken in CPS custody. No outsider to the closed juvenile court system is appreciated, but an outsider who upsets the status quo is especially disdained. At the same time, beneath a show of disdain, family defenders like me sometimes get begrudging respect from a few

State's Attorneys who appreciate that we are fighting for justice for our clients. That's doing our job.

The reality that the CPS system was often destroying families without providing something better has been noticed by people in positions of authority. Several CPS agency directors had become sharply critical of the harm done to children in taking them from their parents and putting them into State-run care.[5] In Ben and Lynn's case, moreover, no one was claiming that their children needed to be raised by better, different parents. The implicit purpose of the case against them seemed to be first to blame and shame them for their son's injury, thus exposing them as child abusers, and then to turn around and return the children to them after they completed whatever course of treatment the State's agents recommended, which in their case was actually *nothing*. In short, the whole purpose of the case wasn't to improve Ben and Lynn's ability to raise their children but to establish that the State was right and they were wrong.

There is a broad consensus nowadays that the foster care system is broken.[6] But there is no consensus yet on why that is—the way that the adjudication of guilt is biased against parents, both in the way it treats the parent from the beginning and in the way it allocates limited resources to the defense. Nor is there consensus on what needs to change or how change is to be achieved.

Beneath this disagreement is the lack of a shared understanding of the proper role of any child protection system. What parenting standards should be enforced, and how should the CPS system enforce those standards? If anything, the consensus is moving in the directions of more conflict and confusion, more intrusion, more presumptions and profiling, and fewer thoughtful individualized assessments.[7] The public seems to want ever more hotline calls at the expense of family life. Calls for expansion of CPS powers are buoyed by legislators looking for a chance to "get tough" on child abusers. One result of the dramatic increase in hotline calling and CPS authority is that parents can no longer let their children play outside or walk to school without fearing that the State might come and snatch their children or label them child neglectors.[8]

Ben and Lynn had stumbled into a system that doesn't know how to treat families fairly, one whose mantra, the "best interests of the children," covers a multitude of mistakes. They were paying a severe price for the child protection system's confusion over the fundamental question of when the State should intervene to take children from their parents.

State's Attorney Bailey proceeded to elicit the private agency caseworker's recommendation to allow Ben and Lynn to return home. Her supervisor supported the recommendation. She and her supervisor, both of whom had master's degrees in social work, had discussed the recommendation several times, so it wasn't an ad hoc, poorly thought-out position. The caseworker believed that the grandparents would be able to protect the children from their parents by providing 24-hour supervision.

If we hadn't wanted Ben and Lynn to be able to go home so badly, it might have seemed terribly insulting. What parents want to have their role with their children second-guessed at every turn by their own parents? This highly unnatural arrangement—giving supervisory control of parents to grandparents—turns normal family dynamics on their head. Fit parents have the right to direct whether their children will have *any* contact with their grandparents,[9] and no one had yet shown that either Ben or Lynn was unfit. So it was odd that a still-unconfirmed accusation of abuse gave the court the power to limit Ben and Lynn's unsupervised contact and impose Ben's parents' supervision on them for weeks on end.

Of course, since the grandparents were 100 percent on the parents' side, we were not going to object to such a step. The caseworker was explicit: having the grandparents supervise the parents in the home, including being available to get up in the middle of the night, would "decrease the risk of harm" to the children. This statement assumed, of course, that Ben and Lynn had put their own children at risk. The presumption of their guilt remained in full force even as the process moved slowly in their favor.

While the caseworker recommended this plan, however, the CPS agency attorney, who had been quiet through the hearing so far, disagreed. Learning of this objection, the judge asked the caseworker about the parents' visits since the case began. "Yes, they visit daily, and we have visiting logs for all the visits," she noted. Ben and Lynn were allowed to come back to their home as early as 5:15 a.m. and leave by 10:00 p.m. They just couldn't stay overnight under the October 2 visitation order. There had been no violations of that order. The parents were always appropriate with the children. The only change the new order would effectuate would be to let the parents sleep in their own home.

The guardian ad litem wanted to make sure that the caseworker had been out there to see the children. She testified that she had been there just four days before, on October 12. The grandmother did not allow Lynn to be alone with the children at all.

"Did you see mom breastfeeding?" the guardian ad litem asked.

"No," the caseworker responded.

Presumably, the guardian ad litem worried that Lynn might have some alone time with Robert. Did the guardian ad litem truly believe that Lynn would turn her opportunity to breastfeed in private into an abusive rampage against her son? It was hard to fathom the depth of distrust of my clients. Yet it was obvious where that distrust had come from: years of headlines about child abuse and a few bad experiences in the courtroom, with parents who took advantage of a liberal court order and then hurt a child. That's what "not taking chances" looked like. Lynn would not be allowed to breastfeed in private.

The caseworker agreed that a detailed written supervision plan would be appropriate; she could prepare one promptly if the parents were allowed back home. Unannounced home visits would continue.

Melissa clarified that others besides family members could continue to act as supervisors. Ben's mother needed some breaks. It was easy for everyone in the courtroom to forget that she had a life, too, beyond her role as the helpful grandma, conscripted by the State of Illinois into mandatory round-the-clock supervision of her grandchildren.

At this point, the CPS attorney jumped on board to question the caseworker. It was the first time the CPS attorney got actively involved in the hearing. She asked if the caseworker had "consulted with her agency's performance monitor" about the recommendation. This mention of the performance monitor, another bureaucrat who supervised the contract between the State CPS agency and its private social service agency contractors who were monitoring Ben and Lynn's family, appeared to be a veiled threat—a warning that, by making this recommendation, the caseworker was crossing a line and that the State CPS agency disapproved.

The governmentally run CPS agency, part of the executive branch of Illinois government, entered into contracts that entrusted private child welfare agencies to deliver basic services for many families. Their contractual duties these agencies assumed including monitoring the families who lived under court orders and reporting back to the court on whether the children's needs were being met and whether parents were following the court's orders. The system depended on trust in the private agency workers to make decisions and render judgments about the families assigned to them. Approval for a specific return-home recommendation by someone who managed the agency's contract seemed entirely superfluous and unnecessary and to be only red tape that served no one's interests, especially not the children's.

Behind the scenes, however, and unbeknown to us as lawyers for Ben and Lynn, the recommendation to allow Ben and Lynn to return home had already been discussed with the private agency monitor, who had already told the caseworker's supervisor that she should retract it. High-level strings within the State's CPS agency were being pulled outside the courtroom to stop Ben and Lynn's return home. The seriousness of Robert's injury was cited as the reason to keep Ben and Lynn away from their children overnight. It was clear, however, that the CPS performance monitor didn't know much about the evidence in Ben and Lynn's favor.

Fortunately, judges are not bound to follow the recommendations of unseen bureaucrats whose knowledge of the facts is unclear. I knew, however, that many other judges, hearing for the first time about a new bureaucratic wrinkle in liberalizing parents' contact with their children, would defer to the unseen bureaucrat and deny the parents' the right to return to their own home.

The CPS attorney asked where the children would sleep. Fortunately, the caseworker knew how to answer: Ben and Lynn could not sleep in the same room as their children. If a child woke in the night, a grandparent would have to wake up. The caseworker hadn't yet discussed the sleeping arrangements with the children's grandparents, however. The caseworker did not know if the grandparents were willing to sleep in shifts. The judge was not aware that Lynn was still breastfeeding Robert, but the caseworker confirmed that she was doing so. Of course, Lynn had been unable to give Robert any overnight feedings since September 11.

By now, Ben and Lynn were reconciled to this level of microscopic scrutiny of their interactions with their children. They had the patience of Job. So did the grandparents. To have their dignity, their integrity, and their privacy rights in their own home under such constant surveillance by the caseworker, the State's Attorney, the guardian ad litem, and the CPS agency attorney was offensive to basic liberties that families have the right to enjoy. They had done nothing wrong that should have caused Lynn to lose the basic right to feed her child in this intimate and healthy way. Despite these indignities, however, the whole family stayed stoic and focused. What kept them going was their love of the children and their single-minded focus on doing what it took to keep them from ever being taken out of their own home.

The conflict we now were witnessing in the courtroom was no longer between the CPS system and the family; it was between the state bureaucracy and the juvenile court judge. That's a classic battle, and sometimes an epic one, but now writ smaller. The executive branch (the CPS agency and its legal representatives) was tangling with the judicial branch (the juvenile court judge) before our eyes. The executive was throwing up roadblocks to the judiciary's use of its judicial power. The representations of the executive branch were saying to the judge, in effect, "If you rule for these parents, it's all on you. We're warning you, Judge. If you take this step, we'll interpret your order as restrictively as possible. We're voicing our displeasure, and we will go up through our own chains of command of command to let you know we do not agree with your plan to let this family have some of its own power and privacy back."

In this battle, the children's representative had tended toward the CPS agency's side. It was remarkable what a united front the State, guardian ad litem, and CPS agency could pull together against a single judge when their own power and control over a family was questioned. Many judges would have backed down. Others judges wouldn't have made the suggestion to liberalize visits in the first place. Parents who want judges to break out of the lockstep process that had become customary in the Cook County Juvenile Court face enormous bureaucratic opposition. It took a special judge to rule for the parents in these circumstances. The exercise of judicial power can be lonely, especially in juvenile court, where the "best interests of the child" mantra can be used to argue for whatever the State wants and where a coterie of well-resourced lawyers stands arrayed against the parents.

After the caseworker testified, the judge asked the parties to state their positions. The CPS attorney spoke up against liberalization. While the agency had no objection to liberal daytime visits, she claimed that overnight visits presented a "risk factor" because the grandparents would be asleep. There was no guarantee they would wake up every time Lynn or Ben woke to feed Robert or change a diaper. State's Attorney Bailey agreed.

The guardian ad litem did not want to take a position yet but wanted to hear from the grandmother first. The judge allowed her to call the grandmother to testify. The guardian ad litem asked Ben's mother if she planned to remain in Illinois caring for the children, through the full temporary custody hearing. Ben's mother admitted that she would like to go home, but she had no immediate plans to leave. She had been supervising Ben and Lynn with their children from 6:15 a.m. until they both left at 8:00 p.m. Lynn stayed home with the children all day but sometimes ran some errands, like going to the grocery store. Lynn was still breastfeeding, but the grandmother remained present when Lynn did so. Ben's mother was used to giving Robert two nighttime feedings. She was more than willing to continue to provide supervision if the parents returned to the home overnight, understanding she'd have to get up during the night if the children woke up. Ben's dad could get up at night if necessary, too.

Ben's mother had just one request. "It would be nice" if the people who came to the home to monitor them would identify themselves. The unspoken point was that she was tired of having a stream of strangers showing up at her door and demanding to see the children, without even showing proper ID's.

Throughout this portion of the hearing, Melissa and I stayed quiet. The drama in front of us was between the judge and the lawyers in his courtroom. "Don't interrupt a judge if he is going your way," is a classic and good litigation rule. It seemed the guardian ad litem was moving slightly onto our side, since the grandmother's testimony answered all of her concerns. The guardian ad litem's neutrality could give the judge the cover he needed to rule in favor of Ben and Lynn's return to their home.

The guardian ad litem now signaled that her objection to the judge's order would not be strenuous. She said that she had "concerns about allowing the parents to move back home" because of the seriousness of the allegations, but she added that if the judge was inclined to grant that order, the supervised visitation order needed to be very clear as to the nighttime feedings: one of the grandparents would have to wake up.

The judge had made up his mind. Reminding everyone that the State and guardian ad litem had asked for a somewhat indefinite continuance and that he had broad discretion to make visiting orders, he was allowing Ben and Lynn back into their own home overnight. He hastened to add that this order was not for the convenience of the parents; it was in the best interest of the children. Robert was a newborn who was still breastfeeding. The parents were already in the home for a great deal of time, so the change he was ordering was not particularly significant. Plus, he did not see the significant risk that concerned the CPS attorney and State's Attorney. At the same time, he acknowledged that having round-the-clock supervision by grandparents was stressful for the parents, and he would not let the hearing drag on for months.

It was already 5:00 p.m. on Friday, October 16. Ben and Lynn returned home that night for the best weekend they'd had since Labor Day.

We had turned a corner in the case. Judges who let parents go home rarely decide to take the children from them after a trial.

ELEVEN

Attacking the Doctor Who Knows Something About Fractures

The judge's ruling took a lot of the family's worry away, although the strain on the family from being constantly supervised continued unabated. Ben's mother still had no idea when she would be released to return back home. Her stay was getting to be much longer than she had imagined. The State and guardian ad litem were not close to resting their cases.

On October 21, we returned to court for the State's cross-examination of Dr. Sheridan. We knew he would acquit himself well, though we hadn't been given advance notice of what the State would try to throw at him.

State's Attorney Bailey started his questions by summarily reviewing the four factors Dr. Felix considered significant. Dr. Sheridan quickly turned the second factor, the severity of the injury, in Ben and Lynn's favor. The more severe an injury, the more a doctor would expect to see other symptoms. If the injury is not noticed, then it's less likely to be severe. Moreover, to Dr. Sheridan's way of thinking, nothing about Robert's fracture *was* severe. He observed worse fractures than Robert's just about every day. The only odd thing about Robert's fracture was his age. The lack of an explanation was a reason to investigate, but that didn't distinguish Robert's fracture from many other cases involving accidental injuries. Unwitnessed accidents happen, and parents don't always notice actions that might cause a fracture to occur. Lots of possibilities could have caused Robert's fracture without the parents' knowledge.

Dr. Sheridan was adept in answering cross-examination questions. He wasn't argumentative, but he was good at turning every question in Ben and Lynn's favor, nailing each point.

Bailey turned next to Dr. Sheridan's own evaluation of Robert's fracture, wanting to know when exactly he wrote his report. In one of the only moments of levity during the entire hearing, Dr. Sheridan mentioned he wrote it when he was in Las Vegas on October 3.

State's Attorney Bailey was quick on the uptake. "Did you win?" "Not this time," Dr. Sheridan replied, smiling.

Bailey asked Dr. Sheridan to use his slide show and pointer again to go through some points on the slides, a step that seemed only to magnify how effective Dr. Sheridan was in explaining X-rays. The State wanted to know how long the fracture was: "five millimeters." The break made Robert's leg shorter by four millimeters, and given the length of Robert's leg, this amounted to a 5 percent displacement. Dr. Sheridan had seen 90 percent displacements. This measurement made the implication obvious; contrary to Dr. Felix's testimony, Robert's fracture was not one any orthopedist would call "severe."

After making no headway on the medical science points, State's Attorney Bailey moved to the heart of his attack on Dr. Sheridan: his customary role as a witness for the defense. In the past 12 years, Dr. Sheridan had probably testified "at least 30 times." Still, testifying as an expert witness was a small part of his practice. As a pediatric orthopedist, Dr. Sheridan spent about 20 percent of his time treating broken bones. But caring for children with congenital anomalies, cerebral palsy, and other disabilities made up most of his practice.

Try as he might, it was hard for State's Attorney Bailey to make Dr. Sheridan look biased, unprincipled, or insensitive. He was hardly a full-time defense expert. And unlike Dr. Felix, his main job was to treat kids, not give opinions about child abuse.

"Do you recall the case of Linda H.?" Bailey asked.

Dr. Sheridan vaguely did recall something. The judge wanted to know where Bailey was going with questions about other cases. Bailey continued, "She was a teenager, correct?"

Dr. Sheridan said he didn't recall specifically; he saw 5,000 patients a year. Bailey dropped these questions but would come back to asking about other cases soon.

Bailey's questions seemed like a clumsy attempt to trap Dr. Sheridan; if Dr. Sheridan remembered the testimony and agreed with Bailey about the opinion he had given in it, that would reinforce the State's position that Dr. Sheridan's testimony for Ben and Lynn was simply his *modus operandi*. But if he had forgotten the case, that made him look inattentive. None of these other cases had anything to do with Robert. Moreover, Bailey never gave us the transcripts he was trying to use to pigeonhole Dr. Sheridan.

I objected. Cross-examination should not be a quiz show or a memory game of "Gotcha!" Dr. Sheridan's prior testimony in other cases was irrelevant unless the State could show a direct contradiction to what Dr. Sheridan was saying now.

Soon the State's Attorney got testy. When Dr. Sheridan started to answer, "Well," the State's Attorney cut him off with, "Doctor, I'm asking you, yes or no?"

That was a bad move. Now the judge called Bailey on his interruption, letting Dr. Sheridan answer as fully as he wished.

Bailey's cross-examination established, simply, that Dr. Sheridan testified for the defense and that the State's Attorney's office didn't much care for his opinions. But the State's own experts, the child abuse doctors, testified virtually exclusively for the prosecution. Just as the State would almost never ask someone like Dr. Sheridan to testify against parents, the defense rarely asked a child abuse pediatrician to give an opinion on parents' behalf. It would be nice and helpful to the cause of justice if the camps were less polarized. Apparently the State's Attorney didn't see much wrong with a doctor being aligned with one side, as long as that side was his.

The State seemed especially bent on undermining Dr. Sheridan's explanation of how Robert's fracture could have been nondisplaced and then become displaced. He wondered whether Dr. Sheridan had ever read anything about this theory. Dr. Sheridan replied confidently, "That's in all the textbooks."

At that point, the State's Attorney started in on a surprising new line of questions, trying his best to score some points through a dramatic demonstration. He pulled out a stuffed cloth doll and handed the doll to Dr. Sullivan in the witness chair. He recited that the doll was "anatomically correct" and stated for the record that it was about 18 inches long. Then he asked Dr. Sheridan to demonstrate the force necessary to cause a nondisplaced fracture on the doll.

There was an obvious problem. Melissa and I exchanged looks of disbelief.

"Objection," I called out. "This is a cloth doll. It doesn't have any bones."

The State's Attorney's response was to note that the doll had a diaper on. That hardly helped.

The judge sustained my objection. Labeling this effort an "improper hypothetical experiment" on a doll that looked like a Raggedy Ann type of doll, the judge stopped Bailey's attempted demonstration of how much force was necessary to cause a fracture on the boneless doll.

There was one dispute on which the State did score a point, however. Dr. Sheridan had said he had reviewed a skeletal survey taken on September 12. But that date clearly was wrong; there was no testing done that day. The State had caught Dr. Sheridan in a typographic error.

To conclude his cross-examination, the State's Attorney challenged Dr. Sheridan about his lack of expertise in child abuse medicine. He asked about Dr. Sheridan's relationship with the child abuse pediatricians at his own hospital. Dr. Sheridan worked with them, and sometimes they sought out his opinions in their own cases. Dr. Sheridan didn't claim expertise in child abuse generally, but he did hold himself out as an "expert on what causes fractures and muscular skeletal injuries in children."

In the big picture and in the larger world, Dr. Sheridan had been part of the slowly succeeding battle to change child abuse dogma about fractures. Spiral fractures had once been thought to be emblematic of child abuse, but while this false assumption had not been eradicated, it was no longer pressed as forcefully it had been just a few years before.

The guardian ad litem's questions of Dr. Sheridan were brief, focusing on how Robert's fracture could have been first nondisplaced and then displaced later. Dr. Sheridan responded that if Robert had been passed from person to person (as we now knew had occurred at the salon), the fracture could have become displaced and started to swell more. The initial signs of swelling would be subtle. It was interesting to hear this, for Dr. Sheridan hadn't been briefed on the stylist's testimony, under the rule that lawyers can't talk to witnesses who are still testifying. Still, Dr. Sheridan was testifying in a manner entirely consistent with Susan, the stylist's, description.

With a minimally displaced fracture, a child's fussiness might not be too great. Babies cry whenever they don't get what they want or need. It might take some time before parents realize that there is something truly wrong with a child's limb needing medical attention.

Again it was my turn to ask questions. I asked Dr. Sheridan about the nerve endings in bones, but he clarified that just the periosteum had nerves. The pain from this rupture in the periosteum might be sharp at first but then turns to a numbing effect. If the baby were breastfed right away, the baby might soothe and fall asleep. A baby can't say, "My leg is killing me." Babies' cries can be mistaken for a number of different things.

At that point, the State tried to stop Dr. Sheridan from testifying about how children cry, proclaiming he wasn't a pediatrician. The judge over-ruled him, pointing out that he "treats children all the time." The judge recalled that the State's expert had based her own opinion on being around families and babies and not on her training as a pediatrician, per se. The judge had been paying attention.

Why do parents give accounts that sometimes seem inconsistent? Once again, Dr. Sheridan gave a common-sense answer. Parents who have no idea how an injury occurred will rack their brains. They may bring up events that didn't seem significant. Coming up with possible explanations and omitting others is what parents do all the time when they bring their kids for treatment.

Dr. Sheridan was excused. Now the judge renewed the discussion of the scheduling challenges that faced us. The guardian ad litem's consulting doctor was still out of the country. The prospects of Ben's mother getting back home before Thanksgiving were starting to look bleak.

The judge could move his own busy caseload around. Dr. Miller, the treating orthopedist who had seen Robert on September 11, was available for the hearing on November 4. Now better prepared than on the previous Friday, State's Attorney Bailey said he expected Dr. Miller to testify that Robert had been irritable when touched; that the distinction between the oblique versus spiral fractures often was impossible to discern; and that she disagreed with Dr. Sheridan's contention that a fracture that is nondisplaced could become displaced.

State's Attorney Bailey had not represented that Dr. Miller held any opinion about child abuse. If Dr. Miller gave neutral testimony, Dr. Sheridan's positive opinion in the parents' favor might carry the day.

Two more weeks passed. It was now November 4. Ben stood before the court's elevated bench with Robert and his twin son at his side. Lynn stood next to her twin daughter. Natalie had come to court, too. Everyone could see that Robert's cast had been taken off; the leg was fully healed. Robert looked healthy and happy in his father's arms, and the twins, dressed in their Sunday best, looked adorable, too.

The nurse who had been unreachable on October 21 was ready to testify. Dr. Miller was set to come in the afternoon.

The nurse recounted examining Robert at about 9:00 p.m. on September 10. When first put on the table, Robert had cried for 10 to 20 seconds. When his legs were lifted to take off his clothing, Robert had cried again briefly, for 20 seconds at the most. The nurse observed that Robert's left leg was about an inch or two larger in diameter than the right—exactly what Ben and Lynn had seen. The left leg was more reddish in color, too, and it rotated more, maybe by as much as 10 to 15 degrees. It looked more unstable.

This was good testimony; brief whimpering when Robert's leg was moved was not what Dr. Felix had described. The nurse soon made the point explicitly: "It wasn't an abnormal-type cry. It was a normal baby cry that you wouldn't necessarily immediately try to comfort."

My cross-examination was brief. "Could you tell from the way you moved Robert's leg and his cry that he had a fracture?"

No, he couldn't tell that.

The nurse's testimony had just demolished the State's theory behind its case against Ben and Lynn.

There was still time for other parents' witnesses before Dr. Miller arrived in the afternoon. Ben and Lynn's friend Mark was there. Mark's apartment was where Lynn had gone in order to feed and change Robert after the audiology appointment on September 10.

Mark had known Ben and Lynn for five years. They got together often for dinner at both apartments, twins included. They trimmed Christmas trees together. Ben and Lynn were "just as loving parents as we could ask for kids." Not once did either parent show signs of any frustration with the children.

Lynn's visit to Mark's apartment on September 10 had been brief—an hour at most. Mark never once heard Robert cry. He had been close enough to have heard crying if there had been any. Robert couldn't have looked happier.

State's Attorney O'Neill then launched into an extraordinarily intrusive cross-examination. Did Mark know how Lynn had conceived the twins? Did they plan to have Robert? How had they gotten pregnant with Robert? Mark seemed to be able to take care of himself and answered these questions just fine, so I let the questions go without objecting.

O'Neill didn't let up. How long Ben and Lynn's apartment had been on the market? When had it closed? Her goal seemed to be to show that Ben and Lynn were under so much stress that they would have snapped and abused Robert, but these questions were falling flat.

Time remained for Ben to testify that morning. He started by describing how he spent as much time as he could with the twins before Robert's birth and how happy they had been when Robert was born. They were just a "very routine family," as he saw it.

The family left Chicago for the suburb's schools and big backyards. Ben reiterated how calm and easy Robert was, and then he reviewed the details of the family's typical schedule from early morning to bedtime. He described the system of time-outs he and Lynn gave the twins if they ever needed redirection, which wasn't often.

Many parents who find themselves in juvenile court do not have much family support, a flexible work schedule, or a gym membership where child-care is available. Many cannot or do not regularly read bedtime stories to their children. Many parents *do* use harsh corporal punishments, rather than child-development–approved disciplinary techniques, often because physical discipline is the only child-rearing system they ever knew. Though often unwelcome, the CPS contract service providers can provide some new parenting skills for some families whose children have been taken into State custody.

By testifying about his own family's routines, however, Ben was proving that his family would do fine without CPS help. Many families with fewer resources than Ben and Lynn also didn't need the sort of help the juvenile court and CPS system provided, even if some parents did appreciate learning some new child-rearing techniques.

Being a parent was central to Ben. Everything he did with the kids was intentional. He said, "I just want the children to grow up with all the opportunities in life that I was afforded. Both Lynn and I grew up in a very loving household." These answers helped show the judge who Ben was.

Ben reviewed his activities during the week of the injury, starting with Sunday, September 6. Ben had taken the kids to the park, putting Robert into a Babybjörn front carrier. This carrier required some leg manipulation. Handing the carrier to Ben, I asked him to demonstrate. There was definitely some leg manipulation to get the baby into it.

Robert had cried out on Monday night when falling asleep on Ben's chest. Constipation seemed to make Robert fussy on Tuesday, but that cleared up on Wednesday afternoon. That brought Ben to Thursday, September 10. He had offered to watch the twins while Lynn went to her appointments with Robert that day.

It was noticeable how respectful Ben was of Lynn and how collaborative they were in their parenting. Each one tried to help the other when possible.

In 38 years as a lawyer, not many people I have run into have been so kind, generous, or respectful of others. With its awesome destructive power, the State didn't seem to understand or appreciate the importance of small kindnesses like Ben's.

Ben had talked to Lynn a few times during her day out with Robert. Their typical daily frequent check-ins were another sign of their close relationship. They were not newlyweds; they had known each other for 14 years. They were a solid team. Lynn had reported Robert's passing marks at the audiology test, but Ben missed her call from the salon. She called back on her drive home, reporting that Robert had been fussy but she thought he was just hungry. Ben arrived back home with the twins at about 5:00 p.m. He wanted to hold Robert right away. Nothing unusual happened at dinner. The first Ben knew of a concern about Robert's leg came just after 7:00 p.m.

Maybe it was a spider bite, they had surmised. With no new pediatrician established in the area yet, they called their neighbor to ask where to take Robert to get medical attention.

When the fracture was discovered at the emergency room, Ben had asked the doctor how it could have happened. "Force," was the only answer he got. When hearing that the hotline and police would be called, Ben said he had nothing to hide. He had said, "If this is protocol, that is fine." Though stunned, Ben was confident that the pro forma hotline call would not cause any serious problems for the family.

After hearing of the fracture, Ben and Lynn conferred. They decided that Lynn need to come to the hospital. The new neighbors who had advised them were able to watch the twins. Ben and Lynn had wanted the best treatment for Robert, so they readily agreed to the hospital's proposal to have Robert transferred to a children's hospital in Chicago. Lynn would go by ambulance with Robert. She wanted to breastfeed him, since he hadn't eaten in a long time. Ben would go home while Lynn would stay with Robert.

Parents like Ben and Lynn often reasonably believe they are doing the best thing by going to the hospital with a strong reputation, only to find themselves in a medical and legal vise when an unexplained injury leads to hotline call by the medical professionals. Similar scenarios accounted for many of the medically complex cases Melissa and I handled.

After I asked Ben to review his contacts with Caseworker Green, I asked him, "Have you ever been violent with anyone, even as a kid?"

While Ben admitted he had fought with his brother, he never had a fight outside the home. He said, "I have never been aggressive towards anybody." As for hurting one of his children, "I can't even think of it and have never, will never, absolutely not." He said the same of Lynn; he had known her since they were both 20 years old, and she would never injure a child. "Absolutely not."

After nearly two months of investigations and hearings, did Ben know how Robert got his fracture? "No." Did he believe it was due to child abuse? "Absolutely not." There was no way child abuse could have caused the injury. It had to be something else.

In her cross-examination, State's Attorney O'Neill probed how Ben had come to seek Dr. Sheridan's opinion. He mentioned a friend's referral. The friend, whom he didn't name, was Mary Broderick. That was a good referral, I thought to myself.

O'Neill probed Ben's memory for information about Robert's crying. She questioned Ben's report to Lynn that Robert was "doing great" when Lynn couldn't see him from her vantage point while dinner was being prepared. O'Neill seemed incredulous that Robert didn't cry at all during dinner.

She asked who was paying for Dr. Sheridan's testimony. For Ben, the question of payment hadn't come up yet. Ben expected to be billed eventually. (In fact, he never was billed.) In the minds of the State's Attorneys, Dr. Sheridan was a hired gun. They just couldn't seem to wrap their heads around the idea that a doctor might testify because he believed he had important medical information to share that could protect children from being taken from their parents without cause. Indeed, such doctors are exceedingly rare; they are heroes, not villains, but the State saw it differently.

The State's Attorney finished with questions about Ben's alleged screaming at Dr. Felix on October 1 when he learned of her opinion. But Ben denied any screaming; his colleagues at work had been close by.

"Did you threaten to sue her?" she asked.

"No," he answered, but he had said that he would "take it to the top" and his lawyers would have "a lot of questions for her."

Ben elaborated, "I saw many of the injustices in this whole process, from the start of the comments by Dr. Felix that this would be a 'multidisciplinary' process. I had reached out to help do their work for them, but she said her opinion would not change, no matter what I did."

O'Neill wanted to know if Ben was still planning to take legal action. But this was none of her business, and the judge sustained the objection to the question. With that conclusion, Ben was done saying his piece.

Dr. Miller was sworn in to testify next. She was in an odd position. No one had talked to her during the investigation, so now everyone was anxious to see what side she would end up on. Usually witnesses help the side that calls them to testify, but there can be surprises.

Dr. Miller was new to Illinois, licensed for only one year, and just two years out of her orthopedics residency. She had finished her specialized pediatric orthopedic training in 2008, and she wouldn't be eligible to sit for her oral orthopedic boards for another year and a half. Nevertheless, because she signed off on treatment for children with orthopedic injuries, we did not object to finding her qualified as an expert in pediatric orthopedics.

Dr. Miller had some training in child abuse, but that training taught her that no fracture is unique to child abuse and no fracture can be ruled out as child abuse. That description seemed objective and scientific.

On September 11, Dr. Miller was the attending pediatric orthopedist on call. A resident told her about Robert and showed her Robert's skeletal survey. She saw a "spiral or oblique fracture," but she couldn't be sure which type of fracture it was without more detail. The X-ray wasn't high quality enough to see. Either way, the treatment would be the same.

Dr. Miller had examined Robert in the afternoon, with Ben and Lynn present. The exam was brief because the clinic was busy. She had taken off Robert's splint and replaced it. Robert did cry vigorously when she moved his leg. She reassured Ben that the leg would heal fully. When Ben asked her what caused the femur to break, all she had said was that there had to be some force applied to the femur or some other trauma given she saw no evidence of metabolic or genetic bone diseases. Suspicion of brittle bone disease was low, and additional testing for it was not recommended.

On September 18, Robert came back to the clinic again. Another X-ray was taken, but the view on it was not good; splint materials stood in the way of visualizing the fracture well. One lateral image did show the fracture better, and that image showed some slight periosteal reaction. So far, Dr. Miller's testimony was tracking Dr. Sheridan's quite closely.

Dr. Miller thought the fracture occurred on September 9 or 10, because the healing visible on September 18 was still very limited.

State's Attorney Bailey started clicking through X-rays trying to find one where the fracture could be visualized well. Slides for September 24 showed more periosteal reaction, appearing like cloudy substances. He tried to get Dr. Miller to say this image established that the fracture occurred on September 10.

She refused to say so, bluntly stating, "This doesn't tell me anything." All it said was that the fracture was healing. Dr. Miller was refusing to let the State's Attorney put his conclusions into her mouth.

While Bailey had forecasted that Dr. Miller would disagree with Dr. Sheridan on the issue of whether a fracture could have been nondisplaced and then displaced, Dr. Miller's answer was direct again. There was no way to tell from X-rays. Someone would have had to go back in time. Whether the child would cry from a nondisplaced fracture would depend on how careful the parent was and if pressure were applied to the leg. She couldn't make assumptions about how all babies would cry.

The State's Attorney pushed Dr. Miller to answer that "changing a child's diaper couldn't cause a nondisplaced fracture to become displaced, could it?"

Dr. Miller responded curtly. "I can't answer that question." Dr. Miller appeared completely uninterested in serving as a witness for the State for a minute longer than necessary.

But Bailey pressed on, "It would take some force, wouldn't it?"

The doctor responded, simply, that you "can't move a child without applying some force." She also refused to call the fracture "major." That wasn't her vocabulary. She was giving the State exactly nothing.

Finally, the State's Attorney went in for the jugular. He asked if you can tell from looking at an X-ray if an injury is accidental or nonaccidental. Dr. Miller's answer was simple: no. Without knowing the circumstances of how the fracture occurred, it was impossible to tell. After getting burned by the witness he insisted on calling, Bailey wanted to make sure that the judge didn't read too much into her neutrality and said, "You're not offering an opinion on whether the fracture was nonaccidental, are you?"

She replied, "No."

The State's next tactic was to try to build up Dr. Felix's superior ability to give the child abuse opinion. Bailey asked, "Would you defer to the child abuse team?"

"Yes, to the *investigating* team," she answered. It was interesting that she used that word; she obviously assumed that a real investigation of Robert's injury had been done by someone. The doctor agreed that she hadn't done any form of social investigation or questioned the parents about the mechanism of the fracture. Her answer suggested, at the same time, that a thorough social investigation mattered.

Bailey pressed on. Why was an investigation important? Dr. Miller answered that there could be other physical signs, including bruising, contusions on the ear, or fractures in multiple stages of healing. She added, "In the case of a single, isolated, long bone fracture in a child, I don't have enough information from my brief interactions with the parents to render an opinion one way or the other."

The conclusion seemed obvious and was hopefully not lost on Judge Sanders. If a doctor who had completed a five-year residency in pediatric orthopedics and who had treated Robert's fracture couldn't say whether his fracture was caused by abuse, then how could a child abuse fellow conclude that abuse was the likely cause? Dr. Miller had strengthened our case. Now the judge wouldn't have to rely exclusively on Dr. Sheridan's opinion.

The guardian ad litem also wanted to minimize the impact of Dr. Miller's very objective testimony. She, too, seemed bent on elevating the opinion of the child abuse doctor. Accordingly, her questions emphasized that Dr. Miller hadn't participated in the investigation. Her role was as a treater, a point to which Dr. Miller readily agreed.

My cross-examination was the shortest one so far. First, I asked Dr. Miller to clarify that *any* kind of impact that causes an injury is a "trauma"; the word "trauma" did not connote "abuse." She also agreed that other bone diseases could have an effect on a child's likelihood of having a fracture. Dr. Miller had not consulted with any other attending doctors on Robert's case, but no one had consulted with her, either.

I had a hunch that Dr. Miller thought the child abuse assessment was something different than what Dr. Felix had actually done. So I asked if the purpose of the child abuse consult was to get biomechanical information, to determine the severity of the fracture, or to determine if there were other fractures. Dr. Miller answered just as I had hoped. The sole purpose of the child abuse consult, in her mind, was for the sort of social assessment Dr. Miller thought the child abuse team was supposed to do.

Dr. Miller had made a reasonable assumption. But she had been wrong in her understanding of what her own hospital's child abuse team's assessment involved. While the social worker had done a social history with Lynn, that history had turned up nothing. There never was a real assessment of the sorts of factors that Dr. Miller had assumed the child abuse team would consider. It was clear in those brief answers that the child abuse doctors and the orthopedists were not talking to each other about child abuse cases. It was equally clear that the child abuse doctors declared child abuse to be likely based on information the orthopedists considered patently insufficient.

How would the parents' lack of any explanation affect Dr. Miller's assessment of the likelihood of abuse? Again, her answer favored Ben and Lynn: the absence of an explanation did not provide an abuse explanation.

Her answers were so good that I took a chance. I went for broke: "What about a unique cry that tells a parent there is a fracture, is there any such thing?"

"No," Dr. Miller responded.

This fourth day of the preliminary hearing ended with minor squabbles over evidence and next steps. The State was on a tear to find Lynn's complete gynecological records, hoping that those records would support the allegation that Lynn had mental health issues. Both the State's Attorney and the guardian ad litem asserted they had been working to get their evidence together with "lightning speed," a claim that was comical if it hadn't been tragic. What *had* occurred with lightning speed was the decision to take the kids on October 1, all while refusing to consider Dr. Sheridan's opinion. We had already expended more than Robert's whole lifetime in court proceedings trying to justify the State's hasty decisions on October 1.

The guardian ad litem still needed court time to present the testimony of her office's medical consultant. We were hard pressed to stop her from calling just one expert to testify. The case law, dripping with language about "fidelity to the best interests of children" as if that were a concept disembodied from children's rights to be raised by their parents, clearly supported her right to present evidence at a hearing.

It was odd but not unusual in Cook County that the guardian ad litem, as the children's own appointed attorney, would weigh in against the parents and seek to label them as child abusers. What if they were wrong? There was something unseemly unfair, almost Soviet,[1] about advocating for the children against their parents. After all, the children had no control whatsoever as to what position their lawyers took in the courtroom. But I was not about to win a fight over her right to present medical evidence.

The guardian ad litem apparently believed that Robert must have been abused. Her institutional allegiance to the child abuse doctors seemed too great to expect her to view child abuse doctors' opinions critically or even with neutral eyes.

The guardian ad litem was conscientious, professional, and intelligent. She was doing what she saw as her job, even if that job had led her to an opposite conclusion about the case against Ben and Lynn. Had she fought for dismissal of the case, she might have been ostracized from her office. A few lawyers I knew had been penalized for consistently and vigorously advocating for children to return home against the wishes of their superiors in the guardian ad litem office.

Some guardians ad litem were especially aggressive in their advocacy for removal of children, asking judges to take children into CPS custody even when the State's Attorney and CPS agency opposed that request. The office attracted some child-saver zealots.[2] We were fortunate that the assigned guardian ad litem had no particular ax to grind against Ben or Lynn. I couldn't fault her personally for trying to present a doctor who favored a prosecutorial position against the parents. That was what her office did in case after case.

Judge Sanders wasn't happy that out of all the pediatric orthopedists in the Chicago area, the guardian ad litem office had picked one who had been out of the country during the pending hearing. When the judge found out that the State's Attorney's office had cancelled a scheduled deposition of this medical expert, he sounded even more frustrated than we were.

"The investigation has been unfolding here in court," Judge Sanders commented. The CPS investigator had brought the case to court "without completing it."

On the spot, without requesting any further testimony, Judge Sanders declared that henceforth Ben and Lynn could be unsupervised with their children as long as they were together and said, "I find the parents have been very credible. If they are together, they are not going to allow anything to happen to their children."

One person in the courtroom, at least, had been paying attention and believed the parents. That person was the only person who really mattered: the judge.

Naturally, the State and guardian ad litem immediately objected. So did the CPS attorney. The three offices that opposed Ben and Lynn moved in lockstep with each other.

The judge had eleven other cases set for hearing on November 19, but he said that he would move all of those cases to 9:00 a.m. in order to hear

Dr. Steinberg, the doctor whom the guardian ad litem could have ready to testify that day. Judge Sanders was moving heaven and earth to finish Ben and Lynn's case before Thanksgiving. He also reserved the afternoon of November 20.

He allowed us to take a deposition of Dr. Steinberg to adequately prepare our questions, because Dr. Steinberg had not written a report. Now, with enough time before the next court date, the judge gave the State its wish: Lynn's gynecological records were to be released. Judge Sanders specified that those records should be sent to the court for its review, not delivered directly to the State's Attorney. This ruling was a tiny nod in favor of a basic right of privacy that Lynn, three years before, had never known she would forfeit, when she had gotten medical care in order to be able to have children.

TWELVE

To the Finish Line

By our fifth day of the hearing, on November 19, it seemed possible that Ben and Lynn's days of coming to juvenile court would soon end. We just needed to get through the rest of the witnesses and final arguments. It had been 10 weeks since the hotline call alleging that Robert had been abused. In juvenile court time, that was a short period of State involvement. In the family's sense of time, it seemed an eternity.

Right away, the State rested its case. Then the guardian ad litem called Dr. Steinberg to testify.

Like Dr. Sheridan, Dr. Steinberg specialized in treating scoliosis. He had been licensed as a doctor in seven different jurisdictions. His credentials were impressive. He was a clinical professor of medicine, with publications on femur fractures. None of his publications, however, were in the area of child abuse, and he rarely treated bone fractures any more. Since he had treated patients at level-one trauma centers for 16 years, however, spending about a third of his time treating fractures there, I readily agreed that he could be certified as an expert in pediatric orthopedics.

I had no idea how the guardian ad litem office had found him, but I couldn't ask. Lawyers have the right to keep that information confidential.

Dr. Steinberg had reviewed all the same X-rays as the other doctors and read their reports. Like Dr. Sheridan, he labeled the fracture "oblique," caused by bending and pulling the leg. A spiral fracture would have required a twisting motion.

Soon he parted company with Dr. Sheridan's assessment, however, and sided with Dr. Felix. "Significant force" was necessary to cause this fracture. Normal daily activities couldn't cause it. It was possible but highly unlikely that the fracture could have been nondisplaced first and then displaced; that would require a significant trauma to Robert's leg twice. Normal daily interaction with Robert wouldn't cause the fracture, either.

He agreed with Dr. Felix; the child would cry inconsolably. An adult intending to use force on the leg was responsible for the injury, although he couldn't say who that was. The person causing the fracture didn't have to intend to cause harm but had to intend an action that wasn't accidental. Dressing the child, putting him in a car seat, or in and out of swing wouldn't have caused the fracture. In sum, Ben and Lynn's lack of an explanation was a real problem.

Dr. Steinberg was, in a way, stating something quite obvious. If Ben and Lynn had an explanation to give, they would have provided it. That would have been the easiest way out of their ordeal.

State's Attorney Bailey asked the questions next and established that if Robert had been passed from person to person, the injuries could plausibly have been accidental. Since this question helped our side, it was a surprise that Bailey asked it. Robert *had* been passed to the stylists at the salon, after all. This expert hadn't been told much about what happened at the salon, we suspected.

Now it was my turn for cross-examination. I brought out Dr. Steinberg's lack of any involvement in child abuse cases because his current employer had no child abuse team or trauma unit. Very few of his patients were under the age of one. None were younger than 30 days old.

Dr. Steinberg admitted that the X-rays alone would not tell him that Robert was abused. It was the job of the CPS agency to investigate. He also didn't know all the explanations that parents might have for what caused the fracture, for he had never spoken to either parent. He didn't have much of a time frame. At his deposition, he had said Robert's fracture could have happened "maybe a week" before Robert was taken to the emergency room. Now, from the witness stand, he compressed the time frame.

When I pointed out the difference, he accused me of "splitting hairs a bit."

I called him on it. "You believe it is splitting hairs as to whether it's three days versus a week?" He was starting to look both sloppy and belligerent.

It was becoming clear that Dr. Steinberg didn't know many of the facts of Robert's case. So I pressed on, asking the same question that was central to Dr. Felix's opinion: how long would an inconsolable cry last? When a witness makes a pivotal claim, an attorney who is trying to undermine that opinion first has to understand exactly what the witness means by the words he or she uses. I wouldn't know what another person means by labeling a cry as "inconsolable." How loud is that, how distinct is that, and how long is that?

Dr. Steinberg admitted that he didn't know how long the child would cry, but he ventured an answer: 15 minutes, 20 minutes, or 10 minutes. He then added, "I'm not sure there is a definite answer." Any parent, he asserted, would first notice the action that caused the injury. Then the child would become inconsolable, and the parent would notice that. If the child's leg was moved, he would become inconsolably fussy for a significant period of time.

Doctors shouldn't testify to things they do not know, and they shouldn't exaggerate. Doctor Steinberg plainly didn't know that the nurse who first had seen Robert and examined his leg said that Robert's crying had lasted 10 to 20 seconds, not minutes.

As to the credit he gave to the parents' claims that Robert never cried inconsolably, Dr. Steinberg's answer was chilling. Without knowing them or their character, he said, "I have a very difficult time believing that's the case."

To his credit, Dr. Steinberg admitted that the case was not entirely clear cut. He acknowledged that Dr. Sheridan and he could look at the same information and disagree. A single, isolated fracture is not an obvious abuse case. He had no information about the family, and he admitted it. He said, "People get upset, and things happen that they don't necessarily intend to happen," but he also acknowledged, "I have no idea, not knowing this family."

The lack of a history for the injury was the "biggest red flag" to him. I wanted to know, "Do you draw the conclusion it's abuse?"

"Yes," he said. It was remarkable that some doctors are willing to reach conclusions with so little evidence, especially when those conclusions so deeply affected the lives of a family they had never met. His certainty was frightening.

Still, his certainty about the duration of the supposedly inconsolable crying weakened his opinion, for it contradicted the nurse's direct observation. At the same time, Dr. Steinberg had managed to make Dr. Felix's opinions seem more reasonable, more grounded in medicine. Indeed, that seemed to be the whole purpose of his being called as a witness.

The guardian ad litem rested. It was time for us to finish.

Lynn testified last, as we had planned from the beginning. It was clear that Lynn was the State's primary target as a suspected child abuser.

Melissa questioned Lynn, allowing her to respond directly to all the innuendos the State had thrown out as potential reasons she would have snapped and abused her son. She had not faced unusual stresses during pregnancy, C-section treatment, or the family's move to the western suburbs. She had no idea where a note referencing "depression" in her gynecological records about came from or whether it was a reference to her.

Next, Melissa handed Lynn family photos one by one, pictures that lovingly documented how Robert was the "sweetest child": at the hospital with the twins and Ben's mom, on the couch showing Robert smiling angelically, in his Pack 'n Play, in his swing, in his Snap-N-Go car seat, in his bassinet, and in his parents' arms. There was one of Robert and Ben both asleep together, with Robert lying on Ben's chest.

Melissa quickly walked through the events of the week before September 10: Robert's startled cry one night after Labor Day, the constipation they had thought Robert had on September 8, his increased fussiness that day, and their decision to give him a warm bath. Prior to that bath, they had been giving him baths just once a week because he hadn't liked bathing. They had a picture of the first bath, of course.

Melissa got to September 10. At the salon, Lynn first had an eyebrow-waxing treatment in the back of the salon for ten minutes. Robert wasn't with her then, and she couldn't see him during the waxing. Two or three receptionists watched him in the reception area.

As I heard this account for the umpteenth time, I realized that Lynn had just identified a gap in time that the entire hearing and the CPS investigation had missed: no one had talked to these receptionists. We didn't even know their names. Lynn couldn't vouch for anything they did with Robert then. Did they roughly handle him while she was getting settled for her hair coloring, and she didn't notice? I doubted it, but it was one of those missing pieces we could never find now, two and a half months after Lynn's hair appointment.

Did Robert's leg get twisted and bent while Lynn got in and out of the salon chair? That was another mystery. It was possible but also seemed unlikely. In fact, no single explanation was likely. But of all the unlikely possibilities, the most probable seemed to be that something had happened to Robert's leg at the salon. The slight swelling, noted by Lynn, started then. The doctors agree that swelling starts to show up within 30 minutes to an hour of a break in the periosteum. Something probably had happened there to start the swelling process when Lynn noticed it.

But that "something" couldn't have been child abuse. It was just too implausible a setting for an act of child abuse to be unnoticed by any other employees or customers. Even if I thought less of Lynn, it's hard to believe anyone would spend a day out with his or her infant son and decide to take time out at a hair salon to break his femur, expecting no one to notice but then asking someone about it as soon as there was the tiniest sign of something wrong.

Why didn't Lynn mention to Ben that she had noticed Robert's leg might be a bit swollen at the salon? When Melissa asked this, Lynn answered honestly; she didn't know. There was lots of traffic when they spoke on the phone, and Robert was hungry. Lynn said, "I was pushing his feeding time. It was close to four, and he had been fed at two." The topic of the possible slight swelling she had seen just before she left the salon hadn't come up during the hurried call on the ride home.

Lynn's flawed memory of seeing an early slight swelling only seemed inconsistent because Lynn had been so conscientious in recounting everything she had done and thought on September 10. The State seemed to be using a double-edged sword against Lynn—first demanding perfect recall and then using any lapse to cut her down.

For the last time, Lynn had to retell her discovery of Robert's swollen leg, her sleepless night at the hospital, and Dr. Felix's questioning the next morning.

To conclude the questions, Melissa asked Lynn about her strengths as a parent, a topic Lynn didn't like to talk about much. In order to protect her future as a mother, Lynn cited her great love of her children and her efforts to provide them a "happy loving home where they will thrive as people." She said that she "tried very hard to answer their needs." Her "job is to be their mother and to be there for them." That was the job, I realized, that the State, the guardian ad litem, and the CPS attorney had been trying to stop her from doing.

"Do you know how Robert got his fracture, Lynn?" I asked.

"No," she responded.

"Have you ever intentionally hurt him?"

"No."

"Do you think Ben would injure him intentionally?"

"That's not possible. He doesn't have it in him. He's the most, kind loving father."

I needed a Kleenex at that moment. It wasn't just Lynn and Ben on trial in the courtroom. The hearing had put motherhood, fatherhood, and the family on trial. *This was what an ideal family looks like*, I thought. And this was what the State, with all its coercive power, had been trying to destroy.

State's Attorney Bailey's cross-examination started with questions as to why Lynn had never mentioned the ten minutes in which the child had been out of her sight at the salon. Of course, no one had asked her for a minute-by-minute account before, and no one had visited the salon to ask questions. Now the State derogatorily referred to the 10-minute gap in her ability to see Robert as a "new story." Bailey demanded to know the receptionists' names, even though identifying them had not come up before. Critical evidence, which should have been sought by an investigator or a State's Attorney, was still missing. How was that Lynn's fault?

Bailey reviewed the hair-coloring process. When Lynn tried to put Robert back into the car seat, he cried, so she held him under the cape while her hair was cut. Maybe his leg hurt then, but he wasn't crying. Then Robert had cried for a couple of minutes going home from the salon; there had been heavy traffic, and the ride home was long.

Bailey wondered about Lynn leaving Robert on the couch a few times while she went to the bathroom. There was no incident of him crying after she returned, and Lynn had no idea how many times this had occurred.

It was unclear what Bailey was going for. An unexplained and unwitnessed incident could have occurred at one of these times. Was Lynn to be faulted for using the bathroom? It was a little absurd.

"Could it be possible you pulled on his leg when getting him out of his bassinet?" he asked.

"No, that's not possible," Lynn replied. "I wouldn't pull on my child's leg. He's an infant. He's my son."

It was hard to make Lynn out to be unknowingly abusive to her son. She was a model of care.

"Could it be possible you pulled too hard while diapering?" Bailey asked.

Lynn firmly answered, "I don't handle my baby infant the way that you are implying. He's a baby infant. You don't yank on their legs." She added that with Robert, "You don't have to control anything. He's a very calm baby."

Lynn's warrior-mother instincts, her firm and strong presence, were coming out. It was easier to see her strength during the cross-examination than during Melissa's direct-examination questions.

The State's Attorney didn't know when to quit. He should have sat down. Instead, he mocked Lynn's answer. "So, he was completely placid when you were with him between September 1 and September 10?"

Lynn responded calmly, "I'm sure there were times he cried, but no, I would not yank on his leg."

"Was it possible his legs were moving and interfering in changing him?"

Lynn said, "It's possible."

That was all the State got from Lynn that day—that Robert legs might move during a diaper change.

The guardian ad litem's cross-examination first established that Lynn was the children's primary caregiver, as if that were still unclear. On September 8, the first day after Robert's birth on which Lynn was alone with her kids while Ben worked, was she stressed or upset?

"No," Lynn answered. She was actually "relieved to just be with her family and kids. I was excited about it. I was never overwhelmed."

"Were you worried about Robert's failing his hearing test?"

"Of course," Lynn responded. "I used to work with kids with hearing loss. It's difficult for anyone. I was concerned, yes."

Did Robert's lack of fussiness concern her, causing her to worry how she would know if something were wrong with him?

Lynn didn't know how to answer. "I don't have a crystal ball. He might cry, or he might not. I don't know."

Did Lynn have an explanation for Robert's fracture now?

"No."

That was it. The guardian ad litem sat down.

We had come to the end, but the case was ending just as it started: with no better explanation as to how Robert's leg fractured. The family had endured a 10-week-long separation, with placement of the children into the

State's legal custody, though thankfully the children never moved out of their own home. The investigation had occurred in fits and starts. Four doctors had weighed in, interrupting their busy schedules caring for other children who more urgently needed their attention. There still wasn't a single answer that was any better than ones Ben and Lynn first gave on the night of September 10 and morning of September 11. If the State really thought that Lynn or Ben had abused Robert, not a shred of evidence had been uncovered to support that theory—except for the lack of an explanation that all the doctors and witnesses in the world also couldn't supply.

Our side couldn't rest the case until written exhibits were all submitted into the court record. The gynecologist's letter was highlighted through Melissa's reading it into the record. There were many other letters from family supporters to introduce. Once again, the guardian ad litem contended that the parents' character wasn't at issue. She objected that all the letter writers could have testified. The State joined in her objection, questioning how the letter writers each came up with their views.

The judge reminded them that they had not agreed to any restriction on the use of hearsay. Judge Sanders would look at the 10 letters we offered to decide whether to admit them into the court record. The final piece of written evidence we wanted the judge to consider was the CPS rule defining abusive bone fractures. The State and guardian ad litem objected even to this, arguing that only statutes count as the applicable law. Their argument was plain silly.

The judge allowed the rule into the record, for it was clearly relevant. It had been used in the hearing and set forth the standards Janelle Green was supposed to meet in her investigation. He also admitted about half of the letters into the record: the ones from the pediatrician, a doctor friend, a nurse who had worked with Lynn, a colleague of Ben, and Ben's mom. But he excluded a letter from Ben's dad as well as ones from a dentist friend, an attorney friend in Wisconsin, and a physical therapist, because these people's opinions had not been referenced in the hearing and they had not testified.

The record was complete. We rested our case.

The judge called us back for closing argument. I had butterflies in my stomach but calmed down when the opposing lawyers started to speak.

State's Attorney O'Neill argued first. She highlighted that Lynn had described the period around Robert's birth as "very stressful." She asserted that Lynn "or someone" had abused Robert, maybe not with intent to break his leg but with an intentional action that caused the break. The parents' "continuing denial" was a concern. She urged that it was self-evident that having a newborn is "highly stressful and difficult for any person to handle." After all, the twins had been screaming in the courtroom on the first day, she noted.

Judge Sanders stopped her. "That's not in the record."

She continued, pointing to other stresses, including the family's recent move to the suburbs. The injury to Robert's leg must have happened very close to September 10. According to Dr. Miller, even if it were initially a nondisplaced break, there would have been more healing signs by September 18 if it happened earlier.

What she said next, though, was startling. "Ben was very credible. His explanations to everyone, all the doctors and everyone involved, were exactly the same."

Lynn, by contrast, has been "highly inconsistent. Most inconsistent of all was her testimony on the stand today." O'Neill pointed to Lynn's inconsistent statements about her observations the salon. She "knew the critical importance of telling the truth," but she had never mentioned the swelling at 2:00 p.m. at the salon.

While the focused attack on Lynn was troubling, so was the sudden exoneration of Ben. A case that started with a focus on both parents had shifted blame to Lynn, but there had been no improvement in the State's treatment of Ben. Now the State was engaging in outright mother bashing. Typically, juvenile court cases overly blame the mother. Even if the father is the sole child abuser, the mother is often blamed for not stopping abuse she was assumed to know about and presumed able to prevent.[1] Often there is little evidence of fault, but the mother is deemed blameworthy when abuse occurs. Still, it was jarring and upsetting to witness the State's demonization of Lynn as a child abuser. It didn't seem to matter that if Lynn *had* remembered her comment about the swelling sooner or recalled the 10-minute gap when Robert was out of her line of sight, it would have helped her.

Still, even with the frontal attack on Lynn, the State seemed not to have any theory of its own to back up its claim that Lynn abused Robert. Did it happen in the bathroom at the salon? At the Panera restaurant where they had stopped for lunch? In the car afterward or at home before Ben arrived? If the fracture had occurred after Lynn left the salon, then why would Lynn have asked the stylist if the leg looked enlarged? But if Lynn had abused Robert, why would she have asked the stylist anything that would bring attention to an injury the State claims she caused? For all the innuendo, the State's claim that Lynn was lying about abuse was riddled with holes and inconsistencies. If Lynn was such a liar, why hadn't Lynn just made up a story about how Robert's leg had been fractured that pointed to an accident so as make the case against her and Ben disappear?

Whatever the theory, the State was now arguing that Lynn had abused Robert and that Ben was innocent. But if that was what the State's Attorneys believed, why hadn't they suggested returning the kids to Ben? Why had they resisted allowing him unsupervised visits? The State had been as willing to restrict Ben's rights as Lynn's.

Every nit got picked in the State's closing argument. The claim that Lynn had said she heard a pop was raised, without mentioning Lynn's clarification that she said she was afraid his leg *would* pop. In closing argument, the State got to use whatever version of facts it chose, as long as those facts were in the evidentiary record. The inferences from those facts are for the parties to argue and the judge to decide.

Soon, State's Attorney O'Neill was accusing Lynn not just of lies but of a deliberate cover-up, too. The more terrible the State made her out to be, however, the more ridiculous the State's version of the case seemed. Part of me wanted the hyperbole to continue, for it is easier to pop a full balloon.

Done attacking Lynn, the State's Attorney moved on to the medical evidence. She labeled Dr. Sheridan's theory about the fracture first being nondisplaced and then displaced as "far-fetched." Not even Dr. Sheridan believed it, she claimed. He was a hired expert who never looked at any CPS investigation records. The lack of an explanation made abuse more likely than not, to a reasonable degree of medical certainty. No one but the parents had been watching the child. Dr. Sheridan shouldn't be believed because he didn't know about Lynn's comment to the stylist and the comment about Robert's leg popping. He simply didn't have the full story. By contrast, Dr. Felix had the advantage of being able to consult with an entire team of child abuse doctors, who all agreed that Robert had been abused.

State's Attorney O'Neill asked Judge Sanders to conclude that there was probable cause to find Robert abused as well as urgent and immediate necessity to take custody of him from his parents. She also asked for companion findings of risk of abuse related to the twins. She didn't utter a word about returning the kids to Ben, even though she clearly didn't think he had done anything wrong.

The guardian ad litem stood up next to argue on behalf of Robert and the twins. She started by agreeing to almost everything the State had argued, including accusing Dr. Sheridan of coming up with hypotheses to fit his conclusions. Because Dr. Miller had no opinion about whether the fracture was accidental or nonaccidental, she urged that Dr. Steinberg's opinion tipped the balance of expert opinion in favor of abuse. The lack of an explanation for the injury, the lack of any history made it a "red flag" for abuse.

"Most of the parents' testimony wasn't credible," she asserted, not distinguishing between Ben and Lynn. Lynn's statement that she wasn't stressed or overwhelmed was "impossible." The evidence that these parents "caused or allowed this injury to be caused to Robert" was "clear." She "certainly wasn't saying that mom is the one who hurt this child," although it had seemed she just said exactly that. Lynn's history as a social worker had nothing to do with the question of whether Robert was abused, contrary to Dr. Sheridan's opinion. She agreed with Dr. Steinberg when he had said that loving parents still could abuse a child.

Still, she hadn't explained anything about how or why Ben or Lynn abused Robert. Nor had she offered any reason why, if they were liars, they hadn't lied to save themselves.

I collected my thoughts. The sincerity of the State and guardian ad litem's arguments frightened me. They had argued that the parents deserved to lose custody of their children. Honest, innocent parents who couldn't explain how their child got an injury would have no chance of keeping custody of their children if these attorneys had been the ones deciding the case.

I started with some observations. The case wasn't complex. What was unusual about it was that the parents had a wealth of evidence in their favor—evidence that was never considered, despite the constitutional duty to consider all the exculpatory evidence. Despite five days of hearing and over a dozen witnesses, four of them doctors, no one knew more about the cause of the fracture than when the case had come in. Robert had a fracture. No one knew why.

I reviewed the State's evidence. Not one of the witnesses disbelieved any of what Lynn said. While it was the State's burden to show what part of the parent's story is false, essential witnesses were never interviewed.

The State was claiming that an unexplained fracture suffices to establish a child abuse. It doesn't have to say who, where, when—either date or time—or what was done. In short, this case raised the question whether abuse is an acceptable explanation for an unknown phenomenon by default. The State had acted as if it didn't have the burden of proof. The State assumed it could win by criticizing Dr. Sheridan rather than showing what happened. But it is their burden to show that the fracture was caused by abuse.

I started to get carried away, launching into seven different reasons why the judge shouldn't credit Dr. Felix's opinion. First, she hadn't assessed child abuse at all. I reviewed each of the factors she looked at, including biomechanics, which she didn't have much training in. What about the factor of the parents' credibility, their mental health? She didn't assess those factors; she just formed an impression. What about their interaction with the children? She wasn't concerned about that, either.

Soon both State's Attorneys were jumping in and objecting, claiming that I was misstating all of the testimony. The judge overruled them three times, letting me continue each time.

Second, Dr. Felix's own investigation wasn't complete; she admitted that investigating the facts was the CPS's team's job, not hers.

Third, she used both the wrong legal standard for her professional opinion and the wrong definition of abuse. Doctors don't give diagnoses on a "more likely than not" standard; they need reasonable certainty. Let's hope, I said, that doctors don't open people up for surgery whenever they think it is just "more likely than not" that the patient has a tumor.

Fourth, Dr. Felix appeared incapable of admitting when she was wrong. She had refused to back down about her note about "depression" in Lynn's family, something that Lynn would know and Dr. Felix didn't.

Fifth, her claim that any parent should have noticed the fracture right away due to the inconsolable cry was based on her personal experience with babies, not her medical training. The claim that Robert must have cried inconsolably when his leg was manipulated was obviously untrue, as the nurse had testified that Robert had cried for 10 seconds and stopped. There's no distinctive "fracture cry."

Sixth, she never was asked about the question that the judge needed to decide: Is there a risk of further abuse from the parents? Are they dangerous? She had no opinion on that subject. Should both parents be suspected or someone else? She didn't know that, either.

Finally, she didn't have comparable experience to Dr. Sheridan or Dr. Miller.

Dr. Steinberg's opinion had similar weaknesses. He admitted that he didn't know much about child abuse. He also didn't seem to want to be bothered with significant factual disputes, labeling a four-day difference (three days versus seven days) as to the outer boundary of when the fractured might have occurred as "hairsplitting." His theory about the inconsolable crying was even more extreme than Dr. Felix's—going out on a limb, he claimed that Robert's crying would last 10 to 20 minutes. The nurse solidly refuted his claim, for Robert cried for just 10 to 20 *seconds*.

If Dr. Steinberg were right about swelling starting within half an hour and if Lynn noticed swelling at 2:30 p.m., that meant the injury happened at the salon. That's exculpatory evidence, for it meant the injury happened unnoticed by anyone and without any inconsolable crying. That disproved the State's theory and refuted abuse.

If Dr. Sheridan and Dr. Miller couldn't find child abuse, how could the other doctors find abuse, knowing the same information? The case didn't turn on medicine at all. It turned on how the State had done its investigation. And the investigation had been utterly flawed.

I listed all the parts of the CPS rule on bone fracture investigations that had been violated. While I shouldn't have to prove the parents' innocence, I pointed to the mountain of evidence in the parents' favor that had simply been ignored. The State's theory was that one of the parents abused their child, suddenly, without warning, and without being noticed. But what kind of an abuser would go to the hospital for an audiology appointment if she had just abused the child? As for the fact that Lynn hadn't remembered the comment she made to the stylist about swelling, it was exculpatory evidence—something she had forgotten that would have helped to exonerate her if it had been considered.

The parents' accounts were detailed and given independently. Ben was interviewed by the police when Lynn was still at the hospital. Everyone who knew the parents spoke to their excellent character and credibility, which Dr. Felix hadn't questioned. It would have been easier for them to make up a story to get people off their backs. Their integrity prevented them from doing that.

The State and guardian ad litem had tried to present their lives as overwhelmingly stressful, including because they had three kids. While Ben and Lynn didn't claim everything was perfect, that was not a reason to take children from their parents.

Every medical witness had agreed that a newborn baby's bones are not very strong. And freak accidents occur. I listed all the ways the fracture could have happened: the car seat, the Babybjörn, the way the father and child rested together, something at the salon, something the siblings did. All of these possibilities had to be considered against the unlikelihood that one of these parents suddenly, out of the blue, when no one was noticing, broke their son's leg through a deliberate action.

To decide this case, the judge would have to decide on the credibility of the parents—a point that no one on the State's side had even considered relevant, let alone probative. I put it bluntly: to rule in favor of the State, you had to believe that Ben or Lynn was a child abuser. But this case had been so hurtful to the parents because they understood exactly what they were accused of. If the State didn't have a reason to accuse them of bad character, we didn't belong in this court. There should be no case. There must be a link to an action by a parent. They had a fundamental liberty interest in the care and custody of their children. The State couldn't abridge that interest without evidence of unfitness.

The whole purpose of the Juvenile Court Act was to return children to parents when safe to do so. But what alternative home did the State want to put these children into? This was a stellar home. These were stellar parents.

I asked the judge to end the State's involvement with this family by deciding that Robert was not abused and the other children were not at risk. I asked him to dismiss the case and allow the family to go back to a normal life.

With that, I thanked Judge Sanders for his patience and all his efforts to hear the case as promptly as he could.

State's Attorney Bailey got up to give the last word. He cited murder cases where motive was never proved. Maybe the injury to Robert was due to neglect; perhaps Lynn had ripped the child from his Babybjörn or car seat. The child screamed, loudly. Lynn wasn't a new mother; she knew the difference between a cry of hunger and a cry of pain.

It wasn't unusual in the juvenile court, he asserted, to have no history of the injury, but that didn't stop the court from finding child abuse.[2] Children couldn't tell us. Parents always minimized. They didn't say, "I crushed the kid's skull," or "I fractured the kid's leg." According to him, "People crack, and that's what we're talking about."

He wasn't insisting that Lynn had a malicious state of mind. This wasn't a criminal case. Dr. Sheridan's theory that a nondisplaced fracture can become displaced was his "modus operandi."

As he concluded, Bailey was starting to sound desperate. He claimed, "The nurse said Robert was screaming," even though that wasn't what the nurse had said. There had to be some kind of screaming and pain. There still should have been some sign of pain even if a nondisplaced fracture had occurred first.

Bailey ended his attack on Dr. Sheridan with a reminder that Dr. Sheridan had trouble visualizing the oblique fracture on one of the slides and claimed to have looked at some X-rays from September 12—an error. He accused Dr. Sheridan of not having the hospital records, which was untrue. I wouldn't get to counter these assertions, as I had no rebuttal time. Dr. Felix had done "everything to figure out whether the child was abused, and Dr. Sheridan did almost nothing."

He conceded that "these parents are loving parents" but still "a mistake was made." Why would Lynn have thought the leg could have popped? Something must have happened already—a pop may have happened in the salon, though he didn't think so. It occurred after the child came back from the audiologist, sometime after the child came home.

As for our contention that the stylist was a neutral party, State's Attorney Bailey said she was "like a bartender." He imagined that Lynn had said to her, "Oh, by the way, did you see swelling on the leg?" and then, he said, "Guess what? The stylist remembers swelling on the leg. That's easy to do."

Bailey's extravagant claim about Lynn's alleged fabrication to her stylist was as cynical as anything I had heard. Nothing about Lynn's character had sunk in. She was still a liar, a fabricator, at least in Bailey's eyes. It was distressing that an attorney representing the State's interest in children's lives had so little regard for parents in general and for Lynn in particular. Bailey's bias against Lynn was deep, although he was hardly alone when he portrayed mothers like Lynn as demons. For her part, Lynn had to be better than a saint to manage sitting quietly in the courtroom and listen to this argument.

Bailey concluded with a final attack on Dr. Sheridan as a hired gun who never saw child abuse when it was plain as day. Even Dr. Sheridan agreed that a "significant force" caused the fracture. The issue wasn't who loved the child, but whether Robert was yanked from a chair or a seat and the parent "didn't do what was necessary to bring the child to the hospital, when the child was screaming and yelling."

He asked that the CPS agency assume custodial responsibility for the three children.

Judge Sanders thanked all of us for our arguments. Aware that we all were eager for his ruling, he asked us to come back the next day at 2:00 p.m. He needed to review some of the exhibits more closely.

The next day, we all assembled on schedule. Judge Sanders handed us his typed-out ruling. It was unusual to get written juvenile court rulings handed from the bench, especially in what was still, technically speaking, a preliminary proceeding. Judges usually read their rulings, and then the attorneys wrote up orders reflecting what the judge had decided. The judge had clearly wanted to give us something to hold on to, something definite and concise.

Judge Sanders summed up the reason the case had come to court: Robert had a femur fracture at four weeks old. He had no other injuries nor did his siblings. Other than the fracture and the parents' inability to explain how it occurred, there was no evidence of abuse. There was no delay in seeking medical treatment. There were no prior findings of abuse. The parents denied abuse.

The judge then summarized the medical opinions: Dr. Felix had considered abuse more likely than not; Dr. Miller said she had no opinions because "a single fracture was insufficient information"; Dr. Sheridan, who treated Robert after his discharge from the hospital, thought the injury was more likely accidental; and Dr. Steinberg could not say it was definitively abuse but thought it was more likely than not abuse.

And then the judge did what trial judges are supposed to do: he decided which witnesses he believed. He found that "Dr. Sheridan is more credible than Dr. Steinberg or Dr. Felix." Dr. Sheridan had superior experience on the issues presented in this case. He testified at great length and remained "calm, logical, and instructive throughout." The judge found "both parents very credible and compelling witnesses," and he "believed their denials of abuse."

With that, he declared that the case was dismissed with a finding of "no probable cause." The children were free to live with their parents, and the grandparents were free to go back home.

Suddenly, there were tears of joy in the courtroom. Melissa and I were crying, too, feeling relief as well as vindication after two months of hard work. We were enormously grateful to Dr. Sheridan. Without his testimony, the family would still have been separated.

An outright dismissal for lack of probable cause in a juvenile court case was rare. This ruling would send a reverberating message throughout the juvenile court building to the State's Attorneys and guardians ad litem, who were unaccustomed to losing a case at the temporary custody stage for lack of probable cause.

We were not sure, however, if the State's Attorney's office would accept the decision. Dismissal orders can be appealed. The order we had fought so hard to obtain could be undone by an appellate court. The guardian ad litem office took many appeals, although we sensed that the State was the more likely party to appeal, given the vigor of their advocacy against our clients. We cautioned Ben and Lynn that we would have to wait up to 30 days before we could be certain that their victory was secure.

Furthermore, the CPS investigation that had begun on September 10 with the hotline call still wasn't finished. Nevertheless, Thanksgiving was sweet. Judge Sanders's ruling had preserved their family. It seemed almost miraculous.

THIRTEEN

Attempts at Recourse and the End of the Investigation

After Judge Sanders decided that Dr. Sheridan's opinion was dispositive, the CPS team and the State's Attorney refusal to consider that opinion on October 1, before the CPS team came to take the kids from their home, continued to trouble the family. Ben and his mother-in-law, Natalie, were the two family members who most wanted to secure some form of redress for the traumatic experience the family had been put through.

The State's Attorney's screener had signed the juvenile court petitions, and Bailey and O'Neill had vigorously prosecuted Ben and Lynn, all without doing a decent investigation first. Attorneys who fail to make a reasonable inquiry into the facts before they sign court papers can be sanctioned through monetary penalties or judicial censure.

Natalie was forceful in arguing for redress. She had never seen such incompetence in her life. Everyone who participated in the fiasco that had wrecked her family should be held accountable, she urged.

Sanctions had never been awarded against a State's Attorney in any juvenile court case we could find. Nor were there reported appellate decisions awarding sanctions against any child protection caseworkers for securing the filing of false pleadings based on a flawed investigation. There were civil rights cases in federal court on these issues but no reported decisions by the Illinois courts.

It was hard to argue with Natalie. We all respected her opinion. She hadn't gotten to be a federal judge by keeping her opinions to herself.

There had been gross negligence at best, if not deliberate indifference to the facts. No "reasonable inquiry" had taken place. The entire cost of the defense had been unfairly foisted onto an innocent family. These were tangible costs that an award of sanctions could recompense.

Moreover, we *had* warned the State's Attorneys and the CPS team. In a strongly worded letter before the hearing had commenced on October 14, we had demanded that the State withdraw its petition, mentioning the possibility that we might seek sanctions later.

So on December 18, 2009, Melissa and I filed with the clerk of the Cook County Juvenile Court a 25-page-long request for sanctions against Bailey and O'Neill and against the screener who had signed the court petitions against Ben and Lynn. We also named five employees of the CPS agency, including all of the CPS team members involved in the decision to take the kids. We named the CPS agency itself for failing to do a proper investigation.

We cited the many respects in which CPS had violated the agency's bone fracture rule for investigations, including its failure to consult a radiologist or an orthopedist, as the rule expressly directed. We cited the obvious failure to investigate the facts supporting the "inconsolable cry" claim, the failure to interview Susan or other employees at the salon, and the rejection of Dr. Sheridan's opinion sight unseen. We brought up the State's indifference to the parents' character letters and the refusal to contact other essential witnesses, including Robert's pediatrician and Lynn's gynecologist, while wasting hours of court time chasing evidence that Lynn had a mental health diagnosis.

The day after we filed our motion for sanctions, we learned that the State was not going to appeal Judge Sanders' dismissal order. Worried that the sanctions request might push the State into taking a defensive appeal, we had delayed filing the sanctions request until the second-to-last day before the State's appeal deadline. To reduce the appeal risk, we put the sanctions motion in the mail, as the rules allowed, so as not to flag it for the State's attention.

An appellate State's Attorney I knew informed me of the decision not to appeal. Our brief discussion showed that a serious internal debate had taken place, and the appellate attorney I spoke with had played a positive role in convincing the line attorneys in her office not to seek to overturn Judge Sanders' order. Win or lose on the request for sanctions, it was relief that the State would not be fighting to take the children or to reverse the conclusion that neither parent had abused Robert.

The request for sanctions soon drew a significant response. The Illinois Attorney General's office appeared before Judge Sanders on behalf of the CPS employees. The State's Attorney's office also wanted ample time to respond, which the judge allowed. The oral argument in favor of sanctions was long. But this time, the judge did not prepare a written ruling. His response was short, and he did not explain himself. The request for sanctions was denied.

It is hard to make the State pay for its mistakes. Perhaps our effort to get sanctions drove a point through to the State's Attorney's office. It made no difference with the CPS agency. CPS caseworkers were frequently sued for incompetence and worse. One more request for penalties—and a losing one at that—would make no difference.

It's easy to forget how difficult it is to hold the State accountable. It's easy to get carried away by righteous anger at injustice. The juvenile court has its own politics, and even the best of judges cannot cross too many lines with the lawyers who appear before them every day.

It was asking too much of Judge Sanders to seek penalties against the lawyers who were assigned to his courtroom every day. State's Attorney's office had a lot of power. For example, the office could stop having any cases heard by any judge its attorneys considered unfair, all without giving a reason or proving any bias. That sort of action could cause a judge to have to be reassigned to another court division, an effective demotion.

Perhaps a narrower focus on CPS's terrible investigation could have worked. Had we focused on Green and Long's incompetent investigation, perhaps the State's Attorney's office would have blamed CPS, too. It's impossible to know if a different strategy would have worked. Litigation decisions are like that: win, lose, or draw, one doesn't know what might have happened had the cards been played differently.

On November 20, although the juvenile court dismissed the petitions against Ben and Lynn, the CPS team still had not finished its investigation of the September 10 hotline call. No final "indicated" or "unfounded" decision had been registered in the Illinois State Central Register. While a juvenile finding of "no probable cause" should have put a stop to the allegations that Ben or Lynn had abused Robert, leading to an immediate "unfounded" decision in the register, no rule directed that the CPS investigation had to be "unfounded" if a juvenile court found "no probable cause" of abuse.

In fact, Lynn was about to be blacklisted in the register. An indicated finding for causing bone fractures would be registered against her for 20 years—unless we could stop it.

During October and November, while the juvenile court case had been unfolding, the CPS team continued to make some investigative contacts. On October 12, Green interviewed Natalie. On October 26, Kirby Long directed Green to "obtain all court orders." He also made a note to himself to request a *"Dupuy* hearing" for Lynn—the special preregistry review by an independent administrator that the federal court rulings from the *Dupuy* case required.[1] This *Dupuy* review gave professionals who worked with children the chance to avoid an indicated finding against them before it would affect their careers.

Early in November, weeks before Judge Sanders' ruling, the CPS team decided to recommend indicating Lynn, but not Ben, as a child abuser, which would put her name in the register for 20 years. No one informed us of this decision, and the CPS team hadn't gotten around to finalizing that decision when Judge Sanders ruled that there was no probable cause to believe that Robert had been abused.

On November 3, Long approved an indicated finding against Lynn for physical abuse of Robert and neglect of the twins, labeling Lynn the abuse perpetrator due to her status as the children's "primary caretaker." A delay in getting a *Dupuy* administrator's conference apparently led to delay in finalizing the decision against Lynn.

Long wanted Green to answer some lingering questions about Robert's fracture, including how long it would have taken for Robert's leg to swell up. So on November 4, Janelle Green paged Dr. Felix, asking her that very question. But Green didn't get through.

Two weeks elapsed. Ben and Lynn now were home, under the juvenile court's order allowing unsupervised contact with their children as long as they were together. But after securing no answer as to how long it would take for a leg to swell following an injury, Janelle Green reached out on November 17 to Dr. Sheridan's nurse, asking her for this information. The nurse dutifully recorded the question, telling Green that Dr. Sheridan was out for the day. Then, Dr. Felix returned her own message, stating there would be some immediate swelling and then more gradual swelling over the next several hours. Dr. Felix repeated her opinion that the fracture was likely due to abuse. Green didn't reach out to Dr. Sheridan again, and she never did speak to him. It remains unclear to this day if she actually ever read his report.

Following Long's additional instruction, Janelle Green asked the police department for its records. The police department clerk told her that they couldn't find the file but promised to look.

As I leaf through the investigative file years after the November 20, 2009, juvenile court ruling in Ben and Lynn's favor, the next page I see in the file still astonishes me. It is a note by Kirby Long's supervisor, CPS manager Kim Ford, dated on November 24. It states that she "agreed with the final finding." So four days *after* the juvenile court exonerated both Ben and Lynn of any abuse, the CPS agency decided to label Lynn guilty of abusing Robert.

The file contains no mention of the juvenile court's order, contrary to Kirby Long's directive to Janelle Green to get copies of the relevant court orders for the file. Once again, the agency was acting heedless of the law, heedless of the facts, and heedless of the consequences of its actions. By now, it was also acting heedless of a juvenile court order.

On December 4, 2009, Janelle Green notified Melissa of the recommendation to indicate Lynn as responsible for abuse of Robert and neglect of the twins. A *Dupuy* administrator's conference—the preliminary review by phone that people who worked with children were entitled to receive before indicated findings got registered against them—would be set for Tuesday, December 8. That gave us exactly one work day— Monday—to prepare for the required *Dupuy* due process review for Lynn.

The case had taken on an *Alice in Wonderland* quality. How could Lynn get out of the rabbit hole? How many times would Lynn have to fight for exoneration? While a court had decided Robert had not been abused by anyone, the CPS steamroller had churned out a new guilty verdict against Lynn.

Responding to the CPS agency was getting to be a financial burden, too. Each time a new major decision was made, the costs of legal representation increased. Melissa and I charged clients fees on a sliding scale when they had incomes above the poverty line. It was uncomfortable to tell the family that our legal representation would cost even more, all after the long juvenile court battle had concluded.

The decision to recommend labeling Lynn as guilty of child abuse caused more than mere indignation. The decision was oppressive, communicating that no matter what Lynn did to exonerate herself, nothing would work. As her counsel, Melissa and I felt discouraged, too. What would it take for this family's nightmare to end completely and forever?

The depth of CPS ignorance and incompetence was mind-boggling. It showed pure ignorance of the law and ignorance of all the requirements that the *Dupuy* case had established. Surely there is nothing that exonerates an accused parent more clearly than a court order that declares their child was not abused. Yet the CPS agency still was bent on destroying Lynn's career after it had tried to destroy her family.

Now Melissa and I needed some extra time to compile records and make a written submission. We requested and got a one-week extension.

On December 15, the assigned reviewer, the area administrator for the Illinois Central Region CPS office, convened the *Dupuy* administrator's conference call. Though not a lawyer herself, an area administrator was supposed to know something about the law that governed the taking of children by the State. She was expected to respect decisions of the federal court and the juvenile court. When in doubt, she was expected to consult CPS's own attorneys about how to interpret a court order.

In Lynn's case, however, the area administrator did exactly what we feared the area administrators might do when we had negotiated the *Dupuy* administrator's conference procedures: she rubber-stamped the CPS team's recommendations.

An administrator's conference is a poor forum for making legal arguments. Some area administrators were better than others in critically assessing the strength of the CPS case, but some still operated under the view that the CPS team just needed a little bit of evidence of wrongdoing by a parent. In effect, the "practically nominal" level of evidence that the federal court had decried in the landmark *Dupuy I* decision continued to operate under the system that was intended to remedy one-sided registry decisions.[2]

The administrator stated that she would consider the evidence we submitted on Lynn's behalf. But she asserted that all that was needed to register Lynn as a child abuser was "credible evidence." After 12 long years to change the "practically nominal" standard for labeling parents responsible for child abuse and ruining their careers, was that work for naught?

On the administrator's conference call, I cited the expertise of Dr. Sheridan and Dr. Miller, highlighting that Dr. Felix, upon whose opinion the CPS recommendation had exclusively relied, was not a board-certified doctor in any field, including child abuse. Of course, I stressed the juvenile court's order, arguing that it legally precluded CPS from finding Lynn guilty of abuse.

The area administrator's questions seemed rote. When I finished, she asked Lynn if she wanted to make a statement. Lynn did. She gave a brief and powerful summation. She mentioned her experience with cases where the CPS agency should have protected children but failed to do so. She said that her "entire career was to help children, and to have them taken from me is very hard. I have worked very hard for my social work degree and license and enjoy working in my profession." She highlighted the many support letters that had been written for her, showing her to be innocent, and she closed saying, "There's no fairness in my livelihood being taken from me." Her statement was more powerful than anything Melissa or I could say.

The area administrator asked to reconvene the call on December 22. When we called in again on December 22, she listed all the materials she had reviewed. She promised a decision by December 31. She had no further questions.

When we received the full investigative file a few weeks later, it showed that the administrator made the decision that very day, December 22. Her summary in the file is brief: "After a deliberate and thorough review, this Administrator CONCURS with the recommendation to indicate Lynn for bone fractures as to Robert and substantial risk as to the twins. All medical professionals agree that a fracture of this type would include objection to any movement of the fractured area. While Lynn maintains no knowledge of how the fracture occurred and denied abusing the child, she was the child's primary caretaker."

That was it. The decision had effectively declared that any mother who is the full-time caregiver of a child can be labeled a child abuser if something happens to her child, even if a court of law says the child wasn't abused.

December 31 came and went as we waited to hear the outcome of the *Dupuy* administrator's conference. The delay in notifying us of the outcome, it turned out, was due to Janelle Green and Kirby Long's delay in entering final notes; Long's superior, Kim Ford, had to press them twice to do so. So it wasn't until January 12 that Janelle Green called Melissa to say that the administrator's conference had upheld the recommended finding.

By then, however, Lynn had gotten a notification directly from the area administrator herself. We already had filed a request for a full administrative hearing on Lynn's behalf on January 11. A legally trained administrative law judge would now hear the case. Lynn's name would be listed as an abuse perpetrator in the child-abuse register, pending a decision at the administrative hearing. That would involve another round of evidence, including medical testimony, all to establish whether or not Lynn should stay listed as a child abuser in the register.

Under the *Dupuy I* due process rulings, Lynn's status as someone who worked with children entitled her to an expedited final hearing decision within 35 days of the date we filed her hearing request. It was hardly a perfect remedy. Permanent damage to careers could occur in the time between the registration of the abuse finding and the final decision from the administrative appeal process, even if that decision exonerated the caregiver. People could be fired as soon as their employer was notified, or they could lose a critical job opportunity. Time was not on the accused caregiver's side.

Once a request for a hearing was filed, however, the burden remained with the State CPS agency to show that a preponderance of the evidence supported keeping their name listed in the register as an abuse perpetrator. Of course, if the parent or caregiver didn't seek this review, then the finding would remain in the register by default, even if there was little or no evidence to support it. Any registry appeal filed more than 60 days after notification of the indicated finding against him or her put the registered person out of luck and out of time; even dispositive proof of innocence wouldn't suffice to clear their name off the register. While the *Dupuy I* decisions had directed massive improvements in the speed at which the full administrative hearings had to be decided, the basic structure of this hearing system was unchanged.

Lynn, fortunately, was not at immediate risk of losing a job. Her social work license was intact for a while. For her, the immediate toll was emotional; she had been labeled guilty for simply being the mother of an injured child, after already being forced to defend herself in an exhausting court battle.

It was an odd system, to say the least. Average folks, including most lawyers who don't specialize in child welfare, often don't know that this vast register exists. The register creates a shadow legal and administrative system that touches millions of children and families in America. To its credit, Illinois at least has a functioning administrative hearing system that allows appeals when parents' and caregivers' names are put into the register as child abusers or child neglectors. But the unfairness of the register—following from the unfairness of investigations—has been a focal point of my own career for the past 20 years. I wish I could say that we have fixed the problems, but I'm afraid all my work has only scratched the surface.[3]

On January 15, 2010, following an instruction to her by Kirby Long, Janelle Green sent a belated letter to Lynn, referring her to parenting classes to remedy her alleged abusive parenting of her son. It was almost comical. No services or classes had been demanded of Ben and Lynn while the abuse case was pending against them in juvenile court. Now, after the juvenile court had decided that the children were perfectly safe at home and there was no reason to believe Robert was abused, the CPS team concluded that Lynn should learn how to parent. Lynn's cooperation with the referral wouldn't result in any change in the register's finding, however. The only way to get off the register was for Lynn to win her appeal.

A week later, I wrote a letter for Lynn, respectfully declining the offered referrals.

As Lynn's administrative appeal was pending, the CPS team finally closed its investigation. Without explanation, Kim Ford waived the requirements of contacts with several witnesses with knowledge of the incident. No one from the CPS investigative team ever interviewed the audiologist, Mark; Susan the stylist; anyone else who had seen Robert with Lynn on September 10; or any other doctor besides Dr. Felix.

Ben and Lynn had been exceedingly unlucky in CPS intervention into their family life and Lynn's career, but they had good luck in their draw of judges. Judge Sanders had been a model of fairness, although we had pressed him too far by asking for sanctions. Nevertheless, we could not have had a better judge for looking at the State's evidence fairly and impartially. Now Lynn had another lucky break: Judge Maloney was assigned as the administrative law judge for Lynn's register appeal. Judge Maloney was highly critical of CPS caseworkers who didn't follow the basic procedures, ignored evidence of innocence, and failed to apply the correct standards for determining whether a parent had abused or neglected a child.

A presentation of lengthy medical testimony shouldn't be necessary. Since we had only a 35-day period in which an expedited hearing was supposed to be decided and a ruling by the juvenile court in Lynn's favor, a judge like Maloney should be able to rule in Lynn's favor as a matter of law.

Legally speaking, it was impossible for CPS to prove that Robert had been abused. The juvenile court judge had found "no probable cause" of abuse. The "probable cause" standard was lower than the "more likely than not" standard that applied at the Lynn's administrative hearing to challenge placement of her name in the register. Since there wasn't probable cause, the CPS attorney couldn't meet his burden of proving a preponderance of the evidence against Lynn. The argument was simple and obvious.

Indeed, it was infuriating that any argument was necessary at this stage. Administrative agencies are required to respect the rulings of courts, as long as those rulings decide the same issue and are final and not still appealable. By deciding not to appeal Judge Sanders's decision, the legal principle of res judicata compelled the administrative agency—CPS—to respect the juvenile court's decision. But we had to argue the point, and the whole time we argued, Lynn remained listed as a child abuser on the register.

Making sense of the State CPS system's decisions had long been an impossible challenge. Clients often ask me to explain the indefensible decisions that CPS investigators make against them, but I am as baffled as anyone. I can write them a book about CPS decision making, like this one, but at the end of the day, the answers come down to two competing explanations for the violations of rights that are endemic to the system: incompetence versus malevolence.

Incompetence explains most of the problems. Bad decisions result from having caseworkers who are not competent to do the job assigned to them. These caseworkers may not be stupid or lazy, although some clearly do not have sufficient analytical abilities, people skills, or work ethic necessary to handle the job. But even the most competent individuals would fail in many investigations, because a great deal of the incompetence results from insufficient training and direction, too many cases in their caseloads, poor supervision, and an unclear understanding of their job duties and CPS's limits, which are not any individual CPS caseworker's fault.

These are systemic failures and result from a failure of the leadership in the CPS agencies.[4] Our society has asked CPS caseworkers to do an impossible job, including but not limited to deciding when kids should be taken from their parents and deciding the guilt or innocence of parents, all without a lick of legal training. Our society has yet to seriously set reasonable limits on caseworkers' authority. Instead, heaped upon overbroad power and unfettered discretion is pressure to make decisions under a deeply ingrained "better safe than sorry" mentality.

Throughout the 13 years that the *Dupuy* litigation was pending, my law partner, Robert Lehrer, consistently argued with me on this point. He advocated the malevolence theory. He considered the CPS system to be "evil." He had a point. Snap judgments about taking children from their parents, deliberate refusal to consider evidence in a family's favor, and oftentimes-abusive behavior toward parents were all indicators of malevolence that went unchecked. Moreover, if one assumes that some of the worst evils are banal, à la Hannah Arendt, then his views may be correct.

I disagreed, for I saw the overwhelming majority of caseworkers as people who were not trying to harm families but who simply lacked understanding and the ability to do better. Some CPS caseworkers supported our clients' claims of innocence but sometimes got overruled by their supervisors. I viewed those caseworkers as heroic and appreciated the need for more dedicated line workers like them.

Justice Louis Brandeis once warned that society should be most on guard when the government's purposes are beneficent, because "the greatest dangers to liberty lurk in insidious encroachment by men of zeal, well-meaning but without understanding."[5] This warning sums up the central problem with the CPS system in America. The CPS system is loaded with beneficent purpose—the purpose to protect children—but operates with far-too-little understanding and far-too-much zeal. Even if there are many good caseworkers, a few bad actors do huge damage. Moreover, incompetence is so rampant that the best caseworkers often leave and the worst ones stay. Beneficent purposes mask the lack of understanding. The public indifference to the plight of families in the system and the utter disdain shown to parents who are accused of abuse contribute to the system's well-meaning but dangerous and insidious encroachments into family life.

The system may also be evil. It was designed and implemented without the essential understanding that a massive system to protect children from their parents cannot work if its powers are unchecked. The limits that the system needs in order to protect children and families simply are not there. "Abuse" and "neglect" have become whatever a CPS caseworker thinks they are. Damage is done under the guise of a child's "best interests" before families have a fair opportunity to fight back.

Lynn's register hearing was set for a prehearing status call on February 3. An expedited hearing was set to commence on February 9 and 16. This timing was a bit delayed already, extending the timing beyond 35 days. The CPS administrative hearing office had not processed Lynn's January

11 hearing request promptly. But after we sent a complaint letter to the chief administrative law judge, Lynn's hearing request was put onto a fast track.

The lawyer for the CPS agency surprised us by filing a witness list that included a plan to call Dr. Felix and her supervisor, Dr. Flannery, to testify. We responded by saying that we planned to "stand on our motion." What that meant was that we considered the claims against Lynn's listing in the register to be so strong that we planned to rely on our legal arguments alone and not present any evidence (other than Judge Sanders' order finding "no probable cause") to the administrative law judge.

Administrative Law Judge Maloney leaned on the CPS attorney to answer the argument that the juvenile court's order precluded the State from putting Lynn's name in the register. She hinted strongly that she thought our legal argument was right.

On February 8, the day before the hearing was set to start, the CPS lawyer filed a written legal memorandum against our position, arguing that the parties to the juvenile court case and the parties in the administrative hearing cases were not the same, because the State's Attorney's office did not represent the CPS agency in the juvenile court.

Actually, it wasn't a terrible argument. The lawyer had managed to find a case to support it—a case holding that two different sovereign governments who are prosecuting a person for the same offense don't need to defer to each other. Inconsistent rulings were permitted in such a case, according to the decision he cited. The CPS lawyer argued that what happened to Lynn was permissible: the "juvenile court had found one expert to be the most compelling and the agency had found another."

On February 9, Judge Maloney announced she would rule on the legal argument before hearing from any witnesses. That was good news. She also gave us one day more to respond to the CPS attorney's "two sovereigns" argument. While this created a significant time pressure, we quickly responded. We argued that the CPS agency and the State's Attorney both represented one governmental interest, not separate governmental entities with different interests. Both represented the State of Illinois, so the "different sovereigns" argument didn't wash.

The next day, Judge Maloney issued a recommendation in Lynn's favor, agreeing to remove her name from the register. The recommendation recited the evidence presented to Judge Sanders and concluded that the juvenile court decision in Lynn's favor concerned the "same allegation." She agreed with us that the CPS agency was not independent of the State and therefore wasn't a separate sovereign. Under the well-established preclusion principles, CPS could not keep Lynn's name in the register.

On February 19, the CPS director approved the recommended decision and issued it to Lynn by certified mail. There were no further appeals possible. The State CPS director can't ask a court to overturn his own final decisions in register appeals. At last, the litigation about Robert's fracture was finally over. It had been nearly half a year since the hotline call.

The family started in on the hard road to emotional recovery, a road that doesn't end with a piece of paper declaring that a parent's name is taken off the register.

FOURTEEN

Partial Answers and Partial Remedies

Soon Ben and Lynn found themselves in the position Mary Broderick had occupied a few years before. Friends who knew of the family's unjust ordeal started sending other families their way for advice and support. After Ben or Lynn had talked for several hours to a distraught mother or father who had just learned of a hotline call against them, I would often get a call from that new person, seeking legal representation. Sometimes the referrals went the other way, too. For parents Melissa and I were representing whose children had a bone fracture or head injury and who wanted to talk to another parent, Ben and Lynn were happy to become those parents' listening ear.

Ben and Lynn wanted to do more to fix the broken child protection system. Ben offered to meet with his elected state representative, a State Senate leader. A meeting with Ben, her constituent, could help us with our legislative reform agenda. We had a practical and immediate interest in getting favorable legislative consideration for measures that could help add fairness to the very unfair system.

After their case ended, how Robert's fracture occurred without Ben or Lynn noticing it immediately remained a mystery. In some cases, the claims against parents clear up magically. For example, several months ago, a father called me for advice during a CPS investigation with a situation that sounded identical to Robert's: a fracture in an infant who wouldn't have been able to cause the fracture himself. The parents had taken the child to the hospital. Because the parents had no idea how the fracture had occurred, a safety plan was demanded on the spot. The couple's children had to leave the home. After several weeks elapsed, the father called the head of the hospital's child protection team, Dr. Chandra, imploring him to put in a word with the CPS caseworkers to let the children come home. The doctor refused to intervene, telling the father that he would just have to wait for the investigation to conclude.

An hour after this call, however, the father got a call from the CPS caseworker. The call had nothing to do with any change of heart or intervention by Dr. Chandra. It turned out that at the same time as the father was begging for his children to be allowed to come home, a day-care center teacher who had been caring for the infant told the CPS caseworker that another teacher had dropped the child. Video footage confirmed the fall.

Suddenly, the mystery had cleared up: another person, not one of the parents, clearly was at fault. Because the parents were not responsible for the fracture, their children came home immediately, the safety plan ended, and the allegations against them were labeled "unfounded." Had the teacher never come forward, this family might have faced a juvenile court ordeal based on nothing more than a fracture the parents never could explain themselves.

There was no such sudden clarifying explanation for Robert's fracture. But there was eventually a clearer explanation for why Robert never had an "inconsolable cry" at the undetermined time his leg was fractured. Ben and Lynn monitored their children's development very carefully, celebrating each milestone and assessing any needs for special care. By the time Robert was a year old, some significant signs indicated that Robert's development was not entirely on track. This notable lack of response to pain and other stimuli seemed related to a medical condition that was becoming more obvious. Robert's demeanor as a very "chill" baby, as Lynn had always called him, was consistent with his minimal reactions to pain that would have bothered other children.

Of special concern was Robert's muscle tone. His mobility lagged significantly. Robert wasn't crawling or walking by the months the child development books reported as average. Ben and Lynn started to seek out more medical and behavioral assessments. They asked for genetic tests. They started seeking special "zero to three" evaluations by the time Robert was 10 months old.

By the time Robert turned one, it was clear that he had hypotonia, or excessively low muscle tone. As the assessments continued to come in, it became clear that Robert had a multifaceted, pervasive and rare genetic condition that impaired his neurological system. Though he was very intelligent, Robert's speech was seriously delayed, and he was very unsteady on his feet when he did start to walk. Even years later, he continued to need supports to walk, and he was prone to falling.

Lynn put the needs of her children at the center of her life. With a wealth of patience and experience with working with children with disabilities, Lynn made obtaining intensive specialized services for Robert her calling. With all the medical and development services and personal care she devoted to Robert, she sometimes worried that her twins were not getting as much attention as they would have received but for Robert's special needs.

When I first learned about Robert's diagnosis, I got angry. Finally, there was a possible medical explanation for Robert's unusual reaction to pain. Alternative explanations as to why Robert might not cry inconsolably had never been considered. Indeed, Ben and Lynn never withheld any of the information about Robert's seemingly unusually high tolerance to pain. They had remarked all along on his calming quickly and showing no signs of significant injury, even when everyone knew his leg was broken. Ben and Lynn had trusted the medical establishment to diagnose and treat their son. Instead of getting answers on September 10, 2009, they were accused of child abuse. None of the doctors they had seen for the fracture had known anything about Robert's neurological condition. That wasn't on their radar screen.

Sadly, child abuse allegations sometimes operate as a smoke screen, providing an explanation that is not only false but also distracting. Instead of securing the fuller medical assessment that should occur, a child abuse accusation disempowers parents in their quest for answers they desperately need. Sometimes, the accusation prevents children from getting care their conditions require. The accusation forces parents to defend themselves from the doctors and the institutions that are supposed to help them find answers. In many of cases where the parents are seeking help for unusual injuries or symptoms they cannot explain, the medical system turns into the family's adversary rather than their friend.

Robert is now in grade school. He still needs some assistance to walk, and his gait is unsteady. His comprehension is excellent, but his speech is markedly delayed, since it requires significant muscle tone to produce intelligible sounds. The family has put into place many specialized therapies, including horse therapy, which has remarkable success in improving the muscle tone of children with conditions like Robert's. Recently, they were thrilled to welcome a beautiful and specially trained therapy dog into their family, which is able to work with Robert in ways humans cannot do. The family also moved to another house so that Robert does not have to manage challenging stairs.

Lynn and Ben still do not have all the answers about Robert's condition. They have consulted with many medical and developmental specialists in Illinois and elsewhere. Robert gets specialized services six times a week. Lynn is Robert's and the twins' full-time caregiver. The twins are finishing middle school. Lynn hasn't been able to return to work yet as a social worker, although she still hopes to do so when the children don't need her attention for so many hours each day.

Lynn tells me that while her life is full of challenges, having her children is something she never takes for granted. She never forgets how close she came to losing what is most precious to her. She and Ben remain eternally grateful to Dr. Sheridan, Judge Sanders, to Melissa and me, and to the family and friends who supported them through the long road to restoration of their family life. The stresses in Lynn's life these days are ones she is grateful to have, and her life, surrounded by the children she loves and a husband, family, and friends who love her, is full of joy.

In the months after the intense litigation, my contacts with Ben and Lynn became less frequent. They stayed active in the community of families who had gotten to know each other through the misfortunate of having allegations against them. Recognizing that lawyers cannot give the same emotional support to a parent that people who had their own family life disrupted can, we actively supported families' connections to Ben and Lynn and other past clients when new clients came to us and wanted that form of support.

Ben, especially, remained unsatisfied that the system had never made amends to his family. He continued to seek remedies. As he was doing so, he uncovered Janelle Green's own personal social media posts. In a series of chats on the topic of corporal punishment, Janelle Green posted the following comment: "My mother tore your butt up. No one threw a better shoe either. I now work for CPS and you know sometimes I am thinking 'they should have tore that butt up!' " The very same person who had investigated Ben and Lynn was *advocating* physical child abuse in her social media posting. Maybe it was just chatter, but it was hypocritical and disgusting.

Ben and Lynn never got the vindication they hoped for. There was never so much as an apology from anyone who worked for the State of Illinois CPS system. Neither Ben nor Lynn had any illusions that they could remedy the wrong that had been done to them. They were far too savvy and too jaded by their experience to expect basic decency from the system that had nearly ruined their family life. Still, they had hoped to make changes that could benefit other families, preventing others from ever going through the fearful episode that nearly destroyed their family.

Natalie also never got to see justice done for Ben, Lynn, and their grandchildren. She died in November 2012, after an extended illness. She spent the evening of her last day with Lynn and the twins. To me, her energy and intelligence never seemed to wane, and news of her death came as a shock.

When I called Lynn shortly after I learned of Natalie's death, Lynn told me that the topic of their juvenile court ordeal had come up in a conversation very shortly before Natalie died. Natalie had expressed gratitude for Melissa's and my help and spoke of her commitment to seeing justice done for other families. Natalie had always wanted to write about the case herself. One day in court, she told me she wanted to submit an article about what had happened to her family to the *New Yorker* magazine. She wanted the world to know of the grave injustice that had shocked her family. She wanted her legacy to include helping to reform the child protection system.

While Ben and Lynn's case was pending in the juvenile court, a related case was pending in federal court. In that case, my office and attorneys from the law firm Winston and Strawn sought remedies for a family who had their son taken from them due to an unexplained fracture of his arm. Eventually that case, *Hernandez v. Foster*, would create an important legal precedent for families.[1]

During the months after the *Dupuy II* case concluded in 2008, I struggled to figure out how to challenge its central holding that safety plans were uniformly voluntary (because the safety plan form so declared) and therefore gave rise to no enforceable due process rights for parents.[2] CPS caseworkers continued to demand safety plans that caused parents to separate from their children. The safety plans that families like Ben and Lynn's were threatened into signing required that relatives or approved friends provide round-the-clock monitoring of the parents' interactions with their children. Children would be taken into foster care, or so parents were told, if the parents did not agree to safety plan demands. These safety plans seemed to proliferate in the wake of the *Dupuy II* decision. Now we, as lawyers for the families, had less leverage when we tried to intercede on behalf of our clients. Families had no available means to challenge these demands which felt much more like threats than voluntary choices.

Judge Posner's *Dupuy II* decision boxed us in. We needed to secure a different decision from the federal courts—a decision that would enable families to fight back against the taking of their children without due process. Getting such a decision seemed a daunting task, however, since the *Dupuy II* litigation had taken eight years of effort and had yielded the terrible results that we had been forced to live with. Still, I was not about to give up. The rights at stake for families like Ben and Lynn's were just too important for me to throw in the towel, tragic though the outcome of our efforts in *Dupuy II* had been.

The Posner decision gave us some openings, but not many. Proving that the State was lying about the evidence it had at the time a CPS caseworker demanded a safety plan was going to be very hard. How was a family to know what evidence CPS had gathered at the time a safety plan demand was made?

The best opening to challenge safety plans would arise if a safety plan were demanded *after* the State had already taken the children, especially if the State's grounds for taking the children were obviously weak. If the State itself decided there was no probable cause to find abuse but the CPS still insisted on keeping the children away from their parents without providing the parents any meaningful opportunity to object, that scenario would present an exception to the paradigm the Posner opinion rested upon. If the child had been taken without probable cause and then a safety plan was demanded, that would make a strong case for showing the family's fundamental rights were violated by the CPS safety plan policies. If the parents were told that they must sign a safety plan in order to see their kids, that would not be voluntary even under Judge Posner's restrictive analysis. In such a case, the parents' bargaining power—their ability to object to a safety plan demand and be no "worse off" for it[3]—plainly would be nil.

It sometimes seems that merely imagining the right test case is sufficient to lead the clients who present exactly that case to walk into the office. Within a year of the final decision in *Dupuy II*, Crystelle and Joshua Hernandez presented that near-perfect case. The *Hernandez v. Foster* litigation, filed on April 23, 2009, would give families some legal tools to fight back against safety plans. The federal court of appeals decision that provided these tools wasn't issued until December 2011, however, which was much too late to benefit Ben and Lynn.[4] And as with most legal victories, while the *Hernandez* decision led to adoption of some important legal principles, implementing those principles required extensive efforts, including several more lawsuits and years of cajoling to get the State to adopt the legal principles and corrective policies into practice.

In 2007, Joshua and Crystelle Hernandez had a baby, Jaymz. Crystelle stayed home to care for him while Joshua served in the U.S. Army in Iraq. After Joshua's discharge, the family moved to Illinois from Texas.

On the morning of September 8, 2008, when Jaymz was just 15 months old, Crystelle heard him crying, via his baby monitor, after he woke from a nap. She ran to Jaymz's room and saw him on the floor of his room, holding his arm. She naturally concluded he must have fallen out of his crib. The Hernandezes had no idea Jaymz could climb out. They quickly lowered the mattress to its lowest possible position so that he couldn't get out again.

New to the area, Crystelle took Jaymz to an unfamiliar doctor's office to have his arm checked. Jaymz turned out to have a torus fracture of his right humerus (arm) bone. During their visit, a nurse wrote a note stating that Crystelle had said Jaymz couldn't "run or climb." If Crystelle had said such a thing, what she meant was that Jaymz couldn't run or climb *since the fall*. But she didn't know that's what the nurse had written until much later, so she had no chance to clarify the point when the nurse made her note.

The doctor treated the fracture and sent Jaymz home. Jaymz was fine except for the broken arm. But the doctor's office called the CPS hotline, viewing Crystelle's alleged statement that Jaymz couldn't run or climb as reason to suspect child abuse.

A CPS caseworker came to the Hernandezes' home that afternoon. She saw Jaymz walking, playing with toys, and interacting with his mother as if nothing were wrong. While she reported to her supervisor that Jaymz looked fine and that she didn't know why she had been sent to the home, the CPS supervisor directed her, over the phone and without ever seeing Jaymz, to take Jaymz into State protective custody.

Fortunately, the CPS caseworker placed Jaymz with his great grandmother, though he barely knew her, since the family had just recently moved to Illinois. Crystelle and Joshua were forbidden from seeing their son. The next day, Crystelle was allowed to attend Jaymz's orthopedist appointment to cast Jaymz's arm. The doctor told the CPS caseworker that it "didn't look like abuse." Indeed, the doctor said that abuse *could not* account for the type of fracture Jaymz experienced, the break could *only* have occurred from a fall.

The same day that Jaymz's arm was casted by the second doctor, the local State's Attorney decided that there wasn't enough evidence to file a petition in the juvenile court to start a case to adjudicate Jaymz as an abused child. Under state law, the CPS agency's authority to keep Jaymz from his parents lapsed as soon as the State's Attorney decided not to file a petition with the juvenile court. Nevertheless, the CPS caseworker told Crystelle and Joshua that they now had to sign a safety plan that would keep Jaymz out of their home; otherwise, they would not be allowed to see Jaymz. The CPS caseworker also told them that they had no parental rights.

Believing the caseworker that the only way they could see their son was to sign the safety plan, Crystelle and Joshua signed it. The plan allowed them only limited supervised visits. Further medical opinions confirmed the lack of suspicion of child abuse. After the parents were separated from their son for nine days under the safety plan, the CPS caseworker finally ended the safety plan. The CPS investigation stayed open for another two months, however, closing finally on November 27, 2008, with a finding that the allegations of abuse were "unfounded."

Terrible and frightening as their experience was, the Hernandez's experience presented a lawyer's dream case: a nearly ideal set of facts from which to challenge the *Dupuy II* decision of Judge Posner insofar as it held that safety plans are voluntary because they represent reasonable "options" for parents. In the context of their case, the Hernandezes had not been presented with any "reasonable option." They could not simply "thumb their nose" at the caseworker's safety plan demand and end up "no worse off" for it,[5] as the Posner opinion had described the safety plan choices given to parents.

If Crystelle and Joshua *had* decided to thumb their nose at the safety plan demand, they wouldn't have seen their child at all. How could such a decision to sign a safety plan be voluntary? Moreover, being misled about their custodial rights added to the coerciveness of their encounter with CPS. That the CPS team knew the State's Attorney had already rejected filing an abuse petition, after concluding that there was not probable cause to believe Jaymz was abused, added to the legal force of this conclusion that the safety plan demand was unlawful.

It followed, further, that if the safety plan was coerced and not a voluntary choice, an opinion in favor of the Hernandezes could drive a big wedge into Judge Posner's across-the-board declaration that safety plans were voluntary waivers of the family's right to live together. Some due process protections would have to be afforded to families facing safety plan demands.

Surprisingly, though, the *Hernandez* case did not receive a favorable response from the federal district court. In a complete about-face from an initial decision that allowed the Hernandezes to proceed with their claims, the federal district court ruled against the Hernandezes when the CPS caseworkers, defending themselves in the suit, requested a judgment in their favor without a trial (i.e., a "summary judgment" request).[6]

It sometimes takes a big loss to lead to a bigger victory. So it was with the Hernandez's constitutional case.

On August 26, 2011, the Court of Appeals for the Seventh Circuit issued a landmark decision and overturned the dismissal of the *Hernandez* case on three of the four claims we had presented.[7] The court first held against the Hernandezes, however, regarding their claims that the initial seizure of Jaymz was plainly illegal under clearly established available precedents. The court of appeals concluded that the CPS caseworkers couldn't be compelled to pay damages for the initial seizure of Jaymz from his parents.

But the decision went on to hold, in favor of the Hernandezes, that as soon as the State's Attorney declined to file the abuse petition with the juvenile court, the CPS agency was no longer authorized to keep Jaymz in its custody. The family's claims challenging the continued withholding of Jaymz should have been considered by the federal court, not dismissed. Then, because the Hernandezes had shown sufficient evidence of coercion when they signed the safety plan, they should have been allowed to prove that their "agreement" to have Jaymz live with his great-grandmother was not voluntary and that it violated their due process rights. The court of appeals concluded that the Hernandezes presented valid claims for unlawful seizure and substantive and procedural due process violations, and the court sent the case back to the federal trial judge for resolution.

The court of appeals also clarified the law going forward. It declared that it was not sufficient for the State to have some evidence of abuse; while having probable cause to believe the child was abused was necessary, it was not sufficient. To take a child from his or her parents without a court order, there also must be "exigent circumstances." In other words, while Jaymz's parents couldn't recover money for the initial seizure, because the law wasn't sufficiently clear prior to the Seventh Circuit's ruling in their case, the Seventh Circuit Court of Appeals would allow *future* children and families to sue the State caseworkers if they were taken from the homes without a court order first, absent an emergency justification for taking the child. The *Hernandez* opinion established a clear and important requirement of due process that families henceforth could rely on.

Following this ruling, the Hernandezes settled their lawsuit against the caseworkers, securing compensation for the trauma they had experienced due to the State continuing to hold Jaymz and coercing their agreement to a safety plan. And a year after the court of appeals decision, the legal team Melissa and I worked with, led by Julie Bauer at Winston & Strawn, won the Seventh Circuit Bar Association's public service award for their legal work on behalf of the Hernandezes.

The case was a very important victory for families, creating an appellate precedent that we could rely on for a fundamentally important principle. It did not entirely undercut Judge Posner's decision that safety plans were "voluntary options." But it provided a critical starting point in reopening a dialogue with the State CPS leadership about safety plan reform.

Following the *Hernandez* decision, other advocacy for safety plan policy changes we started in 2009 finally met with some success. We won a change in state law providing that safety plans had to be in writing, signed by all parties, and spelling out the rights and responsibilities of all of the participants in the plan. That wasn't much comfort to the parents who were still coerced into accepting safety plan separations. But it did set the stage for more changes that would eventually come after Melissa Staas and I, along with the Family Defense Center's attorney Sara Gilloon and teams of lawyers from two major Chicago law firms, filed a trilogy of federal civil rights cases in 2013 and 2014, all relying on the *Hernandez v. Foster* precedent.[8] All three cases settled in 2016 with new stronger policies consistent with *Hernandez*'s holdings.

As a result of the cases that followed *Hernandez*, it is contrary to Illinois CPS policy to threaten parents with taking their children in the absence of evidence of an immediate threat to the child's safety. It is improper to secure a safety plan on the basis of such threats. It is also no longer legally acceptable to hold children at hospitals after they are medically ready for discharge while hospital staff await instructions from the CPS investigator as to whether the children can go home.

It has taken nearly 20 years of legal work to create a legal framework that will stop the involuntary separation of children from their parents under safety plans. But there are some major policy and practice shifts finally underway, at least in Illinois. While Illinois once was at the forefront of using these terrible coercive instruments to separate families and then call the separations "voluntary," I hope Illinois will now take the lead in stopping these abuses.[9]

Safety plans create a shadow foster care system in America—a system in which children are taken from parents for weeks or months and cared for by conscripted relatives and family friends, all under threats and without any judicial oversight. Indeed, safety plan separations do not get counted in state and federal foster care data or other child welfare data reports. Nevertheless, children can remain in limbo for months under these plans, sometimes kept out of school and without access to medical care, since the caregivers have no legal authority to get care for the children. Custody battles between parents and relatives often ensue in the wake of a CPS decision to move a child from one parent into the home of relatives of another, all without court orders.

It took a new CPS administration in Illinois to agree to stop entrenched bad practices because lawsuits are never enough by themselves to make systems change. The work that it has taken to get to this point is a catalogue of fits and starts on a long road to CPS reform. It has been an exhausting and sometimes painful journey, although vital to protect the fundamental rights of children and families live together. There remains substantial on-the-ground resistance to the new policies. Notices of rights, carefully drafted by lawyers working collaboratively for both sides in the wake of litigation and under federal court oversight, are still not delivered consistently to the parents who need to know their rights. The work continues on a local, state, and national level.

Ben and Lynn's case also led directly to another major reform effort in the area of medical ethics.

One day in the fall of 2012, a volunteer lawyer, George Barry, newly introduced to Melissa and me, came to our office seeking ways he could help in the cause of justice for families in the child welfare system. George was a retired tax lawyer with years of service to the State of Illinois. He had also worked for a major accounting firm. These positions gave George extensive experience analyzing complex ethical issues involving professionals who had fiduciary duties to clients. He had a keen eye for conflicts of interest. Soon his sharp analytical abilities would be put to excellent use.

I gave George materials from Ben and Lynn's case to read as background, thinking this material could introduce him to the issues families may face in juvenile court cases. Soon he was asking some very interesting questions on the theme, "Can a doctor do what the doctor did to Lynn at that hospital?" He was especially puzzled about how a child abuse pediatrician at the hospital treating Robert would come to testify against Ben and Lynn.

George's questions stopped me short. The materials I had given George had focused on the conduct of the caseworkers Green and Long, not on Dr. Felix's conduct. But George had read between the lines. The conflict of interest between Dr. Felix's role as a staff doctor at the hospital supposed to treat Robert and her role as an agent of the CPS system prosecuting Lynn and Ben was obvious—at least it jumped out at George.

Although Lynn had brought Robert to the hospital for medical care, Dr. Felix, an employee of the treating hospital, had become the lead adverse witness against the family. Dr. Felix had questioned Lynn after Lynn had been awake all night and then had reported on the interview to the State CPS officials and police. Even if this conduct all were legal, there was something that hit George as unethical about what Lynn and her family had been through on the night of September 10.

I wondered aloud if some significant medical ethical principles had been breached, but I had not studied medical ethics. I knew little beyond the Hippocratic oath that enjoined doctors to "First, do no harm." Still, the Hippocratic oath itself seemed to have been breached in Lynn's case. Research into medical ethics might be used to persuade hospital administrators or doctors themselves that they should take a closer look the practices that put doctors like Dr. Felix at the center of the CPS decisions to take kids from their parents.

Suddenly George had found a project that fascinated him.

It took nearly two years, but in March 2014, George and I published a 120-page paper entitled "Medical Ethics Concerns in Physical Child Abuse Investigations: A Critical Perspective."[10] We sent links to the paper to medical groups, advocacy groups, and journalists. George's research uncovered violations of nine different ethical rules in child abuse cases in Illinois in five representative cases (including Ben and Lynn's) where child abuse doctors served as CPS consultants and oftentimes witnesses against the parents.

Under the Canons of Ethics of the American Medical Association, doctors are expected to be scientists first, not advocates. Doctors are expected to collaborate with other doctors in seeking out the truth, not elevate their own opinions over those of specialists in medical fields in which they are not experts. Unlike lawyers, who are expected to be zealous advocates for their clients' objectives, doctors are supposed to work to achieve consensus about the treatment of a child. Care for a medical condition of the child is the paramount goal, and there is a duty to preserve the decision-making authority of the parent as the person who speaks for the child patient. Doctors also have an ethical duty to provide family-centered care and a duty to mitigate harm to children who are their patients. Each of these duties had been violated in Lynn and Ben's case and the others we analyzed.

The interrogation Lynn experienced in the wee hours of the morning on September 11, 2009, was especially troubling. Doctors are not supposed to participate in interrogations. Given that Robert was not free to leave the hospital at the time the safety plan was demanded, Lynn wasn't truly free to leave, either—not if she wanted to take Robert with her, as she had a right to do throughout the time Robert was receiving services at the hospital. But instead, she was made to answer questions after having been deprived of sleep all night, giving answers that would be shared with police and CPS, all without any warning as to the purposes of the questions or the rights she had in choosing to answer.

Potentially most ethically troubling of all and the clearest of all the violations was that no one had disclosed to Lynn that the doctor who questioned her about Robert's fractures worked under a contract with the State of Illinois, its CPS investigators, its State's Attorneys, and police. Dr. Felix effectively was part of the State's prosecutorial apparatus.[11] It is a basic ethical principle that a doctor who performs an exam on a patient must inform the patient (or the parents, if the patient is a child) who is paying the doctor, especially if that payment creates a duty to anyone other than the patient. Yet no one had told Lynn that Dr. Felix worked under an MPEEC contract with the CPS agency.

George also examined the financial and other incentives involved in the still-new child abuse pediatric subspecialty that became a board-certified field just two months after the hotline call was made against Lynn and Ben. George figured that the child abuse pediatric subspecialty wouldn't have been adopted unless regular pediatricians and other doctors who treated children saw a benefit, both financial and personal. George perceived the incentives clearly. Most doctors, including most pediatricians and pediatric orthopedists and neurosurgeons, didn't want to become embroiled with courts and CPS. They would happily defer unpleasant forensic work to other doctors who claimed to be experts in discerning when a child had been abused. The financial incentives for this deference were obvious. By creating a subspecialty of doctors in the area of child abuse, doctors with medical practices involving children could stay away from courthouses and avoid having to spend uncompensated time talking to CPS caseworkers.

As George and I saw, the child abuse pediatricians appreciated the elevation of their expertise in the eyes of the court. Their board certification in child abuse made them the chief medical authorities the CPS caseworkers were obligated to listen to, which gave them greater power and influence over the outcome of investigations. But the doctor's duty to mitigate harm to families was a duty that the child abuse pediatricians violated in every case we analyzed. Doctors are supposed to be healers. In our cases, child abuse doctors viewed themselves as exceptions to the medical profession's harm-reduction duty. They consistently disavowed any responsibility for the damage to family life their intervention and consultation with CPS caused. Where the child abuse pediatricians took advantage of the family's trust in their hospital and acted as if they were part of the treatment team, it was especially damaging to the family's sense of trust.

Not one child abuse pediatrician I knew of ever admitted his or her opinions about abuse had ever been mistaken. The closest to such an admission any family I represented received was when one of the leading child abuse pediatricians in Chicago admitted that a *colleague* at a different hospital had made a colossal error. The colleague's opinion that a toddler's elbow fracture was due to abuse led to the child's removal from her parents and the filing of a petition in the juvenile court. But when multiple orthopedists determined that it was virtually impossible for abuse to have caused the fracture, the child abuse pediatrician I contacted for assistance helped to correct her colleague's erroneous opinion. She intervened with the State's Attorney's office to get a petition against the innocent parents dismissed. That action was much appreciated by the family.

Of equal concern with the lack of humility and rare acknowledgment of error was the lack of any neutral review of the child abuse pediatrician's conclusions and methods. One head of child abuse pediatrics testified at a deposition that no one at her institution evaluated her. She evaluated herself.

The report George and I wrote was a call for the healers to heal themselves.

The report was noticed in some unexpected places: a TV station in Detroit wanted to tape an interview with me about it, and so did a Christian radio station in Washington state. An emergency room doctor in Connecticut and a law professor in North Carolina wanted to discuss it. Parents with new cases—current as I finish writing this book—called me, saying that they had read the report and wanted to take action to address the policies and practices it highlights as ethical breaches. They also contacted their state legislator to advocate for changes the report advocates. A new family advocacy group, the Family Justice Resource Center, is preparing policy proposals based on the report. One of the hospitals involved in child abuse cases is beginning an independent evaluation of its child abuse program. These are all good steps, the building blocks for momentum that could yield changes in the future.

The American Medical Association and the American Academy of Pediatrics have not taken up any of its recommendations for reform of the child abuse pediatric practice, however. Nor have they declared it necessary for child abuse pediatricians to disclose to parents that they work for the State under a contract and will report what they say about their child to CPS and police.

FIFTEEN

A "Constellation of Injuries" Does Not Equal Child Abuse

Soon after Lynn's name was finally off the register, our office was flooded with new medically involved cases where abuse had been alleged because of a child's injury or symptom. Fortunately, most of these cases ended just as Mary and Tom Broderick's CPS experience ended—with the safety plan lifted after one to two months and an unfounded decision issued at the conclusion of the investigation. While the parents had been compelled to endure long and painful safety plan separations, formal petitions to adjudicate abuse were not filed in juvenile court. Often, after Melissa or I intervened, safety plans were modified so that the parents or children could go home.

In some of the cases, the CPS investigators had labeled the child abused but did not name a parent as responsible. This "unknown perpetrator" determination usually meant that kids would not be taken into the formal foster care system. As a rule, the State's Attorney's office wouldn't file petitions against parents when there was a gaping hole in their claim that the parents were responsible for the child's abuse or neglect.

If the parents admitted, however, that they were the exclusive caregivers for the injured child and if the child abuse pediatrician gave a strongly held opinion that an injury was due to abuse, then petitions might be filed against the parents. The State sometimes removed the children even if there was no specific evidence pointing to either parent as a child abuser. The State didn't have to allege or prove which of the two parents is responsible, just as the State hadn't been compelled to specify the perpe-trator in Ben and Lynn's case.

Two years after Ben and Lynn were fully exonerated, a five-week-old boy named Yohan came to the attention of CPS because of unusual medi-cal findings. His family's resulting ordeal was even more terrible than Ben and Lynn's, measured in cost and duration alone. Yohan and his two-and-a-half-year-old sister, Marika, were separated from their parents, Teresa G. and K.S., for over a year and a half. It took a trip to the appellate court to get justice for the family—justice that never made them whole but did clear them of allegations that never should have been made.

While four-week-old Robert had seemed completely healthy until he had a suddenly swollen leg, Yohan already had an extensive history of medical visits by the time he was five weeks of age. He had exhibited worrisome seizures or seizure-like symptoms for several weeks, symptoms his own doctor observed and couldn't explain.

Yohan was born in May 2011. His birth had been difficult; his umbilical cord had been wrapped around his neck, and the delivery was very sud-den. Stabilizing him after birth took six hours. In his first week of life, he had to see the pediatrician twice due to weight loss. At three weeks, his parents were reporting unusual behaviors, including numerous high-pitched yelps every day and an odd dazed staring look.

At first, the doctor thought that Yohan might have indigestion; she rec-ommended gripe water. But on June 4, 2011, Yohan was especially fussy; while his mother gave him the recommended gripe water, he refused to nurse. The next morning, Yohan woke up and vomited. His parents dis-cussed all of his symptoms with Yohan's pediatrician, who told them to bring Yohan to her office the next day. Teresa G. and K.S. monitored their son closely. Teresa noted a twitch of his left hand and a jerking of his left leg. Later that day, K.S. took a video showing another such incident. Yohan continued to stare, but he also had a twitching of his left eye. The parents noticed two more twitching incidents that day, but otherwise Yohan seemed fine; he had no more vomiting, he nursed normally, and he was alert and playful.

The next day, on the way to the doctor's office, the parents saw another twitching incident. And a nurse at the doctor's office saw yet another epi-sode and alerted the pediatrician. The doctor called it "seizure activity," so Yohan was promptly sent by ambulance to the hospital, where he remained for nine days.

Upon admission, Yohan continued to have observable seizure activity. Physical exams found no notable injuries on his body. CT and MRI scans showed that he had fluid collections on both sides of his brain inside his cranium, which were read as "likely subdural hematomas." There was also fluid in another area, the subarachnoid part of the membranes covering the front left part of the brain, which radiologists read as a suspected hemorrhage.

A special scan of the veins in the head was recommended by a hospital neuroradiologist to rule out thrombosis (blood clotting) leading to stroke, but that scan was never done. Studies of the clotting of Yohan's blood also weren't done. An initial report by the neuroradiologist stated there was no restriction in Yohan's blood flow in his brain, but a later addendum changed that report to identify some evidence of restricted blood flow, low oxygen, or seizures.[1]

These medical findings caused an automatic internal referral to the hospital's child protection team. Any unexplained intracranial bleeding in an infant was viewed with high suspicion for shaken baby syndrome. The child abuse pediatrician began questioning Teresa, asking her to account for whether she had "done anything" to cause her son's bleeding. Like Lynn and other parents who suddenly find themselves questioned by doctors after they bring their children for medical care, Teresa was shocked by the suggestion that she might be at fault and by the new tone of the questions. Teresa believed that Yohan had medical issues that had not yet been diagnosed properly. She asked for a second opinion.

Even though the child abuse pediatrician saw nothing but appropriate interaction between Teresa and Yohan, hospital staff called the CPS hotline. Soon, just as in Ben and Lynn's case, the doctors from whom the parents had sought treatment became the parents' chief accusers.

Yohan continued to show signs of seizure activity, and he was given a sedative. The day after his hospital admission and after the CPS hotline was called, a physical exam of Yohan found that he had normal mobility. Yohan's initial workup listed numerous possible causes for Yohan's bleeding: infection, inflicted trauma, coagulopathy (a bleeding disorder affecting blood clotting), metabolic disorder, or birth trauma, which could still be present three to five weeks after birth. Ophthalmology exams on June 7 and 14 found numerous scattered retinal hemorrhages, first reported by a medical resident as more numerous on the right than the left and then reported by the attending ophthalmologist as more numerous on the left than the right. Which side had more hemorrhages was never cleared up.

A skeletal survey showed some anomalies on Yohan's left lower knee, which were read as a possible fracture. Rib fractures were also suspected but later were ruled out definitively. Doctors reported a concern that Yohan might have a "corner" fracture of his knee—a type of fracture considered by child abuse doctors to be of heightened concern for abuse. The claim about a knee fracture made no sense to Teresa or K.S., however, given that they frequently moved Yohan's knee during diaper changes and he never reacted with any suggestion of pain. Furthermore, no pain or tenderness on either knee had been found at the initial physical exam upon Yohan's admission to the hospital.

Unlike Robert who never got a cast at the hospital though he definitely *did* have a fracture, Yohan soon was given a cast even though it was unclear if he actually had fracture. What was clear was that Yohan kicked his cast off shortly after it was put on, for the cast never immobilized his leg as it was intended to do.

By June 9, Yohan's sedative was removed, and he was smiling and cooing. But two new hematomas, in the subarachnoid area, were discovered, and there were signs of restricted blood flow and reduced oxygen going to his brain.

The State's CPS investigation had begun in earnest on June 8. Just as Ben and Lynn had been unable to explain Robert's fracture, so, too, Teresa and K.S. could not explain the bleeding reported in Yohan's head and within the layers of his retinas. They always suspected that this bleeding was due to the same disorder that was causing the seizures. There were no falls, shakes, or other incidents that could have caused the bleeding.

The CPS team put a safety plan in place, requiring relatives to supervise all of the parents' interactions with Yohan and Marika. This plan remained in place until July 25, making it twice as long as the safety plan for Robert and the twins. And as soon as the child abuse pediatrician finished her MPEEC report, the State filed petitions in the juvenile court, naming Teresa and K.S. as responsible for abuse and neglect of their children. The State sought temporary custody, which would give the State the authority to make the children's placement with relatives or a traditional nonrelative foster care placement. Unlike Judge Sanders, however, the juvenile court judge did not rule for the parents in a preliminary temporary custody hearing. Instead, as usually occurs, temporary legal custody was given to the CPS Guardianship Administrator at the first court date. The CPS Guardianship Administrator and the CPS caseworkers continued the children's placement, fortunately, with Teresa's relatives. Robert's grandparents had come from another state, but Yohan's grandparents came from another continent to care for the children, with no assurances as to when they might be able to return home.

Eventually, the family secured three medical expert opinions, starting with a pediatric orthopedist who reviewed the June 2011 X-rays and reported that he saw only an anomaly, not a fracture. He also saw significant signs of rickets, which was consistent with the fact that Teresa herself had insufficient vitamin D.

In October, an MRI clearly showed enlarged spaces in Yohan's cranium that were characteristic of benign external hydrocephalus (BEH), the same condition that Mary Broderick's son, Ryan, had. Dr. Patrick Barnes, a prominent neuroradiologist at Stanford Medical School, a founder of its child abuse team, and an expert on mimics of child abuse, soon reviewed Yohan's head and leg images and provided an expert medical opinion that Yohan's bleeding was due to BEH. He suggested that the possible medical condition of venous thrombosis might have been responsible for Yohan's hematomas. He, too, did not see a fracture on Yohan's knee but did see skeletal signs of rickets.

A month later, Dr. David Frim, one of Chicago's most highly respected pediatric neurosurgeons, reviewed Yohan's brain scans. He, too, determined that Yohan had BEH, a possible hemorrhage at birth that added to his risk of later bleeding, and connected these conditions to the bleeding surrounding Yohan's brain and the retinal bleeding. Dr. Frim examined Yohan himself in February, finding his growth normal. Indeed, Dr. Frim found that Yohan was developmentally advanced.

Because temporary custody had been given to the CPS agency, the case proceeded to a full trial on the issues of whether Yohan had been abused. The State would have to prove this case by the preponderance of the evidence; in other words, it would have to show that abuse was the likely explanation for the injuries it claimed Yohan had sustained.

The trial didn't commence until May 2012, almost a full year after the hotline call that started the investigation. By the time the trial started, Yohan had lived with relatives for ten months.

Just as in Ben and Lynn's case, a child abuse pediatrician, Dr. Kristin Fortin, had prepared an MPEEC report under the subcontract her hospital held with the State of Illinois Child Advocacy Center. She became the chief proponent of the opinion that Yohan had been abused, asserting that she had ruled out medical conditions as causes of Yohan's injuries. She believed that Yohan had intracranial hematomas, retinal hemorrhages, and a knee fracture, as shown by the periosteal reaction (the cloudy markings indicating healing bone) that appeared on the X-rays taken on June 23. These healing signs had not been visible two weeks earlier when Yohan had come into the hospital. The retinal hemorrhages, in her opinion, were due to "acceleration and deceleration forces"—a fancy medicalized, quasi-scientific way to describe shaking. Yohan, in other words, was the victim of shaken baby syndrome (SBS), the notorious syndrome renamed abusive head trauma (AHT) by the American Academy of Pediatrics.

Both labels, SBS and AHT, spell trouble for wrongly accused parents. The SBS terminology has been superseded for good reason, but its replacement raises numerous concerns of its own. The SBS diagnosis relied on a triad of symptoms—subdural bleeding, retinal bleeding, and signs of increased intracranial pressure or brain swelling[2]—as hallmarks of the disorder. The belief by SBS proponents, including many of the child abuse pediatricians who were seeking board certification for their specialty, was that these hallmarks could only be caused by shaking. But science had shown that this diagnostic triad could be present even when shaking plainly had not occurred.

Child-care givers accused of SBS in celebrated homicide cases were exonerated relying on evidence that the foundation of the diagnosis was unreliable.[3] So child abuse experts started to retreat from the SBS label, although it remains in use by many doctors, lawyers, and CPS casework-ers. In place of the SBS diagnosis, the American Academy of Pediatrics adopted the abusive head trauma (AHT) diagnosis in recognition that the presence of the triad of symptoms did not make for a hard and fast diagnosis.

If anything, the more relaxed AHT label is harder to defend against than SBS. It is easier to label a child the victim of AHT based on a single one of the hallmark conditions in the SBS triad, all without solid evidence showing any abusive treatment of the child. Injuries due to direct impact on the head are now included in AHT, so identifying the specific type of force believed to have caused the children's injury—whether from blunt force or shaking—is no longer required to render a diagnosis of AHT.

Moreover, no other medical diagnosis carries in its name a legal, rather than a medical, conclusion. The word "abuse" in "abusive head trauma" refers to a legal conclusion and not a particular medical condition. The ways of ruling out the alternative diagnoses to AHT are unclear, too, as

Yohan's case would demonstrate. When she diagnosed AHT in Yohan, Dr. Fortin did not clarify which alternative medical conditions she had considered and ruled out.

Neither Melissa nor I had time available to commit to defending the K. family in the juvenile court. We knew from the start that the case would be very demanding, requiring hundreds of hours of time and a longer-term time commitment than we could make, given our other pending cases. Head injury cases inevitably involve several complex areas of medicine. So the family hired Ellen Domph, who quickly became one of our closest colleagues in medically complex cases. Ellen in turn asked us to help the family if the case went up on appeal. Melissa and I agreed to consider it later on, if an appeal became necessary.

The trial commenced in May 2012, 11 months after the CPS hotline call, and continued on various court dates through August. The State called eight doctors to testify, but Ellen Domph, as the parents' defense counsel, was able to secure important concessions from each of them. The ophthalmologist who had examined Yohan conceded that many infants are born with retinal hemorrhages and acknowledged that he didn't know how long retinal hemorrhages would last after birth. These concessions negated the strength of a conclusion that the parents had abusively caused the retinal bleeding.

The neurologist called by the State noted that 25 percent of infants who have precipitous deliveries, as had Yohan, show signs of subdural bleeding at birth and that signs of this birth trauma, including retinal hemorrhages, could continue until an infant was five weeks old. A hematologist testified that Yohan did not have any bleeding disorders that would impede clotting, although testing for clotting disorders that cause excessive clotting (i.e., thrombophilia) had not been done.

None of the hospital's experts considered Yohan's BEH condition to be a significant factor in predisposing Yohan to hematomas. Only one of the State's experts denied that Yohan had BEH, but she used a nonstandard measurement system to reach that conclusion.

The State's orthopedist had diagnosed Yohan with a corner fracture on his left knee, but he admitted on cross-examination that the report of hematomas inside Yohan's cranium influenced his opinion that Yohan's knee had been fractured. He admitted that periosteal reaction seen on the X-rays two weeks after the child came into the hospital did not definitively establish a fracture; rapidly growing infants' bones can show that same reaction. He also acknowledged that fractures ordinarily cause pain, and Yohan exhibited no sign of pain in his leg. He had no opinion as to whether Yohan had rickets.

A radiologist testified for the State that Yohan had no signs of rickets, but she admitted that she had no experience with either congenital rickets or rickets in infants under six months of age. While she believed that Yohan's X-rays were "suspicious" for a fracture, she admitted other causes that could account for the abnormality seen on his leg X-rays.

While the State had called eight doctors, all of whom worked for Yohan's treating hospital, to testify against Teresa and K.S., the parents called three doctors to respond. Sometimes the sheer numbers of witnesses on one side matters, but in Yohan's case, the doctors' credentials and experience turned out to matter more. It was fortunate for Yohan's family that they had been able to secure these doctors' testimony.

Many parents facing charges of abuse would not be so fortunate, although they may be no less innocent. Though the parents were under no obligation to prove Yohan had a medical condition that accounted for his injuries, their expert doctors provided extensive medical opinion testimony, giving alternative accounts of how Yohan came to have the conditions seen on the CTs, MRIs, X-rays, and eye exams. Dr. Frim, whom the appellate court later noted was recognized as a "pre-eminent neurosurgeon" in Chicago and nationally, testified that Yohan was born with BEH. Yohan had both old and newer bleeds, which Dr. Frim believed were due to his seizures. Birth trauma as well as minor impacts after birth could cause the bleeding he saw. The BEH diagnosis made nonaccidental trauma—abuse—less likely than accidental or medical causes. The absence of any marks on Yohan's body, such as bruises or scratches, supported the conclusion that he had not been abused.

Like Dr. Frim, pediatric radiology and neuroradiology expert Dr. Patrick Barnes had extensive clinical and academic experience with BEH, which predisposed infants to hematomas in the membranes surrounding their brains. Based on his review of all of the radiological images for Yohan, he concluded that BEH had been the likely cause of Yohan's bleeding, not abuse. He saw signs of possible clotting, too, that was possibly indicative of cortical venous thrombosis, a condition that Yohan had not been tested for, despite an initial recommendation for a specialized scan to visualize better Yohan's cortical veins. Moreover, Dr. Barnes saw no fracture but, rather, signs of rickets on Yohan's leg. Some features of Yohan's skull and ribs supported the rickets diagnosis, he noted. Congenital rickets, which he believed Yohan had, is one of the mimics of abusive fractures that Dr. Barnes had researched and written about.

The pediatric orthopedist was the parents' last witness. His opinion was that Yohan never had a fracture. The first X-ray, which had been used to give Yohan his cast, showed only an irregularity that would have been more extensive if a fracture had been present. He noted the absence of any clinical evidence of a fracture, including a lack of tenderness in the area where the fracture is believed to be present. The X-rays of Yohan's leg on June 23 also showed classic signs of rickets and no actual periosteal reaction at all.

Judges are laypeople when it comes to medicine. Given all the conflicting evidence as to what doctors thought caused Yohan's bleeding and the conflicting opinions as to whether Yohan ever had a fracture on his leg, the juvenile court judge, in his ruling on August 1, 2012, acknowledged it was very difficult to decide whether Yohan was abused.

But he decided that Yohan had been abused, even though in the same breath, he found that the parents were "loving and responsible." Relying on the opinions of the child abuse pediatrician and State's orthopedist and radiologist over the opinions of the parents' doctors, he concluded that Yohan's leg had a fracture and that Yohan didn't have rickets. Since the parents had offered no explanation for Yohan's supposed fracture (other than claiming that it didn't exist or that the signs seen on the X-rays might be rickets), the judge found the fracture to be due to abuse.

The judge also believed Yohan had no bleeding disorder, based on the State's hematology expert's testimony. Then, in what proved to be a significant error in the eyes of the appellate court, he discounted Dr. Frim's opinion about BEH as a causal link to the bleeding in Yohan's cranium because Dr. Frim had not considered the presence of a leg fracture to be important to his BEH diagnosis.

The juvenile court judge concluded that the presence of injury elsewhere (the leg) was "highly relevant to the constellation of findings" that provided sufficient evidence, taken together, to establish that Yohan was abused. Three possible rare events could be indicated in Yohan's case: birth trauma and BEH could have caused Yohan's intracranial bleeding; benign bleeding could have caused retinal hemorrhaging; and the periosteal reaction on Yohan's leg might not be indicative of a fracture. The judge stated that while he believed that each of these events could have occurred, he thought it was unreasonable to conclude that *all* of these things occurred at once in Yohan's case.

On that basis, the juvenile court judge found that Yohan had been the victim of nonaccidental trauma—child abuse. The judge made findings that Yohan's sister, Marika, was also at risk of abuse. The judge could not name a perpetrator, though, even though the guardian ad litem pressed him to do so.

Two months later, the judge determined that the parents were fit, willing, and able to care for their children. The judge ordered the two children returned home to the custody of their parents. He had found the parents loving and caring. Yohan was then 17 months old and had lived 16 of those 17 months with relatives who were not his parents.

Melissa monitored the case as it proceeded through the trial and attended several of the trial days. Since the family's lawyer, Ellen Domph, was a trial lawyer first and foremost, Ellen had made it clear that she hoped Melissa and I could handle the case if it went up on appeal. Taking an appeal from the abuse finding against them would have been very expensive. More importantly, however, it could have put the stability of the judge's order returning the children home at risk. So the family let their appeal deadline run out, even though it meant that the terrible abuse finding would go unchallenged.

The family's saga, with its bittersweet ending of an abuse finding coupled with the return of the children, would have been over but for a fateful decision by the children's court-appointed guardian ad litem. The decision to appeal the juvenile court's orders was not just the parents' decision to make. As the lawyer for Yohan and Marika, the guardian ad litem didn't accept the juvenile court judge's decision to return the children to their parents. The guardian ad litem decided to appeal that final decision in the parents' favor. The guardian ad litem's chief contention was that the children should not have been returned because the parents never admitted that Yohan had been abused.

It now became essential to mount a defense of the family. Melissa and I quickly took the case on, and we filed a cross appeal on behalf of Teresa and K.S., which allowed the parents to challenge the finding that Yohan had been abused. While the family would have lived with the abuse finding as the price of keeping their kids home, accepting that trade-off was no longer an option. With the parents' right to keep the kids now under assault by the children's own legal representative, we needed to make the strongest arguments, both defensively and offensively, in an effort to keep the kids. The strongest argument was that the abuse finding was wrong.

I didn't expect to win the *In re Yohan K.* appeal. In fact, I repeatedly cautioned Melissa, who took on the laboring oar in the main argument against the abuse finding in our eventual 80-page brief, that she should not expect more than a summary decision to uphold the juvenile court judge's decision. After all, that's how most appeals end up, for appellate courts don't like to second-guess trial court decisions involving child protection questions. The legal principle of deference to the judge who heard the witnesses firsthand has particular force when claims of child abuse were involved.

In the *Yohan K.* case, the juvenile court judge's rationale for finding Yohan had been abused was terribly flawed. But there were many doctors testifying for the State and just three experts who had testified in the defense, so an opinion that recounted the reasonableness of relying on the State's doctors seemed likely. At the same time and partly for the same reason of deference to the trial judge, I didn't think the appellate court was likely to disrupt the return of the children either, because the service providers and caseworkers had been very strongly supportive of the parents. The guardian ad litem was overreaching, I thought, in trying to get the appellate court to disrupt the family for a second time. The State's Attorney's belated decision to join the appeal against the parents didn't change my prediction.

Melissa worked furiously on the brief, mastering the record and digging deeply into the eight different specialty areas of medicine that had been represented in the testimony of the 11 doctors. I wrote the section addressing why the parents were entitled to have the children returned home without being forced first to admit abuse. That argument was strengthened by the reality that the parents were now challenging the abuse findings. Why should parents have to admit abuse if they still had the legal right to appeal the abuse finding?

The work on the appeal was intense. The schedule for briefing had been expedited, and our request for a few extra weeks' time was denied. Cases involving child custody rightly have short briefing schedules and get few extensions of time on appeal. But the record in the *Yohan K.* case was so challenging and the medicine involved so dense and new to us that condensing it into a strong appellate brief presented an enormous challenge. Few lawyers could do half the job that Melissa did on that brief.

Fortunately, Ellen Domph had laid out the evidence in the record masterfully, which helped make the complex puzzle pieces fit logically and forcefully together. Appellate lawyers routinely complain about defects in trial records that they have to work with, which simple objections by the trial lawyer might have cured. Melissa, by contrast, marveled at how Ellen had anticipated every significant issue and carefully laid out the evidence the parents' case demanded.

At the end, we took to calling Melissa "Dr. Staas" in the office, for she had truly synthesized many complex areas of dense medical testimony clearly and concisely. Soon, her help was sought out by attorneys across the country, after the *Yohan K.* appellate decision created an unexpected landmark decision in favor of families.

Lawyers often cannot predict which cases will make a difference to the state of the law. Even though I thought our case for reversal was very strong, I had been burned enough times that I didn't take a win for granted. Especially after my *Dupuy II* experience of having the factual record ignored in favor of arguments that hadn't even been pressed by the opposing side, I had learned to view appellate litigation as highly unpredictable. I didn't want Melissa to feel crushed by a decision that simply rubber-stamped the trial court's ruling. In my book, that would count as a win, since it would mean the children would stay home with their parents.

The Illinois Appellate Court surprised me. Its decision was issued without any argument and with no fanfare. But it proved to be landmark. Instead of summarily affirming the juvenile court's decision, it paid close attention to the defects in the State's experts' opinions due to their failure to consider possible medical explanations for Yohan's symptoms. It also highlighted the strength of the opinions and the credentials of the three experts for the parents. Many appellate court opinions let critical inconsistencies go. Unfortunately, judges in many appellate cases overlook violations of the basic rights of parents in the juvenile court, and lawyers before the appellate court don't always develop the arguments that the cases could present.

Justice Michael Hyman's opinion in the *In re Yohan K.* case is exceptional in its close and careful analysis of the trial court record and its insistence on holding the State responsible for meeting its burden of proof. First, the opinion faults the juvenile court for failing to resolve inconsistencies by deciding which medical expert's opinion was most reliable. The unanimous appellate court's opinion he authored on behalf of the three-judge panel declares that the juvenile court may not use a "constellation" of injuries to prove abuse, absent evidence that any single one of the injuries was due to abuse. Using the sheer number of injuries to reach an abuse conclusion amounted to relieving the State of its burden to prove the abuse case against the parents.

Justice Hyman's opinion also faults the juvenile court judge for failing to credit critical facts in the parents' favor, including the seizure symptoms Yohan had exhibited since birth; the location of the bleeding at the back of the head, which was not common for abuse; and the parents' loving attentiveness to the child, which made it impossible for the judge to name a perpetrator even though the parents were Yohan's sole caregivers.

Comparing the medical backgrounds of the experts who weighed in on the question of Yohan's fracture showed that the parents' experts had vastly more relevant experience. More significantly, the fracture diagnosis was inconsistent with the observations that Yohan had exhibited no pain when his leg was manipulated by hospital personnel. The State's claims about the timing of the fracture were also dubious, since the State's orthopedist had said that Yohan's fracture must have happened on the same day Yohan was seen at his pediatrician's office and was admitted to the hospital.

Either the State's orthopedist was wrong in how he dated the fracture, making his opinion unreliable, or the fracture happened while Yohan was under medical care, making abuse an invalid conclusion. Alternatively, Yohan never had a fracture. In short, there was insufficient evidence of a fracture to make that the crux of the constellation of injuries theory that the State had pressed and the juvenile court judge had endorsed.

Furthermore, there was extensive evidence of rickets that the juvenile court judge failed to credit. The appellate court noted that the many claims that Yohan had normal readings on all his lab tests had been based on tests that were never comprehensive enough to rule out rickets. No doctor at Yohan's treating hospital even considered rickets a possibility, so Yohan had not been thoroughly tested for it, even though his mother had insufficient vitamin D levels and could have passed congenital rickets to Yohan in utero.

The juvenile court judge failed to give sufficient credit, too, to the parents' experts' diagnosis of BEH. Where the juvenile court had faltered, Justice Hyman's opinion declared, was in failing to address whether or not

Yohan had BEH and then failing to consider the condition in assessing its impact on Yohan's bleeding. The appellate court found strong evidence that Yohan had BEH and that it played a causal role in the bleeding. Discounting Dr. Frim's expert opinion about BEH and Yohan's head injuries simply because Dr. Frim had not considered Yohan's leg fracture was "improper."

The appellate court's decision is not an easy read; it is crammed with medical facts and analysis. Still, at its core is a ringing endorsement of a simple proposition: the State must prove cases of abuse. The State bears the burden of proof, and that burden cannot be shifted to the defense by means of unscientific assumptions. The juvenile court judge had allowed the State to evade its duty to prove abuse by relying on a "constellation of injuries" theory even though not one of Yohan's injuries was shown to be caused by abuse. There were well-reasoned explanations for each of Yohan's injuries, even though the underlying medical conditions were rare.

The opinion was, in essence, ratification of a simple point that is basic to our system of justice: parents are entitled to a presumption of innocence. It is not the parents' job to prove they are innocent; the State must prove them guilty. Yohan and his family had to pay a terrible price to get to this simple conclusion. They had also needed a stroke of luck in getting the appellate court to pay close attention to the gaps in the State's evidence, aided by some of the best lawyering I have ever seen, by my friends and colleagues Melissa Staas and Ellen Domph.

After ruling that the State had not proved Yohan was abused, the Appellate Court quickly disposed of the guardian ad litem's argument that the parents should have been required to admit abuse in order to have their children returned to them. The guardian ad litem had insisted that the parents' failure to acknowledge abuse meant that they would fail to protect Yohan in the future. While the parents had been receiving therapy services during the pending juvenile court case, the guardian ad litem contended that these therapy services were not "meaningful" and did not suffice to support the juvenile court's decision to return the children home because the parents had never accepted the juvenile court judge's abuse findings. The appellate court soundly disagreed with the guardian ad litem's contention that the parents were unable to protect their children unless they admitted abuse had occurred, finding that the parents had every right to continue to protest their innocence, especially where their innocence is supported by the evidence.

The appellate court's ruling came down on June 13, 2013—two years after Yohan's hospitalization for his seizure. It was a long time to have family life held in abeyance while complex medical evidence was reviewed by a slew of lawyers. It would have been better for everyone if the child abuse pediatricians had considered alternative explanations for Yohan's symptoms and ordered the right diagnostic tests from the start. It would also have been better, by far, if the many doctors treating Yohan and the CPS system had taken the medical disorders Yohan presented to them more seriously before rushing to accuse the parents of abuse.

As I review *In re Yohan K.* in light of Robert's family's experience, what emerges is how facile the State can be in its assumptions about a child's pain in the face of an injury. In the two cases, the State treated the child's pain responses as a variable that could be manipulated with dramatically inconsistent effect, depending on the specific opinion that the doctor or advocate chose to advance. In Robert's case, the assumption was pressed by the child abuse theorists that Robert would have experienced pain so intense that he would have cried inconsolably. Indeed, this claim became the linchpin of the prosecution's abuse theory. But for Yohan, the absence of any notable pain in his allegedly fractured leg made no difference whatsoever to the child abuse pediatrician and other doctors who opined that Yohan *did* have a fracture. An entire house of cards of a constellation of injuries had been fabricated without any evidence of pain at all.

Melissa and I, along with many family defender colleagues, cheered when we read the *In re Yohan K.* opinion. The decision was also hailed by criminal defense lawyers and members of the SBS innocence network, a growing network of lawyers and advocates who were working to exonerate parents and other caregivers accused of SBS or AHT.[4] After all, if parents can win exoneration from claims that they must have shaken their child under the relatively low "preponderance of the evidence" burden of proof applicable to juvenile court cases, then the implications for overturning criminal convictions, where evidence is needed "beyond a reasonable doubt," were significant.

Celebration did not extend, however, to the Office of the Cook County State's Attorney. The chief of the office's juvenile division, in particular, did not appreciate the *In re Yohan K.* decision. The decision made her increase the burden on her staff to prove their cases involving multiple injuries. Furthermore, the *In re Yohan K.* opinion was getting cited by other jurisdictions. It could hurt the prosecutors' ability to secure criminal convictions, too.

The Cook County State's Attorney's office has significant power and influence. When the State's Attorney's office doesn't like a court decision, it can draft legislation to overturn that decision by rewriting the law so as to make clear that a particular court decision should no longer apply to future cases. So in the 2013–2014 Illinois legislative session, the Cook County State's Attorney's office drafted a bill stating explicitly that child abuse could be proved by showing that a "constellation of injuries" was present. This was as bald an attempt to override a judicial victory of mine as I had seen. The State's Attorney clearly wanted to be able to continue to base its prosecutions on equating more than one unexplained injury with abuse. For our part as family advocates, the prospect of enshrining the elimination of the State's burden of proof into state law was a grave concern.

Our resources to try to defeat legislative proposals were quite limited; we didn't have a full-time lobbyist or well-established relationships with more than a handful of legislators. But we quickly discovered one resource that the State didn't have: Mary Broderick. The State's Attorney's chosen sponsor for its "constellation of injuries equals abuse" legislation turned out to be Mary's local state representative. It is a general rule of politics that representatives listen to their constituents, and Mary was a natural at making the case against a law that would hurt families just like hers.

As soon as Mary met with her legislator and as soon as we explained the legal background of the *In re Yohan K.* case that had invalidated the constellation theory, the sponsor realized that the proposed legislation was not sound. In fact, the State's Attorney's office hadn't explained—or mentioned—the *In re Yohan K.* decision to him when it asked him to sponsor the bill, so he hadn't realized that his proposed bill would overturn a well-reasoned appellate decision. The sponsor didn't call his legislation for a vote. And after meeting with Mary Broderick, he offered to sponsor future legislation on behalf of families to prevent wrongful accusations.

I always had known that Mary Broderick was a force to be reckoned with. I was very grateful that she continued, more than 10 years after the allegations against her were resolved, to fight for justice for other families.

By 2014, the family defense network had grown. Together, we successfully had defended children's rights to be raised by the parents, by defending their families. That defense had worked in the appellate court and in the legislature.

SIXTEEN

We Believe the Children, Except When They Say the Baby *Wasn't* Abused

The ink had barely dried on the *Yohan K.* opinion when another set of parents called seeking help in defending themselves from the terrible allegation that they had shaken their six-month-old daughter, April.

On Saturday morning, August 10, 2013, Tony L. and Tiffany W. had been clearing out of a hotel where they had stayed while Tiffany's home was being fumigated. Tiffany's daughter Veronica, about to turn seven, was having a birthday party, and the family was busily getting ready to make it to the party on time. Tony jumped into the shower, and Tiffany asked Veronica to mind April while she took luggage to the car. April was propped up on the couch with a bottle.

No one but Veronica was in the living area of the hotel room, so when she turned away from April to grab lotion, no one saw April fall. Veronica heard a thump when April tumbled off the couch. Within a few seconds, Tony heard April's loud cries, and he peeked out from his shower. He saw April propped up in Veronica's arms, crying. Tony became alarmed and insistently demanded to know what happened. "She fell," was all Veronica could say. Tony quickly put his pants on and stepped into the living area.

Within two minutes, April's seizures started. Then her breathing stopped. At that moment, Tiffany came back to the room. Tiffany managed to call 911 and began to cry hysterically herself, panicking.

Fortunately, Tony knew CPR. That knowledge might have saved April's life, which suddenly hung in the balance. Tony prayed as he inflated April's lungs over and over, while the couple waited for help.

Fortunately, April began to breathe again just as paramedics arrived.

April was hardly out of the woods. Brought to the nearest emergency room, April soon needed an emergency craniotomy to relieve the pressure from a left-side subdural hematoma. April had retinal hematomas, reported by the ophthalmologist as secondary to the subdural bleeds. And as she was recovering from the surgery, she had to be put into a medically induced coma. Doctors warned Tony and Tiffany that their daughter might not survive. If she did make it, she might have brain damage. Nothing in his life had prepared Tony for this life-and-death emergency for his beloved daughter, although his own childhood had been filled with hardships.

Tony was the oldest of five boys, with an Irish Italian mother and an African American father, who lost all contact with Tony after he was three years old. CPS caseworkers first investigated Tony's home when he was six years old. He had been left alone to watch his younger brothers. When he was 13, Tony went into foster care himself, due to his own mother's by then losing battle with substance abuse. Tony frequently had been hungry and homeless as a child.

Through faith and hard work, Tony became an A student in school and attended college on a CPS-backed scholarship. Several of his brothers were less driven to succeed; they became involved with gangs, and one was shot and killed in 2002. But Tony stuck to the straight and narrow path, never touching drugs or alcohol. He put his energies into education, church, and community.

Tony's father died when he was 16, but he now enjoys a close relationship with his mother, empathizing with the struggles she faced while he was growing up. By the time Tony was a father himself, he had become an extraordinary role model, a mentor for youth in the foster care system. He founded and led a youth service organization to carry out his mission of helping foster youth succeed in life. Because of his professional work and his charisma, he had forged close professional relationships with the state CPS agency director and many community leaders.

The umbrella agency that housed Tony's organization was also Tiffany's employer for 15 years; she had started working there right out of high school as she pursued her bachelor's degree in business. In her position, she facilitated youth workshops for CPS-involved youth. She, too, had a strong faith, deep connections in the community, and many friends.

Tiffany's family was middle-class African American and very close-knit. Like Tony, Tiffany had not known her father. She had been raised by her mother and her aunt, with two siblings.

Tiffany loved being a mother, even though her pregnancy with Veronica was unexpected. Veronica was a bright and happy child, with a strong mind of her own. Tiffany worked hard to instill values of honesty, tolerance, and self control in her daughter. Still, there was plenty of time to play. Tiffany's best memory was taking Veronica on a special one-on-one trip to Disneyland for her fifth birthday.

Tony bears a resemblance to Dwayne Johnson ("the Rock"), and Tiffany is a classic beauty, looking like a contemporary Lena Horne. Together, they made a strikingly handsome couple, and their relationship had been on and off again over the two years prior to April's birth. Still, from the time of April's birth on, they made a very effective and consistent co-parenting team. When April was born, they used to joke together that "this baby is perfect." Both were calm and measured in their demeanor, exuding a sense of patience and strong character.

As well-grounded professionals who worked with youth involved in the child welfare and juvenile justice systems and as devoted parents, the last thing either Tony or Tiffany expected was to find themselves on the wrong side of an abuse allegation.

Being April's dad was Tony's greatest joy. He loved all his time with his daughter. Not knowing his own father, Tony vowed he would be a strong presence in his child's life. He never tired of caring for April. He especially loved to tickle her feet or hold her up, having her kick her legs and pretend to dance to music from his iPad. That's what he remembered doing the evening before the terrible fall changed his family life and shook him to the core.

Veronica loved being a big sister and helping with April's daily care. Earlier Tiffany had been concerned that Veronica might be jealous of April and had proactively enrolled her in therapy three months before April's fall. Tiffany was masterful at managing the children's schedules and daily routines calmly and in a seemingly unflappable manner. Tiffany doted on her children and was proud of how both of them were ahead of schedule on their developmental milestones. Teachers had remarked on how bright Veronica was, but as the case involving April's injury dragged on, it took a special toll on Veronica.

Eventually, Veronica's intelligence, stubbornness, and candor would become factors to be reckoned with for both the prosecution and the defense.

At the hospital, as April struggled to regain consciousness, law enforcement and CPS caseworkers began to work against Tony and Tiffany. Apparently, hospital staff called the CPS hotline on August 10. Hospital notes state "injury not consistent with fall from couch," although it's unclear who first sowed the doubts about Veronica's clear report of April's fall.

As soon as the hotline was called, a mandate worker insisted that Veronica had to stay with relatives, not with Tiffany's friend who had been designated to help care for Veronica while Tiffany was at the hospital. Tiffany was in no position to object at that point, and her family members were more than willing to support her while she attended to April. But while Tiffany and Tony tried to find out as much as they could about April's care, hospital staff gave them little information while their daughter was undergoing emergency surgery.

The mandate worker also interviewed Veronica at her aunt's home, where she started to reside under the safety plan. Veronica recounted how her sister fell from the couch and how her mother had gone to put luggage in the car. Veronica was checked for marks and bruises herself; there were none.

Both Tony and Tiffany were arrested on August 13, 2013. They were held overnight and questioned for many hours.

On August 14, 2013, while both Tony and Tiffany were still in police custody, Veronica was interviewed at a child advocacy center. She stood her ground. After the interview, the police officer labeled Veronica "very well coached." It was an unfair suspicion that would haunt the case. If only Veronica had been believed, not second-guessed for giving an account that supported Tony and Tiffany's innocence, the case might have gone differently from the start. The possibility that Veronica was reporting the truth about April's fall ran counter to his conclusions about the case just four days into it.

During the time that Tony was being held for questioning in jail, detectives falsely reported to Tony that April had died. Left alone to process this shattering news, Tony prayed for the strength to keep going. The police told Tony they suspected Tiffany of abuse, focusing on her because reportedly she didn't cry during her interrogation. Despite police attempts to get Tony to turn against Tiffany, Tony did not budge from his account of what had happened.[1]

The investigation file notes that the police released Tony and Tiffany after a lawyer called the station on their behalves. They were not charged with any crime (and fortunately never were charged as the case unfolded).

Only after hours of believing the worst, Tony learned that April had *not* died but that April was still at the hospital under intensive care.

By the time they were released from jail, the regular assigned CPS caseworker Donna Boyle had taken over all instructions as to the contact Tony and Tiffany could have with April. Tony and Tiffany remained at the hospital while awaiting the outcome of April's major brain surgery, and they continued patiently to wait for several days to be allowed to see their daughter.

Boyle continued the demand that Tiffany had to live separately from Veronica even though there was no court order that stopped Tiffany from caring for Veronica in her own home. The safety plan demand wasn't a choice. Tiffany and Tony begged Boyle to allow them to see their daughter, but she refused to allow it. Boyle started to tell witnesses and family members that April likely had been shaken. As the case progressed, Boyle's statements became more conclusory, with shaking reported as the "only possible explanation," according to some of her case notes.

Caseworker Boyle questioned Veronica again on August 19. Veronica repeated that she had never seen her mother hurt her sister. But according to Boyle's notes and her testimony later, Veronica stopped herself after telling Boyle that she sometimes got spanked for misbehaving, saying, "Wait, are you CPS? I shouldn't have told you that. My momma said I couldn't or you will take me away from her." Veronica's candid statement would prove to be both a blessing and curse as the case progressed.

On August 31, 2013, April had stabilized enough to move to a rehabilitation facility. Though her vision clearly had been affected by the fall, Tony and Tiffany began to hope that she would recover her eyesight and mobility over time. Fortunately, those prayers gradually were answered.

On September 6, 2013, Tony told Boyle that he was about to lose his job in the foster youth support organization he had founded and led. He begged her to call his employer to stop the decision against him. She refused, stating her investigation was "still open." Tiffany was much luckier; she was able to maintain her administrative position, due to her agency director's confidence in her, even though she, like Tony, worked in a youth-serving agency. Tiffany was moved out of child contact work but kept her job.

Slowly, April started to recover. But the family's battle to regain custody of the children had just begun.

Boyle waited for weeks to bring the case against Tony and Tiffany into court. Boyle finally took protective custody of the children on September 27,

2013. Before that, the hospital staff called Boyle several times, checking on the parents' custodial rights and the person to bill for insurance. Though no custody orders limited the parents' rights or directed that Tiffany couldn't live with Veronica, the whole system acted as if the parents had been found guilty of abuse already. Protective custody was timed around when April was ready for discharge. Though CPS had plenty of time to get court orders if they had been following the constitutional requirements laid down in the *Hernandez* case, no one instructed Boyle to seek the filing of a petition before the discharge date.

In support of filing the abuse petition on October 1, 2013, the State's Attorney of Cook County relied on an August 12, 2013, affidavit from the child abuse pediatrician at the hospital that treated April. It recites that she was consulted on August 11, 2013, and she concluded that "violent forces" had been applied to April's head. The State's companion petition as to Veronica asserted that she was at risk of abuse, too.

The doctor's affidavit was baffling. Everything about the story of April's fall held up. Veronica consistently said that her sister fell, telling the same thing to police, CPS, relatives, and her own therapist. No one denied that Tony had been in the shower. Video footage of the hotel showed the exact time Tiffany left to take out the luggage into the car and the time of her coming back, all within the space of 10 minutes. The abuse claim made little sense.

Did anyone seriously believe that during the few minutes before April was experiencing her seizures, either Tony or Tiffany had violently shaken her and then convinced Veronica, who was present throughout, to lie about it? If the abuser were Tiffany, when in relation to Tony's showering did *she* commit this abuse? If Tony, did he cut his shower short to abuse his daughter, all before Tiffany's return to the room? Did they both simultaneously go on a shaking rampage and cover for each other, all while convincing Veronica to lie?

If so, when exactly had they talked to Veronica about all of this, given they had not been alone with her since April's fall? And what of the fall? The doctor did not deny a fall had occurred, so did the abuse occur right after the fall? It was difficult to picture the scenarios the State and its doctor were claiming as the explanation for April's injuries.

Just as with the families who came before them, Tony and Tiffany's character as people and as parents made no difference to the assumption that one of them must have snapped and violently abused their precious daughter and that the other had covered up for the abusive partner. In any event, the State seemed not to need to provide a cogent account that made sense of the actual facts. It was enough to have an injury and officials like the police officer who jumped to an abuse conclusion based on hunches and assumptions.

The dogma that drove the child abuse pediatrician to conclude that shaking rather than a fall accounted for the injury was enigmatic. It rested on the widespread but plainly false belief that children can't get subdural hematomas, retinal hemorrhages, or elevated intracranial pressure from "short falls"—falls from less than two feet. Dogma holds that when children have these injuries and symptoms, they must have been shaken.

A number of child abuse pediatricians have come to believe and repeat this dogma in their written opinions, depositions, and in-court testimony. By contrast, the academic literature and common experience show plenty of examples of freak accidents that cause injuries as bad or worse than April's. A host of factors—not just distance but also speed, angle, and hardness of the floor—affect bleeding in the brain and eyes. One short blow can cause retinal hemorrhages from the impact itself or from the rise in intracranial pressure due to the fall. Children can die from very short falls.[2] Fortunately, April wasn't one of those children.

Fresh from our victory in *In re Yohan K.,* Melissa Staas took on Tiffany's representation under my supervision. But as Tony was now unemployed, he had no resources to expend for legal counsel or medical experts. He would need to have court-appointed counsel. Since Tony and Tiffany were not married and it was uncertain how the claims as to custody of April would evolve during the case, Tiffany and Tony needed separate counsel. Moreover, since Tiffany was the mother of Veronica as well as April, Tiffany's lawyer would be the best person able to present Veronica's potentially essential testimony. After reviewing the possible ways to provide representation to both Tiffany and Tony, both parents agreed that Melissa would represent Tiffany. Tony would ask the court to appoint a lawyer for him.

Soon, Melissa was diving into the medical literature on short falls. The court process depends on medical expert testimony, not lawyers who read medical studies and argue about their meaning, so identifying experts became the most important next step. At the same time, Melissa began to prepare to question the child abuse pediatrician and other doctors at depositions in advance of trial. As in the *Yohan K.* case, temporary custody of the children was taken at the outset of the case, and the matter was set over for trial.

Then the unlucky parents faced an unusual setback. After completing a full report explaining that short falls can and do sometimes cause exactly the sort of hemorrhages April experienced and that there was no evidence of inflicted injury, the family's lead medical expert suddenly died of an injury due to a short fall.

Despite the setback, the case proceeded through pretrial preparation. A second medical expert for the parents provided a solid foundation for the conclusion that April's injuries were consistent with the fall Veronica reported. Meanwhile Tony and Tiffany did everything CPS caseworkers asked of them, and then some, gaining kudos from the family therapists and April's care providers. Glowing psychological assessments of both parents, filed with the court in August 2015, detailed the pride both parents took in their children and described their calm and gentle manner of parenting. As I read both clinical reports, I thought I was dreaming, as every past clinical report that I had ever read had been critical of parents, often nitpicking over minor parenting flaws during an observed visit. But Tony and Tiffany's assessments found no faults in their parenting—none.

As the case continued in a pretrial mode, one CPS error came to the attention of the court. For once, however, the error worked in the family's favor. Without the permission of the court, the CPS caseworker, impressed by both parents' dedication to the children, had allowed them unsupervised visits. But on February 5, 2015, the court ratified the allowance of such contact. The court allowed unsupervised visits to continue during the day, and also explicitly allowed Tiffany to stay with her children overnight as long as she continued to be supervised during the night-time hours if she and the children woke up. This order officially allowing more liberal visits set the stage for a full return home for Veronica on July 2, 2015, prior to the scheduled trial.

As preparation for trial continued, Veronica's status as a witness began to come into focus. Veronica was now eight years old. Veronica still sometimes blamed herself for what happened to April. Though she continued to receive therapy, the trial, no matter what, would be exceedingly stressful for her if she had to testify. Veronica had her own attorney, a guardian ad litem, who was appointed to represent her wishes as well as her "best interests," even if these interests conflicted. Because Veronica consistently reported that her sister had fallen, we were concerned that the guardian ad litem might try to claim that Veronica had been coached, effectively making out her own client as a liar. But we could not direct how Veronica's guardian ad litem handled the case.

All through the 1990s, a common mantra of the child protection system was to "believe the children." That mantra has become less absolute of late, as more child development research has shown that children can be highly susceptible to suggestion, leading to false reports of abuse. Children also can deliberately lie and can be coached to make up allegations against parents, though intentional and successful coaching of children is not particularly easy for a parent to carry off and is quite rare. More subtle suggestions, however, can significantly affect the veracity of children's statements, especially for children younger than Veronica (i.e., typically three-to-five-year-olds).[3]

When she told the CPS worker that she wasn't supposed to tell her about a spanking, Veronica proved herself to be an extremely candid child. While Melissa and I viewed this statement as evidence that Veronica couldn't be coached to lie and had been honest, the State turned it against Tiffany as evidence of her attempt to influence her daughter's reports in order to protect herself. Still, Veronica had consistently told everyone, including her own therapist in private sessions, that her sister had fallen. The State's case for disbelieving Veronica's firsthand account was weak at best, resting on innuendos and intuitions of police officers and CPS caseworkers prone to suspect the worst. The State's police and CPS witnesses' disbelief of Veronica's statements fit with their interests in prosecuting her mother for abuse. Children who report abuse by parents, by contrast, are always to be believed, the inconsistent dogma holds.

Eventually, Tony and Tiffany's solid parenting skills and character won the day, and it was reinforced by Veronica's developmental need to return to her mother's care, which the guardian ad litem appreciated. Advocated by the guardian ad litem and supported by both parents, a staged return of the children ensued. These gradual steps were nominally opposed by the State's attorney, but without a hard fight. Slowly, the children were reintegrated into their parents' now-separate homes, and Tony and Tiffany resumed their collaborative coparenting after they no longer were a couple.

Not willing to concede that the abuse case against Tony and Tiffany was too weak to proceed to trial, however, and with a long trial in the offing, both the guardian ad litem and the State's Attorney agreed to settle the case rather than proceed to trial. The stipulated agreement was entered on November 2, 2015, two years and nearly three months after April's fall off the couch. The juvenile court case was finally dismissed in January 2016, after both parents showed they had fully complied with the settlement agreement.

The agreement and dismissal should have ended the family's long involvement with CPS, but because the parents had been labeled as child abusers in the register, they now needed to clear their names by taking a register appeal. Both Tony and Tiffany were facing abusive head injuries findings in the register for 20 years. Because the juvenile court case had settled without a final decision, Tony and Tiffany could not point to a judgment in their favor that held April wasn't abused. They could not argue, as Lynn had done, that keeping their name in the register violated established basic principles of law. Tony and Tiffany now had to prepare anew for a multi-day-long hearing before the administrative law judge. No longer concerned about a conflict between the parents, however, Melissa agreed to represent both Tiffany and Tony at the register appeal.

For Tony, there was great urgency. Tiffany had been able to maintain employment by being reassigned to administrative duties that did not include direct contact with children, but Tony had effectively given up his exemplary career as a youth services agency leader. He had put his ministry education on hold, too. One thing he hadn't stopped doing was advocacy, however, speaking out and even writing his own story in a chapter of the faith-inspired book called *You Can Make It Too!*[4]

Finally, the administrative hearing occurred on January 19, 2017. And on March 1, 2017, three and a half years after April's terrible fall at the hotel, both Tony and Tiffany won their pleas for exoneration from the abuse claims that had torn their family apart and so deeply hurt Tony's career.

Tony now is back at work with at-risk youth, although he has yet to regain his position as an executive director of a youth services agency like the one he founded. He is working on finishing his ministry degree and works as a consultant to nonprofits. Veronica is doing well in school and is able to enjoy her big sister role again, without questions and blame. Tiffany and Tony continue in their well-developed coparenting plan for April, with a schedule that gives both of them lots of time to be with her.

April is thriving these days, and while her parents are still tearful when they think about the years in which they could not be her primary caregivers, they are immeasurably grateful for the gift of her life and health as well as for the defense they both received through the dark times when their character as people and as parents, as well as their faith, faced the sternest test.

SEVENTEEN

A Statistical Likelihood Doesn't Make Parents Guilty

By 2015, a much stronger family defense legal community had grown up in Illinois and nationally. It was no accident. In 2006, the American Bar Association (ABA) adopted practice standards for parents' attorneys in child protection cases. That effort led to creation of a dedicated Parent Representation Project within the ABA Children and the Law Project (now renamed the National Alliance for Parent Representation). Biannual national conferences for parent attorneys began in 2009, and these conferences helped to build a multidisciplinary family defense movement. Piggybacking on the national network to strengthen work in Illinois, Melissa and I, following state family defender network models from Michigan and North Carolina, started a new Illinois Parent Attorney Network in 2011 with the ABA staff's support.[1]

Still, it often seemed that very little had changed in the practices of the CPS system or at the hospitals generating the cases of alleged abuse. If anything, the system had gotten ever more reliant on the opinions of the child abuse pediatricians, who now had their own board certification process. The MPEEC program was seeking to expand, and there were increasing efforts to exclude or muzzle doctors like Dr. Sheridan from giving opinions to CPS and the juvenile court. The voices of wrongly accused parents, many of them victims of the incorrect opinion of a child abuse pediatrician, were barely heard in these discussions.

As cases continued to come to our attention, Melissa and I sometimes felt we were playing Whac-A-Mole: we would win one important victory for a wrongly accused parent, only to find a new parent calling who faced the same misplaced allegations we had just soundly defeated in the last case. At the same time, each new iteration of the claims against our clients had a slightly different flavor and a new illogic at its core.

Sometimes, the illogic of the wrongful child abuse accusation wasn't based on medicine. It was based on a misinterpretation of statistics.

Thomas was seven months old in January 2016. He was not yet walking, but he already crawled and played actively with his older brother, Daniel, (age two and a half) and the family's dog. Because Thomas's parents worked full-time, a nanny cared for Thomas and Daniel during the work week. While Thomas was fussy, he was teething at the time. Thomas's parents didn't notice anything amiss until it was time for his bath on a Friday evening in January. Thomas's parents noticed he had a swollen right leg. Thomas's mother took him to an urgent care center right away. Medical staff immediately suspected a fracture and sent the mother and child for X-rays.

During a 45-minute wait for the X-ray results, the center's security staff were stationed at Thomas's room. When the fracture was confirmed, the mother was no longer free to leave the center. Instead, she and Thomas were transported by ambulance to the children's hospital for more tests, including a full skeletal survey. That survey found both a healing right femur fracture and single healed posterior rib fracture on Thomas's right side. The report of these survey results was given to the mother in the unwelcome presence of a Chicago police detective.

The parents had no explanation for the fractures. While the interaction between Thomas and his parents was considered entirely appropriate, the hospital still called the hotline, reporting suspected child abuse.

Soon, the parents were told they had to have a safety plan. Just as in Ben and Lynn's experience, the children's grandmother was conscripted to come from out of state to care for the children in their home; otherwise, they would be taken into foster care. The parents had to live elsewhere. The parents weren't given the option of continuing to live with their children.

At the conclusion of the investigation in March, following four safety plans extending for four months, the CPS caseworker screened the case for filing abuse petitions, seeking to appoint the State as the children's legal guardian.

The State had no reason to suspect one parent over another or even to suspect that a parent was to blame. Indeed, the State's lead medical expert, Dr. Chandra, the child abuse pediatrician who now headed the CPS team at the hospital that had diagnosed Thomas's fractures, did not dispute that the injury to Thomas could have been caused by the family dog or by a hard knock by Daniel during play. Still, Dr. Chandra testified that whenever a child has an unexplained rib fracture, it was likely to be due to abuse. His diagnostic opinion of child abuse didn't require any other physical evidence, admissions of wrongdoing, or social history. All that was necessary, apparently, was a misinterpretation of an epidemiological study.

The logic of Dr. Chandra's opinion was brutally cold. A leading systematic review published by Dr. Alison Kemp examines the body of medical literature documenting the characteristics of fractures classified as due to abuse versus accidental causes.[2] While the overall likelihood that any given fracture in a child under 18 months is caused by abuse is very unlikely—just 4 in 10,000 children's fractures are considered to be due to abuse—certain types of fractures had been considered more suspicious than others.

Kemp wasn't studying the overall incidence levels of abusive versus accidental fractures. She wasn't trying to assess how the various studies came to the child abuse conclusion in the first place, either. All she was examining was the specific features of the fractures that doctors considered abusive—which bones, specifically, are most commonly viewed, according to the published literature, as due to abuse? The point was to identify levels of suspiciousness based on fracture type so that doctors could be taught when to suspect abuse and report it for further investigation.

Kemp's study's purpose was never to reach an ultimate conclusion as to whether any specific fracture, on further investigation, was properly put into the abuse category. The study was never supposed to be used to diagnose a patient like Thomas. Nor was it intended to say the level of certainty a doctor should have before labeling any specific fracture as due to abuse.

Of course, how the fractures in the underlying studies Kemp reviewed had gotten classified as abusive versus accidental was often circular; if doctors believe that rib fractures are likely due to abuse, then rib fractures will subsequently be classified as due to abuse. There is no gold standard test or universally accepted diagnostic criteria for abuse; there are just variable degrees of confidence in professional medical and legal opinions. Moreover, the more certain a child abuse expert claimed to be about abuse, even if wrong, then the more likely it is that the expert's opinion would be ratified in a court case, making the certainty and reliability of that opinion appear higher than it is. Kemp herself notes the circularity problem in some of the studies her analysis reviewed.

But Dr. Chandra drew the wrong conclusion from Kemp's reasonable and thorough study and used it outside its intended purposes, concluding that Thomas's fractures were likely to be due to abuse. Eventually, he testified in court against Thomas's parents that because rib fractures were classified as caused by abuse 71 percent of the time and due to accidental causes just 29 percent of the time, therefore *Thomas's* fracture was likely to be due to abuse. Thomas, however, was not alone. Dr. Chandra concluded that abuse is a likely cause of every single unexplained rib fracture in a child, even though the total universe of rib fractures that are due to abuse is unknown. Moreover, Dr. Chandra admitted that he gave the "likely abuse" conclusion in 100 percent of the cases involving unexplained rib fractures in which he testified.

Of course, based on this same logic, Dr. Chandra would have to admit that in 29 percent of the cases in which he provides an abuse opinion, he's wrong. That's a high rate of error in diagnosis. Moreover, he would have to admit that he doesn't know *which* of the 29 percent of cases of nonabusive rib fractures are actually not due to abuse, because he can't distinguish the innocent from the guilty based on statistics. When pressed on the inherent high error rate in his opinion, Dr. Chandra stood by his opinion, claiming that all he was saying was that abuse was "likely" even in the 29 percent of cases in which it wasn't true.[3]

Relying on a statistical generalization, as Dr. Chandra did in Thomas's case, leaves no room for considering specific characteristics of the parents or the children. These statistical studies don't factor out the parents who had long histories of violence from those who were model citizens. Nor did the studies factor out various medical conditions in the children studied, such as whether they had vitamin D deficiencies affecting their bone strength.

In effect, Dr. Chandra's opinion rested on a "constellation of injury" theory pressed to an absurd degree and applied to the statistical universe. Such opinions should have no place in a court of law or in the careful practice of medicine, where the question before the court is, "Was this particular child abused?" Dr. Chandra's theory creates a "constellation" like the one the appellate court had rejected in the *In re Yohan K.*—except that the "constellation of injuries" Dr. Chandra's opinion uses was all rib fractures in the universe of young children. This theory eliminates the need for the State to prove anything beyond the type of fracture that the child has. Dr. Chandra's theory allows for any fractures of a single rib to put the parents into the middle of a juvenile court case, no matter the excellence of their parenting and no matter that they have never hurt another human being. In fact, a full constellation isn't needed; one injury, such as a single rib fracture, suffices.

The doctor basing a claim of child abuse on statistical studies didn't need to identify who caused it, when it happened, or how the child got injured or why. In short, there didn't need to any abuse account that made sense of the facts or any theory of the case against the parent. There just needed to be a fracture and a parent who couldn't disprove the abuse claim or explain the injury.

If Dr. Chandra's opinion were correct, trials in physical abuse cases involving fractures of unknown, uncertain, or disputed origin would no longer be necessary. Children could be deemed to be "likely abused" 100 percent of the time whenever they have been found to have certain types of fractures commonly classified as suspicious for abuse. *Suspicion* of abuse, under this logic, becomes enough for a *conclusion* of abuse.

Dr. Chandra's opinion in Thomas's case didn't look much like a medical opinion. Was Dr. Chandra practicing medicine when he diagnosed Thomas as an abused child? It seems he was practicing statistics, taking epidemiological studies that had an overall descriptive purpose of classification of injuries and misapplying them to the patient he was treating. But a statistics degree wasn't listed on the curriculum vitae he provided during his testimony.

Statistics should not be used in this way.[4] Statistical studies like Kemp's don't factor out the criminals, substance abusers, and utterly reckless and violent parents from the parents who are Eagle Scouts. The statistical studies don't remove the kids who have rickets or other genetic disorders. The statistical studies, in short, don't provide information about any specific child whose risk factors may be entirely different from the majority of the children who have fractures of the same type.

Just as statistical opinions like Dr. Chandra's absolve the State of its burden to prove a case against parents accused of abuse, they give no room for the defense to respond. Since no individual can defend against the claim of statistical probability, there is no need for a costly trial. The specific facts of individual cases no longer matter. Investigations don't matter, either. If a rib fracture is more likely than not due to abuse, there is no need to find out much more about the possible alternative explanations. If the parents don't know how an injury happened, they can lose the kids. Maybe services will help them get the kids back, but maybe not.

To be fair to Dr. Chandra, in Thomas's case, he never told the CPS investigators to take the kids. But he gave his "likely abuse" opinion to CPS and the State's Attorney and then in effect disclaimed any responsibility. He voiced no objection when the CPS system actors, relying on his MPEEC "likely abuse" opinion, decided to take Thomas into state custody.

Kemp's study teaches doctors to be suspicious for possible abuse when ribs are fractured, especially if there is more than one broken rib in different stages of healing. At the same time, the study suggests that doctors can be *less* suspicious of humerus fractures in toddlers, as in Jaymz's case. Calling the hotline and asking for an investigation where a rib and femur have been fractured and the parents have no explanation is a reasonable step in most cases.

Thomas's parents, and most of the families I have represented who get the news of a child's fracture, have accepted that the hotline should be called. But that's as far as Kemp's study should be taken. It provides no support for concluding that child abuse was the likeliest explanation for Thomas's injury. Forcing Thomas's parents to defend themselves from Dr. Chandra's misunderstanding of statistics amounted to shifting the presumption of innocence to a presumption of guilt that no parent could overcome.

After a year of separation from their children, Thomas's parents won their juvenile court trial. By the time the trial was over, Thomas's parents had spent tens of thousands of dollars in savings they had intended to apply to their children's educational needs. They presented extensive medical expert testimony, from four different medical experts, in an attempt to show why Thomas's bones might have been prone to fracturing. But none of this medical evidence turned out to matter.

The judge deemed Thomas's parents, just like Ben and Lynn, to be "highly credible." The judge didn't believe either of them had abused their child.

Still, the juvenile court judge didn't accept the same defense that had won the day for Ben and Lynn. The judge credited the State's claim that the child would have inconsolably cried at the instant his fracture occurred.

The judge concluded that it was the children's nanny, not the parents, who was at fault for failing to notice when the child was injured.

Blaming the nanny provided a relatively easy way out of the more complicated issues of medicine and statistics. The nanny wasn't even a party to the juvenile court case. Months later, the nanny, represented by another family defense lawyer, got her own register finding reduced from twenty years to five, blamed for inadequately supervising the children but not for abuse.

Thomas's family's nightmare of losing the kids to CPS for nearly a year was finally over when the juvenile court judge decided neither parent was responsible for abuse of their children. The family had spent over $100,000 on medical experts, lodging, therapists, and legal bills.

I couldn't help but wonder if Ben and Lynn would have kept their children if their case had been heard by the judge in Thomas's and Daniel's case. In Ben and Lynn's case, there had been no nanny to blame. I also wondered what families would do if they faced the same allegations but did not have the same resources to fight back to keep their kids.

Lawyers in the Cook County Public Defenders' office told us that Thomas's case was just the second one they could recall in which a parent had won a medically involved physical abuse case before that particular judge. But while our clients won their plea for exoneration, their victory was limited to a victory on a different point of law, the point that the State needs evidence of *parental* responsibility in order to succeed in a petition to make children wards of the State. The case did nothing to temper the inferences of child abuse that state witnesses, prosecutors, and judges are quick to draw and slow to question. The family won only after a huge expense and months of traumatic separation of innocent parents from their children.

The judge was considered a fair judge, one who listens and keeps an open mind. And she was fair and careful as she heard the evidence in the long trial. Still, I wondered whether a parent who wasn't perfect and who didn't have another person to blame for their child's fracture would stand a chance of keeping their kids in the face of a child abuse pediatric opinion like Dr. Chandra's.

At the heart of the dispute is a question about how much more than mere suspicion is necessary to establish that a child is abused. Is evidence pointing specifically to a parent's guilt necessary, or is innuendo—"mere suspicion," in the words of Judge Posner—enough to disrupt a family? Is an unscientific assumption about a baby's crying enough? Is the prevalence of a certain type of fracture sufficient to label children "abused" and cause them to be taken from their parents? The court in *In re Yohan K.*, with the benefit of the best set of defense experts a family could have, saw through the State's assumptions that the mere presence of a constellation of injuries sufficed. But is genuine evidence of abuse—a coherent account with an actual incident and a "who," "when," "why," and "how"—necessary to declare a child "abused" and kept in State custody?

More than "practically nominal" evidence should be required. The federal courts have held that the Constitution requires solid evidence before the State can take a child from his or her parent. There needs to be an emergency and identifiable evidence of abuse or neglect. General statistics, constellations of injuries, and unproven assumptions don't cut it.

If children are our future, then their safety in their home life requires that the State should have to prove when their parents are dangerous. All parents—good, average, and even bad ones—deserve a child protection and legal system that requires evidence before they lose their fundamental right to raise their children.

Parents who haven't hurt their children shouldn't lose their children to the CPS system. Parents shouldn't need special access to a family defender to keep their kids at home when a CPS caseworker decides to take them one night. They shouldn't need to spend precious dollars in medical defense. They shouldn't be set up by State-paid child abuse experts whose opinions have been obtained without their consent after they sought help for their child from those experts' hospitals. They shouldn't have to wait weeks, months, or years and hope that they draw a fair judge who will take seriously the requirement that the State needs to prove abuse rather than shift the burden to the parents to prove their innocence.

But sadly, excellent and loving parents do lose their kids. For the CPS system to work, it needs to stop taking children who don't need to be protected from their parents. Parents as worthy as Ben and Lynn but whose skin is a different color lose their children at alarming rates and for longer than Ben and Lynn did, depending on their zip code and their income. Children's right to grow up in their own home with their own parents shouldn't depend on sheer luck in avoiding CPS intervention.

It can sometimes seem like a miracle when families win and the kids come home.

Epilogue: What Needs to Be Done

In the six stories this book profiles and in other vignettes told along the way, State CPS caseworkers took children from parents who were neither abusive or neglectful. Each of the profiled families suffered the worst trauma of their lives after they were unfairly blamed for their children's injuries or medical conditions. Because they had been seeking medical care for their child at the time of the allegations against them, they each felt a terrible sense of betrayal by the systems that are supposed to care about children and families. In each family's case, at least one doctor, and sometimes whole teams of doctors, worked closely with the State to cause the family's separation or delay their reunification. The systems had been put in place to implicate them in abuse. Few established policies and protocols helped them along the way to show their innocence and move on.

After the families were cleared of wrongdoing, they were left to themselves to pick up and go on with their lives. Not one parent to date has received an apology from any of the CPS system's caseworkers, attorneys, or doctors who opined that they or their spouse or partner was a child abuser and turned out to be wrong.

The families responded in a variety of ways after their ordeal was over. For most, the strain remained great. Husbands and wives, grandmothers and grandfathers, struggled to get back to a new normal after feeling their privacy and their dignity had suffered a long-term assault. Their trust in authorities and in medical institutions was deeply challenged. They all lived with anxiety about a next visit to the doctor if their child had another injury they couldn't explain. Some of the spouses and conscripted caregivers refused to talk about their experience, while others made a conscious choice to be open about their CPS experience, choosing not to leave the injustice for someone else to fix.

For Ben and Lynn, the fact that no one knew the cause of Robert's injury led them to work together to find answers long after their CPS case had ended. At the same time as their commitment to caring for their three children and addressing Robert's special needs became an increasingly consuming focus, they found themselves becoming a thoughtful sounding board and caring supporters for over a dozen other families who sought their advice after an injury and a hotline call.

Several of the families have played critical roles in promoting policy changes to benefit other families. A few have joined together to form a new advocacy organization for families like theirs.

Tony was a child and family advocate before his ordeal began and after his exoneration. In addition to his work with youth, he wrote a book chapter of his own and is working on his own book. There is no doubt that he will turn his ordeal into a ministry and an advocacy agenda that will bring positive results for others.

Mary Broderick has stayed involved in advocacy for families with SBS allegations for over 10 years. She became the second board president of the Family Defense Center, and she is a founding board member and the treasurer of the new Illinois family advocacy group, Family Justice Resource Center, where Tony also serves as a board member.[1] Mary remains unflappable. Upon hearing Tony's story and learning that both her son and April had been taken to the same hospital after their respective falls, where a hotline call had turned their search for medical care against them, she declared it unacceptable for this treatment to continue any longer. She continues to advocate with other families in metropolitan Chicago for new policies at the hospitals that apply outdated dogmas instead of science when children present with head injuries.

There is strength in numbers, even if that number is just two. Change can happen when parents with similar stories and vision share their experiences and join together. The stigma of a child abuse allegation silences the accused, but the voices of parents together seeking justice and fair treatment can break through the silence.

I'm sometimes asked how often the stories like the ones in this book occur. Those who ask usually want some reassurance that the problems documented in this book are rare and readily isolated. But the honest answer is that no one knows how many wrongly accused parents there are in CPS systems, especially if, as in all the cases discussed in this book, no criminal charges were brought against the parents. For each family in the book, moreover, Melissa and I know dozens more with similar experiences. Family defenders from Maine to California will recognize the stories in this book as strikingly similar to cases they handle. As this book was written, cases in which Melissa and I helped write friend-of-the-court briefs were pending on appeal in New York and Indiana, and Melissa consulted on a new case from Texas involving the same child abuse pediatrician who had opined that April was abused.

Centralized data on such basic questions as how many people are listed as abusers in child-abuse registers in America, for how long, and for what alleged offenses are not maintained. Safety plans are not counted in published child welfare data reports. The ways this information is kept, state by state and court by court, make it all but impossible to give a good statistical answer that would distinguish wrongly accused from properly charged parents. Counting exonerated families, documenting successful register challenges, and keeping track of the number of safety plans would be good first steps. The shadow foster care system created by safety plans needs to be eradicated by sunlight.

The cases result from policies and practices adopted by policy makers and administrators. Hotlines, investigation procedures, MPEEC policies, safety plans, stipulations to temporary custody, and the public resources available to the State as compared to the private resources needed for the defense—all of these policies are the result of explicit decisions that have led to entrenched practices.

These policies result from the relative powerlessness of the families involved in the CPS system, fed by the stigma and shame of the accusation and the lack of support for family defense in this country. Parents and their advocates are too often not even at the table when decisions about their children and their family's future are at stake.

The families profiled in the book each *did* have the personal resources to fight for their children and to secure expungement from the listing in the register. That's part of the reason their stories could be told here. Each parent was educated, employed, upstanding, and family-focused. Not one of them had a history of violence, criminal complaints, domestic violence, or substance abuse. Several of them had long careers working with children themselves or volunteering in their communities. Most had already been raising older children without incident when their CPS ordeals began. Yet they lost their kids for periods ranging from nine days in the *Hernandez* case to over three years in Tony and Tiffany's case.

Many innocent parents who have their children taken from them lack financial resources to hire a lawyer or pay for medical experts. Most states appoint indigent parents Counsel in these cases; some states do not.[2] Parents' counsel need resources equal to those the State itself enjoys, but such resources are rarely provided. In the face of these imbalances and the presumptions of guilt that this book has documented, parents who have disadvantages of race and class, any history of substance use, disabilities, domestic violence, or criminal conviction may be no more guilty of the allegation of abuse than Ben and Lynn were but may find it impossible to get out from under the assumption that they deserve to lose their kids.

Much of the problem lies outside the juvenile court arena, which is where most family defenders practice. There is no right to appointed counsel during an investigation or to challenge a register listing, so if parents can't afford to hire an attorney to help them navigate the CPS process, they may be plain out of luck, innocent or not. People who work with children may be blacklisted in their careers without any chance to have the evidence against them reviewed first. CPS policies and practices go unchecked when legal counsel isn't available to challenge flagrant abuses.

Such a fallacious system should not be allowed to continue unchecked. Yet even policy makers and child and family advocates remain unaware of the existence of registers, the way they function, and the harm they can cause. Juvenile court processes remain shrouded in secrecy, too. One result is the assumption that "see something, say something" policies have no downside, when the logic of these policies leads to taking the kids without just cause and a massive child-abuse register system with "staggering" rates of error.[3]

If we care about children and if we value families, the risk that children will be taken from parents who love them needs to be reduced. Families deserve to be secure in their own homes, confident that they can raise their children without CPS caseworkers like Green and Long (in Ben and Lynn's case) showing up at their doors one night. Policies that contribute to the acceptance of the high rate of error—including the ways assumptions of guilt have been allowed to take the place of evidence—must be challenged.

Outrage at child abuse needs to be tempered with the understanding that labeling an innocent family as guilty of child abuse hurts the children, too. The goal has to be getting it right. The mantra "erring on the side of the child" has been used to justify many terrible child protection policies that assume no one is hurt when the child abuse hotline gets a false call. But error in the child protection system has no good side. We should all be on accuracy's side, not error's.

The CPS system assumes that it is focused on the "best interests of the child," but the fundamental rights of families to remain together too often are respected in the breach. Over and over, families report feeling as if their guilt was presumed. That feeling is a natural result of a legal system that allows a very relaxed burden of proof on the State and that effectively forces families to defend their innocence rather than compels the State to prove abuse.

It should be unacceptable to adjudicate any State-initiated child protection case based on a finding of the "preponderance of the evidence" standard in the State's favor. With such a burden of proof, risk of error lies almost equally between the parties, but the standard gives the State nearly every advantage, starting with superior resources and a degree of deference that no parent's family defender can hope to achieve. At temporary custody and dispositional hearings, moreover, even more relaxed burdens of proof, with liberal allowance of second- and third-hand hearsay accounts, compound the difficulties families face.

Relaxed legal standards and the practices and customs that force families to go along with demands make it impossible for many obviously innocent parents to get through the court process quickly and with their family rights restored. These defects would be remedied significantly if, instead of the relaxed, ordinary civil burden of proof, "clear and convincing" evidence were required to take a child from his or her parents and make him or her a ward of the court.[4]

But children should not be taken from their homes in the first place except in life-threatening emergencies. It is high time we started to take seriously the constitutional duty of having both probable cause and exigent circumstances before children can be taken from their homes. The CPS system's duty to gather exculpatory evidence and consider it fully needs to be honored at each step of the process.

Some of these recommendations are simply good legal practices and common sense. The CPS system, like the health care system, should start by first doing no harm. The massively erroneous child welfare system gets it wrong from the start when it operates under the assumption that there is no harm and no foul in leveling a child abuse accusation against a child's parent or caregiver.

Before accusing a loving parent of abusing his or her child, the State ought to be able to give a straight answer as to whom the State accuses of hurting the child, when it happened, why, and how. Then, if they have reasonably good answers that could prevail at a trial under the fair scrutiny of a decent judge, it's still important to ask whether the child should be taken and put with someone who will protect him or her better than the accused parent has done. If the State CPS system can't answer these questions, the State should leave the family alone.

I've spent my long legal career fighting for policy changes, including ones this book describes. I'm working to change child-abuse registers and eliminate safety plans issued under baseless threats so that due process is afforded before families suffer the grievous consequences of these practices. This work started in 1997 with the filing of the *Dupuy* litigation and continued for over two decades through my leadership at the Family Defense Center and the National Center for Housing and Child Welfare. Now I am spearheading policy reforms at the federal and multi-state level as the founder and co-chair of United Family Advocates, discovering in the process that many of the ideas this book discusses resonate with strange bedfellows across political lines and racial and social divides.

Work to change an entrenched CPS system takes an inclusive community of advocates. For me and for many others, being part of building such a community of advocates has been a lifelong and never-ending mission.

If it is important to protect children from the loss of their families and families and communities from the loss of their children, then it follows that CPS caseworkers cannot have the awesome and unfettered coercive powers our society has decided to confer on them. Judges operate with more checks and balances than our society provides in oversight of CPS caseworkers. CPS caseworkers are too often allowed to operate as if they are a law unto themselves. Instead of expanding the CPS system, the goal should be to shrink it.

To accomplish this goal, parents need legal defense. Family advocates, including parent advocacy groups, need to be supported.[5] Parents need to have a fair fight to keep their kids, starting with clear notification of the accusations and evidence against them. They need to access fair and balanced second opinions. They deserve to have their own experts treated as professionals, not vilified and derided by State-paid attorneys and consultants who assume they know the truth.

The risk of error that this book documents is staggeringly high—so high as to amount to child abuse and child neglect in its own right. Yet, these are forms of abuse that State child welfare systems inflict every day. Taking children from innocent parents, under policies and practices that deliberately sweep in innocent families along with the guilty, is itself a form of child abuse. The destruction of families that this book recounts should be recognized as a singularly important civil rights issue of our time. Child welfare reform that supports families protects children from the loss of the most precious ties they will ever have. What could be more important than that?

In claiming to be fighting for children, child advocates must be family advocates, too. Family advocates need to proudly proclaim that children's best interests are one and the same as their families' best interests, for there is no other way to protect children but to defend their families—and to fight for the right of families everywhere to raise their own children.

Notes

INTRODUCTION

1. *See*, 705 ILCS 405/2-9, the Illinois temporary protective custody statute in the Illinois Abused and Neglected Child Reporting Act. Illinois laws can be found at http://www.ilga.gov/. Click on "Illinois compiled statutes" to find them by chapter and section.

2. This scenario is drawn from *Hernandez v. Foster*, 657 F. 3d 463 (7th Cir. 2011), which is discussed in chapter 14. Medical opinion later confirmed the parents' account of a fall and contradicted the abuse suspicion.

3. National Child Abuse and Neglect Data System, Children's Bureau, HHS, Child Maltreatment (2016), summary, ix, available at www.acf.hhs.gov/cb/resource/child-maltreatment-2016 (accessed May 29, 2018). There are 73.6 million children under 18 in the United States. *See*, NCCPR Blog (February 21, 2018), available at http://www.nccprblog.org/2018/02/child-abuse-fatalities-keystone-kops-of_21.html (accessed May 29, 2018). A rate of child abuse and neglect reporting of 10 percent of the child population in one year is an extremely high rate, approximately half the cases are screened out from investigations and service referrals. The 1999 Child Maltreatment report (the first such report available online) states that nearly 3 million families were referred to hotlines in 1998. *See*, https://www.acf.hhs.gov/sites/default/files/cb/cm99.pdf#page=15 (accessed May 29, 2018). The growth in numbers of hotline calls has been quite steady.

4. *Id*.

5. *Id*. at ii and summary p. xii.

6. U.S. Department of Health and Human Services, Administration for Children and Families, Administration on Children, Youth and Families, Children's Bureau. *See*, https://www.acf.hhs.gov/cb (accessed June 26, 2018), The AFCARS Report (2016), p. 1.

7. *Id.* at ii.

8. There is no comprehensive federal definition of abuse or neglect. *See*, U.S. Department of Health and Human Services, *Assessing the Feasibility of Creating and Maintaining a National Registry of Child Maltreatment Perpetrators* (Washington, D.C.: Office of the Assistant Secretary for Planning and Evaluation, 2012). This source discusses the challenges of having a national child abuse registry in the face of nonuniform definitions of abuse or neglect across states and recommends against a national database in part for that reason.

9. *Id.* at ii.

10. *Id.* at summary p. xii. The statistic is based on dividing 2.3 cases "referred in" by 676,000 "child victims."

11. *Id.* at ii, which cites 1,750 reported deaths due to abuse or neglect in 2016.

12. This phrase is commonly used in CPS. *See*, L. Beller, "When in Doubt, Take Them Out, Removal of Children from Domestic Violence Victims Ten Tears After *Nicholson v. Williams,*" *Duke Journal of Gender Law and Policy,* 22, 205–39 (Spring 2015).

13. Two principal federal statutes set requirements for state CPS systems. The first is the Child Abuse Prevention and Treatment Act of 1974, requiring hotlines and investigations, which has been reauthorized and amended eight times and was codified at 42 U.S.C. 5101 *et seq.* The second is Title IV-E, funding foster care and adoption assistance, now called Title E, of the Social Security Act, most recently amended through the Family First Prevention Services Act, codified at 42 U.S.C. § 671 *et seq.*

14. *See,* V. Sankaran and C. Church, "Easy Come, Easy Go: The Plight of Children Who Spend Less than 30 Days in Foster Care," *University of Pennsylvania Journal of Law & Social Change,* 19, 207 (2017), available at http://scholarship.law.upenn.edu/jlasc/vol19/iss3/2 (accessed May 29, 2018).

15. *Dupuy v. McDonald (Dupuy I),* 141 F. Supp. 2d 1090, 1136, *aff'd in relevant part,* 397 F. 3d 493 (7th Cir. 2005). Discussed in chapter 4, this decision concluded that the child-abuse register operated as a blacklist, that the Illinois system was rife with error, and that it employed policies and procedures that magnified the risk of error. The author was co-lead counsel in *Dupuy.*

16. The seminal work on this topic is D. Roberts, *Shattered Bonds: The Color of Child Welfare* (New York: Basic Books/Civitas, 2002). Two shorter recent features are S. Clifford and J. Silver-Greenberg, "Foster

Care as Punishment," *New York Times*, New York Regional Section (July 7, 2017) and E. Ketteringham, "Live in a Poor Neighborhood? Better Be a Perfect Parent," Op Ed, *New York Times* (August 22, 2017). *See also*, National Coalition for Child Protection Reform, "Child Welfare and Race," Issue Paper #7, available at https://drive.google.com/file/d/0B291mw _hLAJsVURqdktmOFRjOG8/view (accessed May 29, 2018).

17. I. Chasnoff, H. Landress, and M. Barrett, "The Prevalence of Illicit Drug or Alcohol Use During Pregnancy and Discrepancies in Mandatory Reporting in Pinellas County, Florida," *New England Journal of Medicine, 332*, no. 17, 1220 (April 26, 1990).

18. A variety of different terms refer to the courts where CPS-initiated petitions to remove children from their parents are heard, including "dependency court," "juvenile court," and "family court." The stories in the book all arose in Illinois, where proceedings are governed by the state's Juvenile Court Act, 705 ILCS 405-1, *et seq.*, and where the term "juvenile court" is used for both child protection and delinquency/juvenile justice cases. Sometimes, I use "child protection court" or "dependency court" interchangeably with "juvenile court."

CHAPTER 1

1. An internal memo by the Family Defense Center law clerk Ryan Shellady in the summer of 2017 found that 37 states used a version of the process described in this paragraph. An article by Shellady in the 104 *Iowa Law Review* Issue 3 (2019 publication date) discusses the due process issues with safety plans.

2. 325 ILCS 5/7.16 limits appeals of registry decisions to named "perpetrators."

3. Quotes in the family-story narratives have three sources: my recollection of conversations, investigative files, and transcripts in my personal possession. Except for chapter 15, which is told from published sources, each of the families in the cases presented here have reviewed the narrative about them.

CHAPTER 2

1. *See*, American Board of Pediatrics, "Child Abuse Pediatric Certification," available at www.abp.org/content/child-abuse-pediatrics-certification (accessed May 29, 2018); Council of Pediatric Subspecialties, available at

http://www.pedsubs.org/SubDes/ChildAbuse.cfm (accessed March 2, 2018). Before 2010, these subspecialty fellowships were two years long; since 2010, they are three-year programs.

2. *See,* Chicago Children's Advocacy Center, "Our Response to Child Physical Abuse," available at https://www.chicagocac.org/what-we-do/our -response-to-child-physical-abuse (accessed March 2, 2018). This source explains the MPEEC program, including its history.

3. 325 ILCS 5/5. Illinois practice gives only police, doctors, and specific investigative CPS caseworkers considered "designated employees" authority to take protective custody. Foster care and intact family caseworkers do not have this power.

CHAPTER 3

1. *See,* https://www.illinois.gov/dcfs/aboutus/notices/Documents/cfs _1441_child_endangerment_risk_assessment_protocol_(fillable).pdf (accessed March 2, 2018) for a sample of this form. This assessment has been required by Illinois law since 1994.

2. Rules governing child protection investigations in Illinois are at 89 Ill. Admin. Code 300. Specific allegation definitions are at Appendix B to this rule. Procedures implementing the rules can be located on the DCFS website at https://www.illinois.gov/dcfs/aboutus/notices/Documents /procedures_300.pdf (accessed May 29, 2018) and Appendix B thereto. Illinois has more detailed rules and procedures than many other states do.

3. 89 Ill. Admin. Code 300/App'x B-9/59.

4. 325 ILCS 5/7.12.

5. *Id.; see,* 325 ILCS 5 *et seq.* generally, which contains no requirement for a court finding of abuse prior to listing in the register. *See,* Children's Bureau, HHS, Child Maltreatment (2016), n. 4, 15, for an explanation of the classification system for "indicated" and "unfounded" reports. Most states use the term "substantiated," and some states have various levels of substantiation.

6. The same child abuse pediatrician was later excoriated by the federal court for failure to reveal a contrary medical opinion of which she was aware in a case that had led to the imprisonment of Jennifer Del Prete for 12 years. *Del Prete v. Hulett,* 2010 cv. 5070 (N. D. Ill, 2012), available at https://law.justia.com/cases/federal/district-courts/illinois/ilndce/1:201 0cv05070/246383/26/ (accessed May 29, 2018). *See,* D. Tuerkheimer,

Flawed Convictions: Shaken Baby Syndrome and the Inertia of Injustice (Oxford: Oxford University Press, 2014) and B. Pope, "Woman Previously Freed by Medill Justice Project Investigation to Sue Alleged Conspirators," *Daily Northwestern* (August 25, 2017), https://dailynorthwestern .com/2017/08/25/campus/woman-previously-freed-medill-justice-project -investigation-sue-alleged-conspirators/ (accessed May 29, 2018).

7. *Dupuy v. McDonald,* 141 F. Supp. 2d 1090, *aff'd in relevant part sub nom Dupuy v. Samuels,* 397 F. 3d 493 (7th Cir. 2005) ("*Dupuy I*"). *Dupuy II* opinions are at *Dupuy v. Samuels*, 462 F. Supp. 2d 859 (N.D. Ill. 2005), *aff'd,* 465 F. 3d 757 (7th Cir. 2006), *subsequent appeal,* 495 F. 3d 807 (7th Cir. 2007*), cert denied,* 128 S. Ct. 2932 (2008).

CHAPTER 4

1. *See, Goldberg v. Kelly,* 397 U.S. 254 (1970). Procedures to challenge state actions may be required either before or promptly after the action that takes away a protected individual liberty interest, including the familial associational interests of parents and children. *See also, Matthews v. Eldridge,* 424 U.S. 319 (1976).

2. *Meyer v. Nebraska,* 262 U.S. 390 (1923). *See also, Prince v. Massachusetts,* 321 U.S. 158, 321 U.S. 166 (1944). In *Wisconsin v. Yoder,* 406 U.S. 205 (1972), parents' fundamental rights were affirmed in the context of the religious freedom of Amish parents to avoid the compulsory education laws. In *Stanley v. Illinois,* 405 U.S. 645 (1972), the Supreme Court reinforced the requirement that a father could not be deprived of custody of his child without a hearing.

3. *May v. Anderson*, 345 U.S. 528, 533 (1983).

4. *Troxel v. Granville,* 530 U.S. 57 (2000).

5. *Quilloin v. Walcott*, 434 U.S. 246 (1978).

6. As discussed in detail in chapter 14, *Hernandez v. Foster,* 657 F. 3d 493 (7th Cir. 2011) clearly established this constitutional principle in the federal Seventh Circuit Court of Appeals.

7. *Miranda v. Arizona,* 384 U.S. 436 (1966), for example, establishes this stringent test for waiver of the zealously protected right against self-incrimination under the Fifth Amendment of the U.S. Constitution. Other waivers, like waivers of the Sixth Amendment right to trial by jury, are scrutinized closely by courts to assure that these decisions are knowing, intelligent, and voluntary. Given the fundamental rights of families, it is

244   Notes

unclear why any less zealous scrutiny of the waiver of familial rights to live with their children should be acceptable.

8. *Schneckloth v. Bustamonte*, 412 U.S. 218 (1973), sets out a multifactored "totality of the circumstances" test for voluntariness; whether the decision was made under threats or promises is particularly relevant to the overall assessment of whether consent, or any decision to give up a right, is "voluntary." *See also, Ashcroft v. Tennessee*, 322 U.S. 143, 153–54 (1996), which applied more objective external factors tests for voluntariness.

9. These terms come from *Duchesne v. Sugarman*, 566 F. 2d 817 (2nd Cir. 1977), a federal court challenge to a lengthy removal of a child without affording the mother an opportunity to challenge retention of her child in State custody.

10. There were other restrictions imposed on legal services programs by the Gingrich Congress in 1996. Numerous attorneys left LAF at the same time, including John Bouman and a team of housing and welfare lawyers who became the core staff of the Sargent Shriver Center on Poverty Law. *See*, www.povertylaw.org. Several of the other departing lawyers worked with Robert Lehrer and me on these cases after we formed our firm.

11. 42 U.S.C. § 1983 (Civil Rights Act); 42 U.S.C. § 1988 (Civil Rights Attorney's Fees Act).

12. *Dupuy I: Dupuy v. McDonald,* 141 F. Supp. 2d 1090, *aff'd in relevant part sub nom Dupuy v. Samuels,* 397 F. 3d 493 (7th Cir. 2005). *Dupuy II: Dupuy v. Samuels,* 462 F. Supp. 2d 859 (N.D. Ill. 2005), *aff'd,* 465 F. 3d 757 (7th Cir. 2006), *subsequent appeal,* 495 F. 3d 807 (7th Cir. 2007*), cert denied,* 128 S. Ct. 2932 (2008). Two additional trips to the federal court of appeals in *Dupuy* concerned attorney's fees issues.

13. *Dupuy I,* 141 F. Supp. 2d 1090.

14. *See,* D. Redleaf, "Child Abuse Registers Abuse Due Process," *Verdict,* 24, no. 2, 2–12 (April 2018), available at https://files.acrobat.com/a/preview/45d0172f-8241-4ee8-bffa-cdd679854179 (accessed May 29, 2018). This is the magazine of the National Coalition of Concerned Legal Professionals. Sex offender registers at least have the virtue of requiring a criminal conviction as a prerequisite to being listed. For an excellent review and critique of the juvenile sex-offender registry laws, *see,* E. Lehrer, "Rethinking Sex Offender Registers," *National Affairs,* 35 (Winter 2016), available at www.nationalaffairs.com/publications/detail/rethinking-sex-offender-registries.

15. *Dupuy v. McDonald*, 141 F. Supp. 2d at 1130.

16. *Dateline NBC* also later ran a full-length feature called "Clearing Names" that focused on the Dupuys' personal story.

17. *Dupuy v. McDonald*, 141 F. Supp. 2d 1090 (N.D. Ill. 2001).

18. *Dupuy*, 141 F. Supp. 2d at 1130. The reported error rate applies to cases that had a neutral due process review. Because the burden is on the indicated person to request review and navigate the appeal system and no neutral review takes place otherwise, there is no way to determine an overall error rate for all indicated findings, including those that were never appealed.

19. *Dupuy*, 141 F. Supp. 2d at 1130.

20. *Dupuy v. Samuels*, 462 F. Supp. 2d 859 (N.D. Ill. 2005).

21. *Jordan ex rel Jordan v. Jackson*, 15 F. 3d 342 (4th Cir. 1994) held that for due process purposes, five days was the "outer limit" on how long a child could be kept in state custody without affording a hearing to the parents.

22. 465 F. 3d 757 (7th Cir. 2006).

23. 465 F. 3d at 760.

24. *Id.*

25. *Id.*

26. *Id.*

27. 465 F. 3d at 761.

28. *Dupuy*, 141 F. Supp. 2d at 1130.

29. 465 F. 3d at 62. It wasn't a truism but another unwarranted threat: if the State possessed no evidence against the family, then the possibility of removal was not lawfully authorized. The form itself intimidated parents into signing agreements in cases where there was no specific evidence amounting to probable cause.

30. 465 F. 3d at 762.

31. *Id.*

32. 495 F. 3d 807 (7th Cir. 2007).

33. 128 S. Ct. 2932 (2008).

CHAPTER 5

1. *See, Dupuy v. McDonald*, 141 F. Supp. 2d 1090, *aff'd in relevant part*, 397 F. 3d 493 (7th Cir. 2005).

2. *Hernandez v. Foster*, 657 F. 3d 493 (7th Cir. 2011).

CHAPTER 6

1. Illinois' child representation system is somewhat unusual in requiring appointment of both an attorney and a guardian ad litem for children in dependency cases and in providing for legal representation of the guardian ad litem if that person is not an attorney. The roles have been allowed to be collapsed into one person under Illinois case law. *In re K.M.B.*, 123 Ill. App. 3d 645 (1984). *See,* American Bar Association (ABA), Center on Children and the Law, "Standards Of Practice For Lawyers Who Represent Children In Abuse And Neglect Cases" (Approved by ABA House of Delegates, February 6, 1996), available at https://www.americanbar.org /content/dam/aba/migrated/family/reports/standards_abuseneglect.auth-checkdam.pdf (accessed May 29, 2018). These standards do not expressly disapprove of dual appointments, but note that the child's legal rights should be the focus of representation.

2. Twelve states do not provide a right to counsel for indigent parents in these cases. *See,* Public Justice Center, National Coalition for a Civil Right to Counsel, at civilrighttocounsel.org/map (accessed May 29, 2018).

3. Assistant State's Attorneys and guardians ad litem usually didn't know a lot more than the parents' counsel at this initial court date, although their access to the CPS caseworker, the primary witness against the parents, was superior. They, too, were very recently assigned to handle the petition that a different State's Attorney had screened for filing with the court.

4. These restrictions were part of amendments to the Legal Services Corporation Act, which authorized federal funding for legal services for the poor. 42 U.S.C. § 2992 *et seq.* The *Dupuy* class action suit, see chapter 4, thus could not have been filed at the Legal Assistance Foundation after 1996.

5. I left the Family Defense Center, www.familydefensecenter.net on October 31, 2017, and affiliated with the National Center for Housing and Child Welfare. I continue to co-lead a bipartisan child welfare reform advocacy coalition. *See,* www.unitedfamilyadvocates.org. In November 2017, I also opened a small private consulting practice. *See,* www.familydefenseconsulting.org.

CHAPTER 8

1. 89 Il. Admin. Code 300, App'x B-9.

2. *See, Dupuy v. McDonald,* 141 F. Supp. 2d 1090 (N.D. Ill. 2001), *aff'd in relevant part,* 397 F. 3d 493 (7th Cir. 2005).

CHAPTER 9

1. *See,* P. Barnes, "Imaging of Non-Accidental Injury and the Mimics: Issues and Controversies in the Era of Evidence-Based Medicine," *Radiologic Clinics of North America,* 49, 205–29 (January 2011). There is extensive medical literature on child abuse mimics.

2. S. Sherl, L. Miller, N. Lively, S. Russinoff, C. Sullivan, and P. Tometta, "Accidental and Non-Accidental Femur Fractures in Children," *Clinical Orthopedics and Related Research,* 376, 96–105 (July 2000).

3. *See,* 705 ILCS 405/2-3(2) for the definition of an abused child; 705 ILCS 405/2-18 for evidence at the adjudicatory hearing or trial; and 705 ILCS 405/2-21 for findings and adjudication.

CHAPTER 10

1. A judge since 2000, Hon. Patricia Martin served as the chair of the National Counsel of Juvenile and Family Court Judges from 2011–2012.

2. Nationally, Title IV-E funding for foster care and adoption services was over $7.7 billion in fiscal year 2016. E. Stoltzfus, Congressional Research Service, "Child Welfare: An Overview of Federal Programs and Their Current Funding," 20 (January 20, 2017), available at https://fas.org /sgp/crs/misc/R43458.pdf (accessed May 29, 2018). Over half of Illinois' $1.1 billion child welfare budget in 2014 came from federal funds. Child Welfare League of America, "Illinois's Children 2017," available at https:// www.cwla.org/wp-content/uploads/2017/04/ILLINOIS-revised-1-1.pdf (accessed May 29, 2018).

3. The average length a child remains in foster care in the United States is 31.2 months. *See,* Children's Bureau, HHS, "The AFCARS Report Preliminary FY 2016 Estimates as of October 20, 2017," no. 24, 1, available at https://www.acf.hhs.gov/sites/default/files/cb/afcarsreport24 .pdf (accessed May 29, 2018). Illinois consistently has reported longer than average reunification delays.

4. There is extensive and growing concern about the racial disproportionality in child welfare intervention, starting with D. Roberts, *Shattered Bonds: The Color of Child Welfare* (New York: Basic Books/Civitas, 2002). Two shorter features are S. Clifford and J. Silver-Greenberg, "Foster Care as Punishment," *New York Times,* New York Regional Section (July 7, 2017) and E. Ketteringham, "Live in a Poor Neighborhood? Better Be a Perfect Parent," Op Ed, *New York Times* (August 22, 2017).

5. For an excellent example of a child welfare director who has forcefully argued for radical reshaping of the foster care system, *see*, M. McGrath Tierney, "Rethinking Foster Care," TEDx Talks (Baltimore, January 2014), https://www.google.com/search?q=molly+tierney+ted+talk&oq=Molly+Tierney&aqs=chrome.1.0l6.4764j0j4&sourceid=chrome&ie=UTF-8 (accessed May 29, 2018).

6. The Illinois Governor referred to the state CPS agency as "in shambles" prior to the "transformation" he claimed to direct. *See*, C. Kelly, "Press Release: DCFS Transformation Applauded by Governor," March 21, 2016, available at https://www2.illinois.gov/dcfs/aboutus/newsandreports/news/Documents/DCFS_Transformation_Applauded_by_Governor_032116.pdf. Analyzing misguided child protection policies is nothing new to the National Center for Child Protection Reform, which has an at least weekly blog highlighting a major CPS system failure somewhere in the United States. *See*, www.nccprblog.org.

7. The recent discussion of expanding the use of "predictive analytics" in child protection investigations portends a huge expansion of the use of demographic assumptions, including stereotypes and unconfirmed data in child protection databases, to draw conclusions about which parents should keep their children, in effect ratifying racial profiling in a child protection context. *See*, NCCPR Child Welfare Blog (October 19, 2017), available at https://www.nccprblog.org/search?q=predictive+analytics (accessed May 29, 2018).

8. Lenore Skenazy writes extensively on this topic, including on the Web page www.letgrow.org. My own report, with Caitlin Fuller, "When Can Parents Let Children Be Alone" (August 2015), available at www.familydefensecenter.org, addresses policy recommendations (accessed May 29, 2018). *See also*, D. Redleaf, "When Parents Can Let Children Alone," TedX (Chicago, May 6, 2017), available at https://www.youtube.com/watch?v=cv5JIuOk8yA (accessed May 29, 2018). After Utah recently changed its law to allow children to play outside without their parents facing neglect charges, I wrote a comment published in *The Atlantic* (April 12, 2018) that discusses why laws like Utah's benefit families across class and racial lines, available at https://www.theatlantic.com/letters/archive/2018/04/letters-free-range-parenting/557558/ (accessed May 29, 2018).

9. *Troxel v. Granville*, 530 U.S. 57 (2000).

CHAPTER 11

1. Denunciation of parents was encouraged for Soviet schoolchildren, who were taught to emulate a boy named Pavlik Morozov. Morozov

denounced his father to Soviet authorities. *Encyclopedia Britannica,* "Pavilk Morozov, Russian Communist Youth" (February 1, 2018), available at https://www.britannica.com/biography/Pavlik-Morozov (accessed May 29, 2018).

2. *See,* R. Wexler, *Wounded Innocents: The Real Victims of the War Against Child Abuse* (Buffalo, NY: Prometheus Brooks, 1990), which discusses the harmful impact of "child saving" policies and practices that assume children are better off "saved" from their parents by child protection intervention. *See also,* J. Doyle, "Child Protection and Child Outcome: Measuring the Effects of Foster Care," *American Economic Review* 97, no. 5, 1583–1610 (2008), which documents greater harm to abused children's long-term development from foster care than remaining home.

CHAPTER 12

1. *See,* D. Redleaf, "Protecting Mothers Against Gender-Plus Bias," *Children's Rights Litigation,* E-Newsletter (October 2011–July 2012) (three part series), available at https://apps.americanbar.org/litigation /committees/childrights/content/articles/fall2011-protecting-mothers -gender-plus-bias.html; https://apps.americanbar.org/litigation/committees /childrights/content/articles/spring2012-0312-protecting-mothers-gender -plus-bias.html; and https://apps.americanbar.org/litigation/committees /childrights/content/articles/summer2012-0712-protecting-mothers-gender -plus-bias.html (accessed May 29, 2018).

2. Bailey cited *In re Simmons,* 127 Ill. App. 3d 943 (1974) as support. In that case, an unexplained spiral fracture in a three-year-old led the trial court to conclude there was insufficient evidence of abuse, but the appellate court reversed, saying there did not have to be proof of intent.

CHAPTER 13

1. *Dupuy,* 141 F. Supp. 2d 1090 (N.D. Ill. 2001), *aff'd in relevant part* 397 F. 3d 493 (7th Cir. 2005), which directed a preregistry review process called an "administrator's conference."

2. *Dupuy,* 141 F. Supp. 2d at 1130.

3. *See,* D. Redleaf, "Child Abuse Registers Abuse Due Process," *Verdict Magazine* (April 2018), electronic version available at https://www .familydefenseconsulting.com/article-page (accessed May 29, 2018). *See also,* D. Redleaf, "The Impact of Abuse and Neglect Findings Beyond the

Juvenile Courthouse: Understanding the Child Abuse Register System and Ways to Challenge Administrative Child Abuse Register Determinations," in M. Guggenheim and V. Sankaran (eds.), *Representing Parents in Child Welfare Cases: Advance and Guidance for Family Defenders* (ABA, 2015); D. Redleaf and S. Pick, "Challenging a Child Abuse Listing," Children's Rights, ABA, vol. 12, no. 4, 3 (Summer 2010). Part I is available at hpps.americanbar.org/litigation/committees/childrights/content/newsletters/childrens_summer2010.pdf (accessed May 29, 2018), and vol. 13, no. 1, 1 (Fall 2010). Part II is available at http://apps.americanbar.org/litigation/committees/childrights/content/newsletters/childrens_fall2010.pdf (accessed May 29, 2018).

4. CPS directors do not last long in many CPS systems. My legal career has spanned the tenure of well over a dozen different Illinois CPS directors, including eight directors since 2006.

5. *Olmstead v. United States*, 227 U.S. 438 (1928) (Brandeis, dissenting).

CHAPTER 14

1. *Hernandez v. Foster*, 657 F. 3d 493 (7th Cir. 2011).

2. *Dupuy II*, 465 F. 3d 757 (7th Cir. 2006).

3. 465 F. 3d at 762.

4. *Hernandez v. Foster*, 657 F. 3d 493 (7th Cir. 2011).

5. *Dupuy II,* 465 F. 3d at 762.

6. *Hernandez v. Foster*, 2010 U.S. Dist. LEXIS 3815 (N.D. Ill., Jan. 15, 2010).

7. *Hernandez v. Foster*, 657 F. 3d 493 (7th Cir. 2011).

8. *See,* http://www.familydefensecenter.net/fdc-cases/2016-safety-plan-settlements/ (accessed May 29, 2018).

9. Pennsylvania also has had extensive litigation on safety plans. *See, Croft v. Westmoreland County Children and Youth Services*, 103 F. 3d 1123 (3rd Cir. Jan. 1997); *Starkey v. York County,* No. 1:11-cv-00981, Doc. 28, 2011 WL 11071762 (M. D. Pa. Sept. 21, 2011) (Jones, J.); and *Billups v. Penn State Milton S. Hershey Med. Ctr.*, 2012 WL 1392294, 2012 U.S. Dist. LEXIS 56414 (M. D. Pa. Apr. 12, 2012) (Kane, C. J.). Mark Freeman has brought a number of challenges to safety plan practices in Pennsylvania, and Carolyn Kubitschek and I worked on another Pennsylvania case, *D.M. v. County of Berks*, 929 F. Supp. 2d 390 (E.D. Pa. 2013) with lead counsel Benjamin Picker of Philadelphia.

10. The report is available at http://www.familydefensecenter.net/wp
-content/uploads/2016/04/Medical-Ethics-Concerns-in-Physical-Child
-Abuse-Investigations-corrected-reposted.pdf (accessed May 29, 2018).

11. *Mohil v. Glick*, 842 F. Supp. 1072 (N.D. Ill. 2012) holds that child
abuse pediatricians act under color of law in preparing MPEEC reports, at
the same time as it holds that qualified and absolute immunity protected
the child abuse pediatrician from liability for damages in that case.

CHAPTER 15

1. The report identified "hypoxic-eschemic" effects, which can result
from extended seizure activity or from stroke or a combination of the two.

2. The third prong is variously described as symptoms of brain swelling (encephalopathy) or axonal injury.

3. The famous trial against Louise Woodward in 1997, the so-called
Boston nanny, contributed to doubts in the minds of experts as to the validity of the SBS paradigm at the same time as the general public was led to
view it as incontrovertible fact. Dr. Barnes reconsidered his prosecution-side
abuse opinion following the trial in that case. *See,* D. Tuerkheimer, *Flawed
Convictions: Shaken Baby Syndrome and the Inertia of Injustice* (Oxford:
Oxford University Press, 2014) for a thorough history of the development
of the SBS and AHT paradigms and their impact on criminal convictions
of wrongly accused caregivers. *See also*, R. Balko and T. Carrington, "Bad
Science Puts Innocent People in Jail and Keeps Them There," *Washington
Post* (March 21, 2018); R. Balko, "Dr. John Plunkett, RIP, He Told the
Truth About Bad Forensics and Was Prosecuted for It," *Washington Post*
(April 10, 2018), which discusses the impact of Dr. Plunkett's research on
short falls and his work as an SBS expert for the accused. The 2016 movie
The Syndrome (M. Goldsmith producer/director, S. Goldsmith, reporter)
chronicles prosecution attacks on the doctors who have questioned the SBS
paradigm, including Dr. Barnes and Dr. Plunkett.

4. This network is coordinated by Katherine Judson at the Wisconsin
Innocence Project, which is housed at the University of Wisconsin Law
School.

CHAPTER 16

1. For several compelling stories of intimidating questioning in SBS
cases leading to false confessions, *see,* D. Tuerkheimer, *Flawed Convictions:*

Shaken Baby Syndrome and the Inertia of Injustice (Oxford: Oxford University Press, 2014).

2. J. Plunkett, "Fatal Pediatric Head Injuries Caused by Short-Distance Falls," *American Journal of Forensic Medicine and Pathology,* 22, no. 1, 1–12 (2001).

3. For an excellent overview of issues in children's testimony about abuse, Prof. Maggie Bruck's lecture and writings, including studies with Stephen Ceci, *see,* D. Goleman, "Studies Reveal Suggestibility of Very Young Children As Witnesses," *New York Times* Archives (1993), available at https://www.nytimes.com/1993/06/11/us/studies-reveal-suggestibility-of -very-young-as-witnesses.html?pagewanted=all (accessed May 29, 2018); and M. Bruck, "Science in the Courtroom," Cornellcast (March 26, 2013), available at ww.cornell.edu/video/science-in-the-courtroom-with-maggie -bruck (accessed May 29, 2018).

4. "You Can Make It Too," The Inspire Me Collection (Get it Done Publishing, 2017), gidpubservices@yahoo.com.

CHAPTER 17

1. Mimi Laver directs this national project. I serve on its steering committee. For more information, *see,* https://www.americanbar.org/groups /child_law/project-areas/parentrepresentation.html (accessed May 29, 2018).

2. A. Kemp, "Patterns of Skeletal Fractures in Child Abuse: Systematic Review," BMJ, 337, a1518 (2008), accessed at https://www.ncbi.nlm. nih.gov/pmc/articles/PMC2563260 (accessed May 29, 2018).

3. I am indebted to my son Brian Libgober for pointing out that three statistical paradoxes (or more) may be at play in Dr. Chandra's statistically based opinion: Berkson's Paradox, Simpson's Paradox, and the Prosecutor's Fallacy. Rather than put myself in the company of lawyers who practice statistics without a license, however, I will leave it to statistical experts to analyze the specific categories of statistical misinterpretation in which Dr. Chandra's opinion falls, beyond its clear misreading of Dr. Kemp's study.

4. *See,* D. Faigman, J. Monahan, and C. Slobogan, "G2i Inference in Scientific Expert Testimony," *University of Chicago Law Review,* 81, 417 (Spring 2014) for analysis of leading precedents and a recommended legal framework for the admissibility of scientific "framework" evidence and "diagnostic evidence."

EPILOGUE

1. The organization incorporated in January 2018. Michelle Weidner is the executive director of this new organization. I'm its president, and Melissa Staas is its vice president. For more information, *see,* www .famjustice.org.

2. *See,* Public Justice Center, National Coalition for a Civil Right to Counsel, at civilrighttocounsel.org/map for a list of states that provide counsel to parents in child protection court cases.

3. *Dupuy,* 141 F. Supp. 2d at 1136.

4. The same imbalances in power, coupled with the rights at stake, as documented in this book, were viewed as strong reasons for requiring the State to adhere to a "clear and convincing" burden of proof to terminate parental rights. *Santosky v. Kramer,* 455 U.S. 745 (1982). The finality of the parental right termination was also a major factor weighing in favor of the higher burden of proof, but as this book has shown, there also are severe and irreparable consequences for children being taken from their parents and adjudicated "abused."

5. Public and private foundations, as well as individual philanthropists, could do much more to support family defense work and parent advocacy. Unfortunately, only a tiny number of foundations support the critical work of the advocacy groups mentioned in this book. Fewer still make family-centered child welfare reform a high priority in their giving portfolios. For many years, pathbreaking advocacy was supported generously by the relatively small and exceptional Child Welfare Fund administered by the legendary David Tobis. *See,* D. Tobis, *From Pariahs to Partners: How Parents and Their Allies Changed the Child Welfare System* (Oxford: Oxford University Press, 2013). More individual donors and foundations are needed to take up the cause. Protecting families from separation by the State should be seen as a centrally important civil and individual rights issue, requiring much broader support for both policy advocacy and representation.

Index

Ethics, legal, 78, 193; comparison with medical ethics, 193. *See also* Sanctions

Ethics, medical. *See* Medical ethics

Exculpatory evidence: duty to consider, 42, 57; failure to consider, 54, 82, 93, 95, 161, 163, 173; policies in the wake of *Dupuy I*, 97; recommendation as to importance of, 235. *See also Dupuy I*

Exigent circumstances (requirement for seizure of child), 189. *See also Hernandez v. Foster*

Explanations (for injuries), 31, 54, 62, 111–113

Family court, 241 n.18. *See also* Juvenile court

Family defender, 15, 57–59, 76, 211, 222, 228, 229, 233, 235, 236; importance of empathy/ engagement of, xxv, 68, 76; introduced in stories, 5, 32, 202, 218, 223; network, 211, 222, 233, 236; role in explaining system, xxii, 34; role in preventing child removal, xxii, 58–59, 229; role in reframing narrative, 68; separate counsel for two parents, 65, 218, 220

Family defense: field in general, xxiii; as viewed by outside, xxiii, 39, 57, 129–130; workloads, xxv

Family Defense Center, 51, 54, 73–74, 190, 232

Family Justice Resource Center, 195, 232, 236, 253 n.1

Federal court. *See* Civil rights litigation; *Dupuy I*; *Dupuy II*; *Hernandez v. Foster*

"Felix, Dr. Sandra" ("Robert" story/child abuse pediatrician), 13, 14, 15, 17, 24, 27, 28, 30, 55–57, 78, 83, 88, 92, 95–99, 104, 110, 144, 146, 152–155, 162, 165, 166, 171, 173, 176, 192, 193; testimony in juvenile court, 106–119. *See also* Fracture(s); "Robert" story "Lynn"/mother; "Dr. Sheridan"/orthopedist; Medical ethics

"Flannery, Dr." ("Robert" story/ child abuse pediatrician supervisor), 108, 179, 242 n.6

"Ford, Kim" ("Robert" story/ casework manager above "Kirby Long"), 57, 100, 172, 175, 176

Fortin, Dr. Kristin (*Yohan K.* story, child abuse pediatrician), 201–203

Foster care, 15, 48, 63, 126, 244 n.9; duration of stays, 247 n 3; oversight of, 126; parents' view of threat of removal to, 44, 213, 245 n.29; as potential outcome of Hotline call, xix; rates of placement, xix; Tony L. ("April" story/father) as youth in care and youth services leader, 213 216, 221

Foster parent, 63–64. *See also* Relative Caregivers

Fracture(s): age of child as a factor, 118, 136; alternative explanations

also *Dupuy I*; *Dupuy II*; *Dupuy v. Samuels*

Pediatrics, 197; role of non-child abuse pediatricians in child abuse cases, 28, 31, 95, 158, 169, 197. *See also* Child abuse pediatricians; Orthopedists

Periosteal reaction, 145–146, 201, 204. *See also* Fracture(s)

Periosteum, 112, 139. *See also* Fracture(s)

Petitions (in juvenile court), 66, 75–79, 188, 199, 217, 224

Physical abuse, definition and frequency, xix, xx, 76, 86, 108, 111, 147, 153

Placement case, 82. *See also* Foster care

Police: arrest of parents, 215; comparison of CPS powers with, 39, 79; questioning of parents, 215; role in child protection investigations, 21, 95;192, 215, 223; role in stories, 10, 28, 31, 58, 122, 172, 215

Politics (of CPS), 130. *See also* CPS system critique

Posner, Judge Richard (as judge in *Dupuy II* appellate case), 47–52, 186, 188, 189, 228. *See also* *Dupuy II*

Preclusion (aka res judicata/estoppel), 177, 179–180

Preponderance of the evidence, 72, 175, 176, 200, 210, 235. *See also* Burden of proof

Presumption of innocence, 6, 131, 209, 227, 228

Private agencies (role in CPS), 126, 131, 132–135

Probable cause, 35, 69, 71, 80, 166, 170, 171, 176–178, 186–189; rarity of dismissals for lack of, 167

Prosecutor, 66, 193, 211. *See also* State's Attorney

Protective custody: authority under Illinois law, 242 n.3; decision to take, 15, 56–57, 62, 91, 92. 95, 187, 217; lapse/release, 76, 188, 189 (See also *Hernandez v. Foster*); legal requirements for, 35, 56–57, 69, 245 n.21; role of child abuse pediatrician in decision, 25, 57, 62; role of MPEEC report in decision, 25, 55–57, 62; statutory citation, 239 n.1; threats of taking, 21, 43, 46, 49–50, 56; timing of court action following, 77; voluntary agreements (claims as to), 35, 46. *See also* Safety plans

Radiologists, role in cases, 26, 88, 96–97, 123, 169, 203

"Reasonable efforts" to prevent child removal, 76

"Reasonable inquiry" (into facts of case), 169

Recommendations (of author), xxv, 228–229, 233–237

Register (administrative listing of child abuse decisions), xxi, 25, 28, 40–41, 170–173, 180, 221, 234, 241 n.2, 244 n.14; as blacklist for employment,

About the Author

Diane L. Redleaf has been a leading family defense attorney and policy advocate for over three decades. After graduating from Stanford Law School in 1979, Redleaf began representing poor families at the Legal Assistance Foundation in Chicago. She became a partner in the law firm Lehrer and Redleaf in 1996. From 2005 until 2017, she served as executive director and legal director of the Family Defense Center in Chicago, an agency which she founded. In 2017, she expanded her national child welfare reform efforts through United Family Advocates, a national bipartisan child protection policy advocacy network that she initiated in 2016. Redleaf has taught at the University of Chicago Law School and Loyola Law School. She has led dozens of class action suits and appeals and has won several awards, including the Chicago Bar Association Alliance for Women's Founder's Award and the Distinguished Alumni Achievement Award from her alma mater, Carleton College. For more information, see www.familydefenseconsulting.com and www.unitedfamilyadvocates.org.